Yale Publications in the History of Art, 24

Vincent Scully, Editor

THE ARAGONESE ARCH

AT NAPLES

1443–1475

GEORGE L. HERSEY

NEW HAVEN AND LONDON: YALE UNIVERSITY PRESS

1973

The Leopold Schepp Foundation provided assistance for
the research and publication of this book.

Designed by John O. C. McCrillis
and set in Garamond type.
Printed in the United States of America by
Connecticut Printers, Inc., Hartford, Conn.

Published in Great Britain, Europe, and Africa by
Yale University Press, Ltd., London.
Distributed in Canada by McGill-Queen's University
Press, Montreal; in Latin America by Kaiman & Polon,
Inc., New York City; in Australasia and Southeast
Asia by John Wiley & Sons Australasia Pty. Ltd.,
Sydney; in India by UBS Publishers' Distributors Pvt.,
Ltd., Delhi; in Japan by John Weatherhill, Inc., Tokyo.

To Charles Seymour, Jr.

Contents

List of Illustrations

Preface

HERE WERE two chief artistic events in Naples in the second half of the Quattrocento. One was the erection, at mid-century, of the Aragonese Arch by Alfonso I and his successor Ferrante. The other was the renewal of the city planned and partly executed by Ferrante's son, Alfonso II, from 1485 to 1495. I have discussed the renewal in an earlier volume. In the present book I turn to the Arch. Eventually I plan to complete my studies with a volume on Don Pietro of Toledo, the sixteenth-century viceroy whose patronage in many ways formed the climax of these earlier events.

The Arch has features in common with the renewal. Any study of either must deal with intentions rather than achievements, and with patronage exercised far from the main artistic centers of the time. Both projects were at once grandiose and provincial. In each case Parthenope, mythical foundress of Naples, and her tradition of royal rule, were invoked. Alfonso II, namesake of a famous and even legendary grandfather, thought of himself as Alfonso I's continuator, and therefore of his renewal as a sort of continuation of the Aragonese Arch.

Yet one cannot ignore the differences between the two events. The actual building of the Aragonese Arch began only after ten years of planning. The historian must therefore approach the monument slowly, and readers will find they have penetrated a third of the way through the book before they come to its execution. On the other hand Alfonso II's building campaign for new walls, gates, fortifications, and palaces was begun without prelude, was carried on feverishly for ten years, and then as suddenly abandoned. Alfonso I's patronage was concentrated overwhelmingly on a single work while that of his grandson involved a variety of projects. Alfonso II's patronage entails a considerable literary and historical background while the Castel Nuovo Arch is in this respect somewhat isolated. The methods used by the artists, too, were different: the Arch was erected in the contemporary Roman manner by a changing tribe of anonymous workers, while Alfonso II's program was mostly the work of individualistic Tuscans. The earlier program was carried out in a medieval industrial way, the latter in a more consciously "artistic" fashion.

These differences in historical fact have necessitated differences in methodology. For Alfonso I, I can (as I should) quote the documents in full; for Alfonso II, I had to be more circumspect, since there are so many documents. Similarly, the bibliography for this volume is an attempt to be fairly exhaustive, whereas that for the book on Alfonso II was not. And since the artists who worked for Alfonso II are all well known I did not feel the need for the short biographies I have inserted here, in appendix 2, which will provide readers with most of the known facts about Il Magnanimo's sometimes obscure assistants.

In the writing of this volume, my first thanks go to G. A. Kubler and Charles Seymour, Jr., who suggested in 1961 that I write a Yale M.A. thesis on the subject. To them, and in later years to Egbert Haverkamp-Begemann, Sheldon Nodelman, William L. MacDonald, David Cast, and Vincent Scully I owe the fact that my early studies were reasonably fruitful.

Since that year I have spent a good deal of time following out the strands of my argument. In this later work Professors Roberto Pane, Giancarlo Alisio, Alfonso De Franciscis, Raffaello Causa, Alfredo Parente, Riccardo Pacini, Amedeo Viuti, and Ottavio Morisani, all in Naples, deserve many thanks. I am particularly grateful to Ing. Luciano Balsamo for arranging for me to study the Arch from the scaffolding erected while it was being cleaned in 1963. In Spain, meanwhile, Professors Federico Udina Martorell and Josefina Font have been most cooperative, and so too in England were Sir John Pope-Hennessy, the late Professor Roberto Weiss, and Dr. John Moores, in Holland, H. R. Hoetink, and in this country Walter Cahn and Philip Foster. Photographs were supplied to me through the kindness of Guido Spinazzola and Alberto Cotogni. I must also thank Robin Bledsoe, Cynthia Brodhead, and John O. C. McCrillis of the Yale Press for their patience and good ideas.

I regret that I have received Gabriel Alomar's *Guillem Sagrera y la arquitectura gòtica del siglo XV* (Barcelona, 1970) and Hanno-Walter Kruft's *Domenico Gagini und seine Werkstatt* (Munich, 1972) too late to make use of them.

Finally, I have received three useful grants, one from the Fulbright Commission for study in Naples in 1962, one, for photographing the Arch, from the Yale Graduate School in the same year, and a Morse Fellowship, also from Yale, which enabled me to spend the spring and summer of 1967 on the work. Portions of chapters 3 and 5 have appeared in *Master Drawings,* and I am grateful to the editors for permission to reprint that material here.

G. L. H.

New Haven, Connecticut
June, 1972

Chapter 1: THE PROBLEM

HE ARCH OBSERVED   The Aragonese Arch, frontispiece of the Castel Nuovo in Naples, turns away from Vesuvius and the Bay, and faces northward toward the gentle slope of Mont'Echia (*fig. 1*). In the fifteenth century even the city proper was shouldered aside, and one approached the castle chiefly from the harbor or by a wide new avenue, the Strada dell'Incoronata, now via Medina. By any route one had to walk out toward the countryside to see the Arch with its white and gold Betulian marble glistening between the castle's reddish-gray towers.

To the modern eye the Arch hardly looks like an ancient Roman one. But for the Quattrocento poet Gonsalvo Cantalicio, Alfonso's monument was fully classical: "The royal triumphal gate tells of the deeds of the first Alfonso, like that in Rome which witnesses Septimius's victories, or as the worthy Flavian arch [i.e. of Titus] shows forth. This noble gate looks northward to Monte Sant'Elmo and to Virgil's tomb."[1] Nonetheless the modern eye is right. The Arch is anything but classical in conception and siting. Unlike the arches of antiquity, it is neither freestanding nor visible and approachable from many directions. And, of course, it actually consists of two triumphal arch facades, one on top of the other, which in this setting would have looked odd, perhaps even grotesque, to a visitor from ancient Rome. But then, the Aragonese Arch, or Arch of Alfonso I as it is often called, was built not only as a triumphal monument, but as a castle gate and cenotaph as well. To make matters worse, it has always been incomplete and for most of its life was only partly visible: the upper part, the cenotaph, is empty, though meant to be filled with a colossus, and the lower part was blocked soon after it was built, by a barbican erected by Alfonso's son Ferrante. Other outworks were added, culminating in enormous torrioni, curtains, and casemates designed by Francesco di Giorgio about 1492. The Arch remained thus, semivisible and swallowed by the castle's defenses, until the 1870s.

But even now that it is again completely visible, it is full of disparities and contrasts, most obviously in its relation to the castle. One notes the large curves of the castle's towers, the solid rectangles of wall linking them, the slope of the scarps sinking into earth or sea, the battlements along the crests of the building (*fig. 13*). These forms, whose logic depends on their continuity, quite illogically break to form a thin slot. This is filled by the Arch. But the Arch hardly seems part of the castle. It possesses, especially at a distance, precisely the opposite effect of its setting. Rather than being an ornamental emphasis, it is simply a small rich building heavily clamped into a large plain one.

This formal disparity matches a historical one. The upper parts of the Castel Nuovo, the round towers and curtain walls, are of a traditional type which Alfonso had known in his native Spain. But the scarped, battlemented ravelins around the bases of the towers and walls were an experiment. To contemporaries they would have appeared strange and improvisatory. Thus the traditional upper part of the Castel Nuovo is quite literally protected by the novel lower outworks; and it is within this double protection, in turn, that the Arch is fitted, itself neither experimental nor traditional but, rather, an exotic relic or trophy. In contradiction to the normal tendency of Renaissance architecture, which was toward unity of style, the Castel Nuovo here not only uses three different formal languages but does so in a logical manner, each language making statements proper to its own origin or purpose. Thus the lower facade functions visually as an open-membered support. It is emphatically vertical in articulation, with its tall filigree of pedestals, columns, and ressauts. The upper arch on the other hand is flat and full. In its original setting it flowed up into a loose curve against the sky. Its dominant elements are horizontal: a cornice, an entablature, and a tympanum, while its verticals—columns and pilasters—are correspondingly telescoped.

The sculpture, insofar as it acts architecturally, increases this differentiation. The figures of the lower arch are embedded in a dominant architecture. Those of the upper are contrastingly colossal, more than equal to their setting; indeed they are released by it and move forward from it. At the same time these upper statues and reliefs, especially the recumbent river gods, increase the sense of relative weight, of forms held aloft by the frame of verticals below. All this gives the sense of a procession of sculpture moving throughout the monument. Because the two triumphal arch facades are the same height and their openings the same width, it is even possible, rather fancifully, to read them as the reassembled back and front of a freestanding structure. Perhaps this superimposition was thought necessary in order to form a tall gate that would also include a cenotaph; yet even so the original triumphal arch idea, of a double-faced object through which a procession moves, is preserved—especially if we envisage a real-life procession entering the lower opening, and then the colossal statues emerging, as a transformed part of that procession, above.

The visual contrasts are matched in the Arch's use of sources. The lower section is a fairly strict copy of a Roman monument, the Augustan Arch of the Sergii at Pula, Yugoslavia, while the upper is freer and more characteristically Quattrocento. Thus, both stylistically and iconographically, the present stands on the shoulders of the past: or, one might say, the lower arch is a vestibule to the upper, an entrance from the past to the present.

The king's employment policy emphasized such expressive differentiations. As with the styles of architecture, so too the workers and artists were typecast in appropriate or at least logically contrasting roles. The traditional Spanish towers and walls of the Castel Nuovo were built by Alfonso's Catalan followers, his fellow invaders of the city. Then, having consolidated his position, the king turned to local masons for the "modern" ravelins. Still a third work force of artists from Lombardy, Dalmatia, and other foreign parts carved the Arch itself. Its lower part was in all probability designed by an architect and antiquarian, and its upper part, the proposed cenotaph, by a specialist in tombs.

Even the two inscriptions, referring to the two parts of the monument, point out role

differences. On the lower, "antique," architrave is ALFONSUS REX HISPANUS SICULUS ITALI-
CUS PIUS CLEMENS INVICTUS: Alfonso appears in the guise of a Roman emperor, his con-
quests and qualities given as his names. On the middle architrave is ALFONSUS REGUM
PRINCEPS HANC CONDIDIT ARCEM, which gives the king his modern title, "first among
kings," and stresses his modern achievement, the New Castle. This appears just beneath
the "modern" half of the Arch.

These historical and visual diversities, however consistent they may be, create problems
for orthodox criticism. I have mentioned the disparity between the Arch and the Castle, and
have suggested that similar things appear within the Arch. Thus the ressauts of the lower
part do not carry on up. The tympanum, niches, and columns are not dictated by continuous
coordinates. The upper cornice has no frieze or architrave. In contrast to this ambiguity, the
lower half is taut and spiky, as in the way the frieze clings to the ressauts. While the lower
arch detaches itself crisply from the towers, the upper sags back. A more orthodox architect
would have proceeded differently, it seems to me, letting the lower horizontals be minor,
that is, stringcourses or friezes, but making sure that the crowning entablature was very tall.

Still, there are enough consonances in the design to demonstrate that principles of some
sort were followed. The scarped bases of the towers are echoed in the tall, flowing plinths
of the lower arch, which thus has its own, ceremonial scarps. The two outward-curving
volumes of the towers are answered by the arches' upward-curving voids. The flanking towers
themselves are daintily echoed by the paired columns on either side of the entrances, so that
these metaphorically become miniature coupled towers. In other words, the Arch mimics the
forms of the Castel Nuovo. It thus becomes even more a building within a building, not
uniting itself with its matrix but distinguishing itself, accenting its difference by translating
the castle's language into a denser and more ornate idiom.

But there is one crucial point at which the mimicry stops: the castle has a singularly narrow opening, the Arch wide ones. Therefore, because it is a restatement of the castle, and yet
void-positive rather than volume-positive, its columns seem to be holding the upper and
lower arches temporarily open. This returns us to the idea of a procession—a real-life one,
passing in or out, which has now also the sense of forces kept at bay for its benefit. In the
lower arch, in turn, the archivolt has dropped from its normal position to accommodate the
counter-rampant griffins who push it down and stretch the spandrels they occupy, adding to
this effect of a temporarily created opening.

THE SCULPTURE   As noted, the lower arch has a miniature sculptural population of
about three-foot-high figures. On its two inner flanks knights-at-arms in high relief stand
watchfully in coffered rooms (*figs. 35, 37*). Above these on either side are pairs of niches,
small versions of those in the upper arch (and, though empty, perhaps at one time intended
for dwarf versions of the upper Virtues; *fig. 46*). Beyond the niches the angel and flower-

studded vault curves upward, the cross of Calabria embedded in its crest (*fig. 47*). Rising in front of the observer over the inner portal, is the now-fragmentary coronation relief of Ferrante (*fig. 48*).

There is no impression of perspective distance in the lower reliefs. Rather one has the sense of being watched by tiny spectators. Their smallness isolates the observer, increasing his scale, magnifying him into a colossus.

The figures in the attic frieze are slightly larger than those below. They depict the proto-type of all the daily-life processions that occurred in Alfonso I's reign, the king's entry into Naples on 26 February 1443. Though they move horizontally between the two enormous full entablatures of the Arch, they are not crushed by the incredible contrast in scale, but weave dominantly in and out of their architectural background.

The upper population makes up a third world, of allegory rather than fact, and at colossal scale. On the left of the nicchione is a draped military personage, stiffly projecting its armed shoulder, possibly intended to guard the equestrian portrait of Alfonso planned for the central opening. The latter statue would presumably have been immense, larger than the Gat-tamelata, perhaps as huge as Leonardo's later projected statue of Francesco Sforza. A similar guardian would have gone on the right. Above, in four niches, are the Cardinal Virtues at even greater scale, and next, the truly Cyclopean river gods. Finally, above the segmental margin of the gods' tympanum there were originally three giant saints, though only one, Saint Michael, is now in place. The upward jumps in scale are dissonant when the Arch is seen from afar, but as the observer approaches and enters the figures soar most impressively overhead.

As in the architecture there are sculptural correspondences or similarities that bridge over or interlock with these zone-by-zone sculptural variations. The same small heads that watch from the lower vault stare down from the upper. The one large figural element in the lower arch, the pair of griffins, is repeated in miniature on the upper frieze. The spandrel figures here are also miniatures—eager, handsome Victories leaning forward to lay wreaths on the victor's brow. Such lapses in the overall scale-increases create hostages of a sort, placing pygmies among the giants and vice versa.

Framing these three distinct populations is a fourth group of bouncing erotocamps, dol-phins, naiads, and putti, swarming along fibrillated canals or bedded on garlands. They buoy up the weightiness of the architecture, tethering its solids gently together. Such crea-tures perfect, in the Arch as a whole, the sense of a ceremonial that has risen upward and frozen into silence.

The changes of scale are not only eloquent in themselves, they fit the styles of the archi-tecture. The miniature spectators stand in the "antique" supporting pavilion, their signifi-cance to be completed only by the presence of the actual entrances and exits. The procession of 1443, nearer life-size, occupies the space between the two architectural worlds of past and present, the space of History. And the colossi, expressing the Eternal, move forward out of the Present, that is, the upper tomb.

EARLY HISTORIOGRAPHY   Historians and critics of the Aragonese Arch have concentrated on explaining these stylistic and formal disparities and on identifying its designer. In this process the Arch has been subjected to the standard assumptions of post-Vasari scholarship, whereby works of art are conceived by a single mind and executed in an individual style. Thus for long the relation between the Castel Nuovo and the Arch was held to be somewhat fortuitous. Despite Alfonso's inscription the fortress was almost unanimously attributed to Charles of Anjou (who did in fact build on the site in 1279), and while Alfonso was called the Arch's builder, even for this his responsibility was limited, according to many. Thus, after the triumphal celebrations of 1443, says the sixteenth-century historian Costanzo:

> The *eletti* [rulers of the municipal districts] had a great quantity of white marble brought, and also the best sculptors of the time, to make a triumphal arch to place before the steps of the cathedral's smaller portal; and when it was ready . . . Cola Maria Bozzuto, who had well served the King in the war, went to complain, saying that the arch blocked off the light from his house; and the King, laughing, said Cola was right, and then sent to thank the eletti of the city, and to tell them he would see to it that the arch was moved to the Castel Nuovo, where one now sees it at the entrance to the inner gate.[2]

In other words—and the story is far from being an utter fabrication—the Arch was a white elephant, offered by the well-meaning citizens and suffered by their kindly king. In later times another tale sprang up, which implied that the Arch had suffered several additions. According to this story, some or all of the upper colossi were erected in the mid-sixteenth century, and it was even said that they had been carved by Giovanni da Nola.[3] Such stories, repeated down through the nineteenth century, explained the Arch's disunities while absolving the revered Alfonso of bad taste.

The idea that a single artist was responsible for the whole does not, of course, square with the theory that the Arch is an agglomeration. Nonetheless attempts to identify a single creator began early. The first such is rather ambiguous, merely a statement that the "best part" of the Arch was by Andrea dell'Aquila, a pupil of Donatello.[4] A slightly later poem by Porcellio Pandone, a member of Alfonso's court, claimed that the Roman sculptor Isaia da Pisa was the monument's designer.[5] A third artist, Pietro da Milano, asserted in his epitaph that it was he who had "cleverly built" the Arch, and that Alfonso had knighted him partly for this reason. In 1524 Pietro Summonte, a Neapolitan humanist, claimed Francesco Laurana as the artist involved,[6] and later still Vasari maintained that the Arch was the creation of Giuliano da Maiano.[7] Subsequent writers have simply repeated these assertions, and for three hundred years the Arch was as deeply buried in controversy as it was in barbicans and bastions.

After the middle of the eighteenth century, however, attitudes changed. To the eye of the Neoclassicist the Arch was a different object, and a far handsomer one, than it had been to the baroque taste. This can be illustrated by comparing a 1697 portrayal (*fig. 2*) to one made at the end of the eighteenth century by Séroux d'Agincourt (*fig. 3*). In the earlier print, from a guidebook by Pompeo Sarnelli, the image of an antique triumphal arch is greatly softened. There is an exaggerated plasticity, with thrusting pedestals and zigzagging recessions, while figural detail shrinks within its boundaries. Behind the display of energy the towers flatten into a "ground," while the inner arch and its bronze doors are brought forward to the front plane, completing the illusion of a south Italian eighteenth-century frontispiece. Séroux on the other hand, in a much larger and handsomer print, isolates the arch from its towers as if it were a relic of antiquity. And having freed it he drastically widens its proportions. The radiating and vertical energies in the Sarnelli turn horizontal. The inner arch and bronze doors are completely omitted, thus increasing the effect of antiquity.

At about the time Séroux's book appeared, Leopoldo Cicognara published engravings of the triumph frieze and of one of the inner reliefs (*fig. 4*).[8] These are couched in the omnipresent linear style of the era, and in them the Arch's sculpture becomes as Neoclassical as its architecture had been for Séroux. With their wary *disinvoltura,* their hose worn like the trousers of Bourbon courtiers, Alfonso's barons are transformed even as they are admired by Neoclassicism.

Such graphic focus on the Arch matched a desire to free it from its physical setting. Antonio Niccolini, greatest of the Neapolitan Neoclassicists, wanted to demolish the Castel Nuovo and reerect the Arch, which he called a "bella e magnifica porta," as the focal point to a new marina in the harbor (*fig. 123*).[9] Niccolini's praise anticipated that of Séroux:

> The arch of triumph which occupies the principal part of this plate is certainly the most magnificent monument of this type which Architecture and Sculpture have created in the long interval of time that has unfolded from the Decadence of Art to its Renaissance. But it would be difficult to find for it a less favorable place. Stuck between the two towers of the fortress which is still called the New Castle, even though it dates from the period of Charles I [*sic*], and surrounded by a corps-de-garde and various other structures, its situation makes it so little striking to view that many travelers have visited Naples without having noted it.[10]

This was an age of archaeology. Students now began to examine the Arch with more care, and earlier tales about it were checked and criticized. An excellent article, the first of real scholarly merit, was written in 1836 by Mariano d'Ayala,[11] and in 1843 R. Liberatore published drawings and details that corrected Séroux's too-great latitude.[12] In 1850 G. V. Fusco dealt with the problem of authorship.[13] Indeed, rather more interest was shown in the nine-teenth century than in our own period. No doubt this was partly because the Arch included a fairly close copy of an antique prototype—though the actual model had not yet been spotted.

At about this time, and in line with Niccolini's and Séroux's ideas, the Arch began to be unwrapped from its outworks. In 1823, under the supervision of Louis Bardet de Villeneuve, the Castel Nuovo as a whole was restored. Then in 1854 a restoration of the Arch proper was undertaken by Liberatore and Orazio Angelini. Between 1872 and 1889 most of the outer bastioned walls were demolished.[14] Restoration continued in 1876 after the left-hand entrance tower collapsed, damaging some of the Arch's sculpture and gravely threatening its stability. In 1904 a more definitive restoration, under Adolfo Avena, was made;[15] capitals and other details were recut, and the extreme left-hand lower column was replaced com-pletely. A building on the right, however, blocking the Torre della Guardia, was left stand-ing. Finally, in 1921, this and other outer buildings were removed as part of a controversial restoration by Riccardo Filangieri and Pietro Municchi, under which the whole of the Castel Nuovo was returned to its supposed appearance during the reign of Alfonso I.[16] Those who claimed that the castle was really the work of Charles of Anjou protested, of course, and not without effect: the building is still known, in Naples, as the "Maschio Angioino."

MODERN SCHOLARSHIP   Modern writers have sought to attribute the sculpture and identify a designer. For the title of designer a pair of distinguished new claimants has come forward: Pisanello and Alberti. Unfortunately the only old contender who has been removed is Giuliano da Maiano. There is equally little agreement as to the attribution of the sculpture.

Until recently there were two main collections of documents on Alfonso's artistic patron-age. One still exists in the Archivo de la Corona de Aragón, Barcelona; the other was for-merly in the Archivio di Stato di Napoli but was destroyed during World War II. These documents began to appear in print in the 1870s. Among the archival writers were Camillo Minieri-Riccio, Erasmo Percopo, and Giovanni Ceci. A vast collection of abstracts compiled by Gaetano Filangieri appeared in the 1880s and 1890s, and this is still a principal source of documentary information on Neapolitan art.[17] Various other documents affecting the Arch have since been published.[18] Indeed, the number of ancient records that have been connected with the Arch is an embarrassment of riches. I have drastically pruned the list and reprinted in appendix 1 only those documents, along with certain sources, that I feel really do belong.

The earliest important modern monograph that includes a thorough analysis of the litera-ture, was published in 1899 by Carel von Fabriczy.[19] Fabriczy claimed that construction be-gan some time before 1455 and that it continued, with an interruption from 1458 to 1465, until 1467/68. He identified the designer as Pietro da Milano. His study is marred mainly in that he confuses this Pietro with a similarly named artist who worked in the 1450s in Rome and Orvieto. Fabriczy says almost nothing about Alfonso's patronage or about the

Arch's imagery or influence, but he does, as a point of interest, go into the matter of the triumphal procession. As the reader will have guessed, this idea of a procession is essential to my own interpretation.

The next writer on the subject, Emile Bertaux, was the first to introduce the august names of Pisanello and Alberti.[20] He suggested that the original conception was the latter's, made for the cathedral site, and that Pisanello reworked this design for the Castel Nuovo. The connection with Pisanello was established through a group of fifteenth-century drawings in the Louvre known as the Codex Vallardi; Bertaux was able to point out correspondences —mostly rather general—between these and certain of the Arch's architectural details.

In 1902 Fabriczy published a document showing that Pietro da Milano had been working in Ragusa (Dubrovnik) in 1452,[21] and as a result he abandoned the idea that the other Pietro, the Rome–Orvieto one, was the Arch's author. Fabriczy's discovery also raised the interesting question of Dalmatian sources for the Arch. At the same time Ettore Bernich, in *Napoli Nobilissima* and elsewhere, revived the Alberti attribution, even claiming that the medallion on the Arch's left inner pedestal (*fig. 42*) was a portrait of the Florentine architect.[22] Bernich repeated Bertaux's theory about Alberti's original design for the cathedral site and Pisanello's revision, and even boldly presented a reconstruction, based entirely on intuition, of this revision (*fig. 5*). Whatever its lack of historicity, Bernich's design does show how the Arch appealed to a mind trained under Neoclassicism. This same spirit brought forth a more genuine archaeology in Avena's famous drawing of the Arch before restoration, stripped of additions, its wounds fully exposed (*fig. 6*). This enormous rendering, 4 by 1.3 meters, was shown at the Paris Exposition of 1900.

Now we are in the richest period of Arch scholarship. In 1907 two monographs on Laurana appeared. One, by Wilhelm Rolfs, contains the most exhaustive description of the monument that has so far appeared. Rolfs scanned its surfaces with the vigilance of radar and described the figure sculpture like a physiologist.[23] He also printed a prodigious list of Roman "sources," but he ignored the iconography, the Neapolitan background, the historical situation, and the architectural influence of the monument; nor did he attempt much critical evaluation. Rolfs concluded that while Francesco Laurana was the most important artist involved, Pietro was the actual builder. He also pointed out, I believe for the first time, the use of the Pula prototype for the lower half. In the other monograph[24] Fritz Burger analyzed a number of drawings by or connected with Pisanello, aside from those in the Codex Vallardi, and linked them with the Neapolitan monument.

In 1908 the agglomeration theory crumbled definitively when Giuseppe De Blasiis proved that the whole of the "Maschio Angioino" had been built in the period of Alfonso I or later.[25] In the same year Avena published his restoration report, including a reproduction of his drawing, and useful diagrams of the individual blocks that make up the structure. He also made a thorough block-by-block analysis, concluding that the Arch was built in four campaigns, but not dating them.[26]

After this the scholarship became more fanciful. In 1914 Leonello Venturi, in the midst of his Urbinese studies, attributed the Arch not to Francesco but to Luciano Laurana, the architect who in 1465 had been summoned by Federigo da Montefeltro to build the ducal palace in Urbino[27] and who was later in Naples. The analogy of the latter's belvedere with the Castel Nuovo entrance, and various supposedly Lauranesque carvings in the interior of the palace at Urbino, filled out Venturi's case and prepared for the controversies that arose in the 1920s with Riccardo Filangieri's restoration.

Most of these latter were set at rest by Filangieri's masterly article of 1932 which presented, with a documentary history of the Arch, an artistic analysis that is far more trenchant and convincing than any earlier one. Filangieri also published a document showing that on 17 July 1453 Pietro da Milano, Francesco Laurana, and Paolo Romano were paid for contributions to the Arch, thus pushing back the beginning of work on it at the Castel Nuovo site by about two years. On the other hand Filangieri curiously agreed with Fabriczy that there was no overall meaning to the Arch's imagery.[28]

In the following year, 1933, a fifteenth-century drawing turned up which was assumed to be a preliminary elevation of the Arch (*fig. 16*). It was first published by Leo Planiscig, then by Riccardo Filangieri.[29] Planiscig affirmed that all possible designers but Pisanello were now excluded, so clearly did the drawing (now in the Boymans Museum, Rotterdam), fit in with the work of this artist; Filangieri avoided such extremism—prudently, as we shall see. This important discovery helped complicate all the earlier issues and added yet another element to the Arch's long prehistory.

In the later 1930s the various candidates for the post of architect continued to be discussed. In 1937 W. R. Valentiner took up Andrea dell'Aquila's case, reanalyzing and reattributing much of the sculpture. Also taking a connoisseur's approach, Raffaello Causa in 1954 proposed Guillermo Sagrera, the Catalan sculptor and architect who for a time had been protomagister of the Castel Nuovo, as the Arch's designer and as a major contributor to its sculpture.[30] Causa made a fascinating case for much of the sculpture constituting a sort of Gothic Revival. More recently Eileen R. Driscoll has returned to the Alberti question, claiming that the Arch's proportions derive from his precepts.[31] More convincingly, she documents the funerary character of the Arch's imagery, emphasizing its partial function as a cenotaph. She, like Riccardo Filangieri, would give to Alfonso himself responsibility for the basic program. More recently still, Gianni Carlo Sciolla, in an article in *Critica d'Arte,* distinguishes between the different styles of architecture and relates them to two different aspects of the program, one ideal and medievalizing, the other archaeological.[32] He denies both Pietro da Milano and Guillermo Sagrera as possible designers of the whole. He says instead that the Arch is "the result of a long and tortured period of preparation in which numerous designs were used and changed about." Dr. Sciolla's article anticipates parts of my interpretation, and I am only sorry that it appeared too late for me to incorporate all its insights into my own work.

Despite this assortment of documents, analysis, and speculation, however, none of the main issues raised by the Arch has been settled. The disparities of style and scale are still inexplicable, the identity of the designer, or designers, is as shadowy as ever. No convincing iconology has been put forward. All that has really been shown, in fact, is that a monument resembling the heterogeneous accumulation of centuries was in fact a single conception. These two facts—the unity of Alfonso's intent, and the heterogeneousness of the result—will be the foundation of my own investigation.

Chapter 2: THE BACKGROUND IN 1443

LFONSO AND HIS COURT   Alfonso of Aragon was born about 1396 and educated at the court of Henry III of Castile at Medina del Campo. The piecemeal character of his empire is reflected in his early titles. On 2 April 1416, he succeeded as King of Aragon, Valencia, Mallorca, Hungary, Catalonia, Sardinia, and Corsica, as Count of Barcelona and Cerdaña, and as Duke of the Athenians. To these he later added the titles of Count of Roussillon and King of Jerusalem.[1] On 14 June 1420, as a stepping-stone to Naples, he landed in Sardinia, and then moved on to North Africa; on 5 July 1421 he was in his future capital. There he was warmly greeted by the queen, Giovanna II, last of the Angevin dynasty and sister of the great King Ladislas. Giovanna adopted him, making him Duke of Calabria and heir to the throne of Sicily. His entrance into Naples was the occasion of a regatta and triumphal procession.

But all this was only an abortive prelude. Giovanna, allying herself with Filippo Maria Visconti of Milan, changed her mind about her new heir, who was thereupon driven from the city. Besieged in the Angevin fort that stood on the present site of the Castel Nuovo, Alfonso managed to escape to Marseilles and thence to Spain where he spent eight years rallying his resources. He was creating a new démarche with Giovanna when he returned to Italy in 1432, but his efforts to win her back failed, and at her death on 2 February 1435 she left her kingdom to her cousin, René of Anjou. Alfonso now found that the pope, Milan, Venice, Genoa, Florence, and other Italian states were determined to keep him out of Italy. His fleet was defeated at Ponza, on the way to Gaeta, and with his brothers Henry, King of Navarre, and Giovanni, he was taken prisoner to Milan.[2]

In Milan he was able to profit from the virtuousness of his captor. Pontano describes the situation: "Alfonso having been taken in a naval engagement with two of his brothers, one of them also a king, and with many nobles, not only did Francesco Maria Visconti order them to be freed, he withheld from them no kind of liberality, courtesy, or clemency" (*De liberalitate* 32).[3] Alfonso in fact made a secret pact with Filippo, dated 8 October 1435, renouncing claims to Corsica and to bases he had acquired in Tuscany and pledging his support against Filippo's rivals, the Sforza. At this crucial moment the unhappy René of Anjou was in prison in Lorraine, so Alfonso was the more easily able to attract support from the barons in the south. After defeating the Angevin forces he entered Naples in June 1442 to be its master for the next fifteen years.

At this point the secret pact with Filippo Maria Visconti was renewed,[4] with the result that power in the peninsula was henceforth balanced between the southern kingdom and the northern duchy. On this basis Alfonso made peace with the pope, Eugenius IV. Leaving the government of his Iberian possessions to his queen, Maria, he now concentrated more and more on Italy and the eastern Mediterranean,[5] fighting for the Visconti during the wars of Milanese succession, 1447–53.[6]

Alfonso found in Naples a municipal structure that matched the fragmentary character of his dominions. The city was divided into five *seggi,* the Capuana, the Nido, the Porto, the Portanova, and the Montagna. A sixth, citywide seggio, that of the Popolo, included the tradesmen.[7] The seggi had a great deal of power, being in fact tribes of a sort, with their own laws and customs and their own administrative headquarters. The civil service was similarly subdivided into independent bureaus manned by hereditary officers.[8] During the early part of his reign Alfonso simply added to these "tribes" in creating his military and administrative machine. Thus the court humanists were divided into Spanish and Latin (i.e. Italian) contingents,[9] while his captains and ministers were mainly Catalan and Castilian. The greatest of these ministers were Iñigo d'Avalos, in charge of the powerful Reale Camera della Sommaria, and Francis Siscar, Viceroy of Calabria. But Alfonso utilized local noblemen to head the famous group of seven military and administrative bureaucracies, the "sette grandi uffici del regno" that he also brought into being. Finally there were distinct Florentine, Catalan, Milanese, and other national groups among the city's general population. Each had its own special occupations, its own quarter, and often its own administrative and legal machinery, tax structure, marriage customs, and, on the occasion of public ceremonials, its own costumes and forms of theatrical expression.[10]

As time went on Alfonso gradually tried to replace this imperialism and tribalism by building a unified Italian state.[11] It is true that he continued his push to the east, fighting the Turks with the help of Scanderbeg in Albania and reinforcing his claims in Dalmatia at Ragusa. He even planned a crusade.[12] But on the whole by 1455 the scope of his intentions had swung from a horizontal Mediterranean axis to a vertical one along the peninsula. Already in the 1440s the alliance with the Visconti would have helped to dictate this change. Alfonso even began to give away the more detachable parts of his empire and to concentrate on that part of it for which he had sacrificed the most.[13] Thus his brother Henry was made King of Navarre, Maria became his permanent *locumtenens* in Barcelona, and the other brother, Giovanni, was promised the island of Sicily. When Alfonso died in 1458, his son Ferrante became king of the Italian mainland provinces only. Furthermore Alfonso's dying injunction to Ferrante was to get rid of the remaining Spanish power in his realm.[14]

The Arch was conceived and begun in the tribal/imperial period of 1445 to 1452, but it was moved and reconstructed in the 1450s, when Alfonso had turned to the idea of a local Neapolitan kingdom.[15]

Alfonso's court was a brilliant one even by the standards of the age. A lover of learning, he founded the University of Catania, instituted a school of Greek in Naples at the Basilian monastery, and sent promising youths to study at the University of Paris.[16] The "Latin" intellectuals at court included Lorenzo Valla (in Naples from 1435–48), Pier Candido Decembrio, Giovanni Pontano, Antonio Panormita, Bartolommeo Fazio, Porcellio Pandone, and (for a time) Aeneas Sylvius Piccolomini. There were also Greeks, among them Giorgio di Trebizonda.[17] Alfonso's library contained exquisite works of the bookmaker's and book-decorator's art, including the famous manuscript of Xenophon's *Cyropedia* translated into Latin for Alfonso by Poggio Bracciolini for 500 ducats. Valla wrote a historical work in praise of Alfonso's father, *De rebus gestis Ferdinandi primi,* and Alfonso's copy was among the most sumptuous books of the period. Pontano says that the king gave an even more princely sum, 1,000 *monete d'oro,* to Panormita for writing *De dictis et factis Alfonsi arago-num,* modeled on Xenophon's life of Socrates (*De lib. 30*).[18]

Alfonso's patronage did not stop short with Greek and Latin books and authors but extended to classical "temples," Gothic paintings and tapestries, and oriental gems. He commenced his reign by building three votive chapels marking his entry into the city, and there is reason to believe that all three were small temple-form buildings with pilastered exteriors,[19] perhaps somewhat in the manner of the church of Sant'Andrea, Ostia. One of the chapels, built near Poggioreale (at the present vico Pacella al Mercato) to the east of the city, was dedicated to Santa Maria della Pace and had an altarpiece by the Catalan painter Jacomart Baço.[20] For Emperor Frederick III's visit to Naples in 1452 with his wife Eleonora of Aragon (Alfonso's niece), a magnificent set of tapestries depicting Solomon and the Queen of Sheba was ordered from Flanders.[21] Pietro Summonte mentions further patronage of northern ateliers, including three paintings possibly by Roger van der Weyden, for which Alfonso paid 5,000 ducats.[22] A painting of the Adoration of the Magi by Jan van Eyck, says Pontano, was prized by the king as much as any object he owned (*De mag. 19*). He had another van Eyck, a painting of the Passion with Mary, Gabriel, the Annunciation, John the Baptist, and Jerome in his study;[23] and the Medici had sent him paintings by Fra Filippo Lippi, we are told.[24] Pontano asserts that "In his day King Alfonso outstripped all the kings of that age, both in acquiring and exhibiting the things used in the Mass and for the adornment of the priests, and in regard to statues of the male and female saints, of which he possessed many, including the twelve apostles made of silver" (*De mag. 13*).[25] This love of brilliance led the king to collect jewels, in a way that surpassed even the famous Duc de Berry, according to Pontano. And he had all manner of richly wrought oriental curiosities brought from the East.[26]

Perhaps the chief expression of his love of variety in art was the court ceremonials. Even the tournaments staged in front of the Arch, in the Largo del Castello, or on the southeast side of the Castel Nuovo in a special moat, were as theatrical as they were military, with participants speaking prepared parts, and elaborate scenographic facilities, effigies of men and animals, music, and the like.[27] The first and greatest of these ceremonies, of course, was the triumph procession of 1443.

THE TRIUMPH OF 1443   In a sense this event did duty in Naples for the coronation that had already occurred years before in Spain.[28] The classical sources for such processions

are mainly in Suetonius and Livy, and they are well known.[29] Pontano mentions the triumph
of Aurelian (*De mag.* 17), which featured Gothic tribes in their native costume and bearing signs or emblems of their countries—an Alfonsine touch. In the Middle Ages similar
processions occurred differently. Instead of the general or emperor who had conquered a
distant land returning home to receive the plaudits of his fellow-countrymen, the medieval
conqueror was more often a foreigner who had sacked and captured a city, and who now
passed through it as its new ruler, entering each district and receiving the obedience of its
leaders.[30] Such, probably, had been the famous "triumph" of Charles I of Anjou after the
Battle of Benevento in 1266, and doubtless also the more stylistically antique triumph of
the Emperor Sigismund in 1433, in Rome, for which decorations were supposedly prepared
by Donatello and Simone Ghini.[31] This was also the reason for Alfonso's triumph, and
similar processions were made on their accession by his successors.[32]

Imaginary triumphal scenes probably also contributed to the conception. The triumph of
Caesar or Alexander was a common theme for marriage *cassoni,* for example. A Florentine
panel of about 1450 in the Courtauld Galleries, London, *fig. 7,* is typical of these. As was
the case in Naples, the emperor is seated on a draped curule chair mounted on a float shel-
tered by a canopy borne by attendants, with nobles behind and, in front, mounted trumpeters
(cf. *fig. 64*).[33]

A more immediate prototype was Alfonso's earlier triumph on 25 June 1421, which
probably whetted his appetite for such things—all the more since it proved abortive.[34] On
that occasion Alfonso, the new Duke of Calabria, was greeted at sea by flower-laden barges
and saluted with artillery salvos, fanfares, and a mock sea-battle. His entry into the city took
place at the eastern end of the harbor through the Porta del Carmine. Accompanied by
nobles and clergy he visited each seggio, ending up at the Angevin castle that stood on the
future site of the Castel Nuovo.

The triumph of 1443 was even more elaborate. The Florentine contingent led off with
great brio. First came twelve horsemen wearing carmine *giupponi* and embroidered violet
sollecti (cloth footwear) decorated with studs or rings and with very long points. Then
came a float bearing two allegorical females, one standing "over the head" of the other. Another float had a portal above which stood a damsel dressed as Justice before a brocade-cov-
ered throne. Above this in turn were three more figures holding an imperial crown. A third
float had seven allegorical ladies and a turning globe, the latter presided over by a standing
armed figure of Caesar, carrying a scepter and with his head wreathed in laurel. He saluted
the new king in verse as a second Caesar, and presented him with his throne and crowns.[35]

The next part of the procession was prepared by the Catalans, whose float displayed the
Arthurian siege perilous, the chair whose seat flames unless the one worthy ruler sits in it.[36]
The siege perilous was surrounded by five Virtues, with Justice presiding over Fortitude,
Prudence, Charity, and Faith. Justice apostrophized the king while Charity distributed coins
to the spectators. The Catalan merchants followed.

Alfonso rode on a gilded four-wheeled chariot decorated like a fortress with battlements and corner turrets. It was drawn by four or five snow-white horses in red and white silk harnesses bearing the arms of Aragon. Around his neck was the collar of his Order of the Lily, with its symbol, a golden griffin. He carried his scepter and orb, and the hem of his crimson houppelande swept the ground. In front were placed the crowns of his six kingdoms, and across the back of his chair was a mantle that had once been René's. Before him, now displaced from the throne's seat, burnt the fire of the siege perilous. A magnificent baldacchino with twelve poles, each carried by a representative of one of the seggi, was raised over his head. Other nobles led the horses. Immediately behind the royal chariot came the most important members of the court, Giovanni Antonio del Balzo Orsini, Grand Constable and Prince of Taranto, Raimondo Orsini, Chief Magistrate and Prince of Salerno, and the other *grandi ufficiali.* There were also Sidi Ibrahim, ambassador of the king of Tunisia, and his suite; the humanists Valla, Panormita, and Porcellio, prelates and noblemen, and finally the common people. In all there were thirty-eight dukes and counts, one hundred barons, and numerous bishops, nobles, and knights. There were also trumpeters and other musicians, people from exotic places including two Ethiopians on horseback, and odd sights such as "laughing horses."[37] The city too was magnificently decorated. The headquarters pavilion of each seggio was draped with banners. Here noble and beautiful virgins and matrons danced to the sound of tibia and stamping feet.[38]

In the Largo del Mercato was

> an arch corresponding to the triumphal car, all of gilded and colored wood. The car passed beneath [the Arch] and was made to fit the streets it passed through. And the arch rose with four faces and four arches; at the top of each corner it had trumpeters dressed in silk, with the arms of Naples, and on the walls were flags with different symbols and writing, saluting the prosperity and good fortune of King Alfonso, and narrating his origins and royal heritage in the Catholic faith; then, on top of the said arch, six young boys sang like angels, dressed as winged nymphs.[39]

The triumphal car became a key relic of the triumph. It was preserved until about 1580 inside San Lorenzo Maggiore, over the main door,[40] and its general character seems to have been known afterwards from a drawing belonging to M. A. Cavalieri, which was engraved in Summonte's *Historia* (fig. 8).[41] Both the Aragonese manuscripts of the *Cyropedia* and the *De rebus gestis Ferdinandi primi* (fig. 9) illustrate it, though perhaps only with the loosest historicity. It also appears in medallions by Pisanello (Hill, *Corpus of Italian Medals,* nos. 43e, 43d), and in drawings for medals in the Codex Vallardi. A fresco in the ceiling of the Sala dei Ricevimenti in the Palazzo Reale, Naples, painted by Belisario Corenzio in the early seventeenth century, shows it in what seems to be a fairly accurate reconstruction probably based on Cavalieri's drawing, and it appeared earlier in a relief of about 1455 (now destroyed) in the Sala dei Baroni in the Castel Nuovo.

After visiting each of the five noble seggi, the king dismounted at the cathedral and prayers were said. It was here that the permanent marble triumphal arch was being erected, by the seggi but also at Alfonso's desire, in honor of the event;[42] 8,000 ducats had been raised for it. In the weeks before the procession Panormita had busied himself composing an epigram for it.[43] But, as we have seen, before it was completed it had had to be moved to the Castel Nuovo.[44]

There is actually little in this picture, aside from the breached wall and some ambiguous costume details, to make us think of the triumph as a serious revival of antiquity. There is no mention of the pagan sacrifices, Roman dress, prisoners, or other features of antique triumphs that would have been perfectly well known. On the contrary, the stress was on the king's Christian virtues and modern lineage, on his knightly order, and on such medieval symbols as the siege perilous. As far as one can tell the ornament on the triumph car and its "corresponding" arch was Gothic (fig. 8). Only one float, the Florentine one with Caesar, was at all "antique," and this only in part, since the turning globe, the three allegorical women, and the imperial crown are not necessarily Greek or Roman. The actual procession, while it did contain a few antique elements, was in reality a more or less folkloristic expression of the tribal structure of the city and, less strongly, of Alfonso's empire.

On the other hand, the later humanist accounts of the triumph do paint the picture of a genuine antique revival. The earliest and most elaborate of these is Porcellio's poem, *Parthenope capta,* which recasts the procession in the trappings of the classical epic. Alfonso appears as Caesar and his empire as a new Rome. Porcellio's poem thus forms a kind of literary correlative for that other ex post facto antique version of the triumph which is the Castel Nuovo Arch.[45]

REBUILDING THE CASTEL NUOVO   Like the original procession, the Castel Nuovo was a mosaic of styles. As soon as the celebrations were over—perhaps before—Alfonso appointed the Catalan Francis Bonshoms to rebuild the old Angevin fortress. Bonshoms was at work at least as early as 1 May 1444,[46] and the present castle may owe its trapezoidal plan to his use of part of the foundations of the earlier fort. Parallels for Alfonso's round towers and high walls are to be found in castles then being erected in his native Castile by such masters as Juan Pacheco: Belmonte, for example, with its curious hexagonal plan and outer bailey, which bore a superficial likeness to the ravelins of the Castel Nuovo. Other Spanish examples are Mombeltràn, Avila, and, in the same neighborhood, Barco de Avila.[47] But the Spanish castles have complicated walling that zigzags over the terrain, very different from the Castel Nuovo with its towered volumes. They also lack the deep scarps that anchor the Neapolitan building to its site.

Other countries provide fewer and less convincing prototypes. In Provence, Villeneuve-les-Avignon and René's castle at Tarascon do have similar towers,[48] but again, the immense balconied ravelins do not appear. In Italy at Bracciano (1470), for example, and Senigallia (end of the fifteenth century) we see Castel-Nuovo-like forts, but they are apparently all later than the one in Naples. Senigallia shows one more advanced feature than the Castel Nuovo, the pent-roofed casemates (*fig. 10*). On the whole, however, it seems Alfonso was following a current Iberian tradition when he began the Castel Nuovo, introducing it perhaps for the first time on Italian soil.[49]

As to the composition and setting of the Arch proper, paired towers flanking a sculptured entrance gate had appeared on the Porta Romana, built by Frederick II Hohenstaufen at Capua, and at Frederick's Castel del Monte in Apulia (*fig. 11*). Another example, also close to Alfonso, is at the Aragonese pantheon, Poblet. Even more striking is one that unfortunately I cannot illustrate adequately: the two-towered gate at Barco de Avila, which in the fifteenth century apparently consisted of two superimposed arches.[50]

These prototypes and parallels all lack the curious ravelins and the rounded battlemented balconies of the Castel Nuovo (*figs. 1, 12, 13*). Such features are clearly involved with current attempts to build fortifications that would counteract, in defense, the new giant cannon that shot missiles in flat trajectories, as well as providing emplacements for the offensive use of such guns. Alfonso had been able to destroy the old Angevin fort with the help of these weapons, so it is logical that he would be among the earliest to take them into account in his architecture.[51] Another novelty, even more curious, is the galleries in the upper walls. Riccardo Filangieri says that these were intended to go all around the landward sides of the castle, and that they were to function as firing platforms.[52] Finally, the immense ditches of Castel Nuovo are striking. These were as much as fourteen *canne* (30 meters) wide, about twice the width of the old Angevin ones they replaced.[53] Some of them formed courts for underground stables, and we have seen that the southern ditch was used for tournaments.

The Castel Nuovo's combination of low ravelins and deep, wide ditches anticipated the late fifteenth-century fort that was to replace the tall medieval type. Therefore, by building this experimental base, this platform or serrated masonry cup emerging from a cavity,[54] Alfonso set the stage at Castel Nuovo for the even more immense fortifications built by Alfonso II in the 1490s. More important, these forms were "modern" in the sense that they were neither antique nor traditional, neither Roman nor Gothic. Alfonso's sense of the Castel Nuovo's modernity is implicit in an epigram he is said to have composed: "If the name given this place be other than 'new,' let not a single one of its stones remain."[55]

The "modern" features of the Castel Nuovo were erected by Italians, not by the Catalans who had built the more traditional parts. Thus in February 1447 Bonshoms was joined by a certain Luigi Castello as administrator of the works. In September 1448 another Italian mason, Pertello de Marino, was given a supervisory function of some sort, though payments to Bonshoms continued. In March 1450 the Catalan Guillermo Sagrera appeared briefly in Pertello's post, but by 20 December 1452 Sagrera had been put in charge of the great Gothic meeting hall, the Sala dei Baroni.[56] Even before that, in the spring of 1451, Alfonso had contracted with Onofrio di Giordano and other Italians to build the scarps and ravelins according to designs furnished by the court (Doc. 5).*

The most significant Gothic contribution to the Castel Nuovo is the Sala dei Baroni, which with its immense Gothic vault and central eye is a kind of medieval pantheon (*fig. 14*).[57] The room is twenty-six meters square at floor level, and around the upper part are grouped balcony openings, between which the ribs reach up into the octagon, which is also supported on squinches. The ribs form a jagged star whose crest is twenty-eight meters above the floor. One of the largest of Gothic rib-vaults, it is related to Catalan prototypes such as the vault in the old chapter house by Arnau Bargués in Barcelona cathedral.[58] Originally the Sala dei Baroni was far from being the drab room we see today. The junctions of the ribs were decorated with the arms of the countries under Aragonese rule. The floor was covered with *azulejos,* a brilliant display of Hispano-Moresque tile, and the walls were hung with Flemish tapestries.

Sagrera's countrymen, such as Pere Joan and his followers, filled other parts of the castle with Flamboyant Gothic doors, windows, staircases, and rooms, carved with interlaced moldings. In the 1440s Bartolomeo Prats and Bartolomeo Vilasclar created the Arch's rib-vaulted vestibule,[59] and in the 1450s Antonio Fraburch and Antonio Gomar rebuilt part of the chapel.[60] Altogether the Catalan contributions formed an elegant display of Gothic virtuosity; and it should be noted that the only elements in the Castel Nuovo that we would today call "Renaissance" were its four ceremonial portals—the Arch, Ferrante's inner portal, the entrance to the chapel (which dates from after Alfonso I's death) and the Porta del Trionfo in the Sala dei Baroni, leading to the royal apartments.

In sum, the Castel Nuovo was formed out of three vigorously and appropriately differentiated languages: private life and relations with the barons were Gothic (or, in Alfonso's mind, no doubt, Aragonese); defense was "modern," and Italian, and ceremony was antique. This parallels the different verbal languages used by the court: Castilian for domestic purposes, Catalan for business, Latin for religion and law.

AN ANGEVIN PROTOTYPE FOR THE ARCH   In much of this Alfonso was only imitating the Angevins, who with Boccaccio, Petrarch, Giotto, and Tino da Camaino had established such a reputation for patronage. Alfonso may even have been influenced by the legend that René himself was a painter[61]—a possibility that adds interest to attempts to identify the Aragonese ruler as the Arch's designer.

The Angevins' influence on the Arch itself stems from the tombs they built for their kings and queens. The most important of these is in San Giovanni a Carbonara, the work of Andrea and Marco di Nofri da Firenze (*fig. 15*).[62] It is the burial place of Ladislas (d. 1414), the last important member of the dynasty. Ladislas, like Alfonso, had entered

---

* See appendix 1, p. 65.

Naples as a triumphator, and in fact he was legally Alfonso's uncle, being brother to Giovanna II. His tomb, based on a tradition going back to the monuments of the Emperor
Henry in the Camposanto, Pisa, and of Charles I of Anjou formerly in the Duomo in Naples
(now destroyed),[63] consists of two superimposed arches, the upper complexly Gothic and
the lower more neutral and classical. Together these form a tall palanquin that climaxes in
an equestrian statue of the king. The lower part, with its colossal caryatids who carry the
whole structure, is a gate. Two gabled pavilions unfold like polyptych panels from the
second zone. The tomb was considered impressive even in the later Quattrocento, for Sannazaro praises it:

> Admire the floating stone in snowy columns,
> Visitor, and the horseman who sits upon its crest.[64]

There are two principal styles of sculpture. The effigies of the king and his sister, the
sarcophagus group, and the four niched kings on either side of the upper opening are
strongly Gothic. The tensions of their bodies are evenly distributed, their draperies curl in
decorative coils around their ankles, and the cusped niches contain the forms of the smaller
figures as gems are set in brooches. But other figures are active, turbulent, rhetorical, classicizing. The caryatids are conceived in the rounded, heroic manner of Nanni di Banco. One
of the prophets on the left of the lower arch is at least partly derived from Donatello; he
has the intensity and the heroic hands of the Duomo Saint John the Evangelist. The seated
virtues flanking the royal couple are equally Florentine, while—and this is a different sort of
classicism—the head of another prophet, below the Donatellesque figure, is borrowed from
an antique portrait of Socrates.

Such classicism makes a significant counterpoint to the Gothic effigies of the tomb: the
part of the monument that has to do with death's humanist anagoge is active, verging
toward the Renaissance. The more sacred and conservative part, the portrait effigies and
sacramental figures, is traditional and medieval. The tomb of Ladislas is thus like the Arch
itself a layered procession or ascending series of tableaux in which styles play expressive
roles. At the base are the caryatid-virtues who carry the palanquin with its royal personages,
the king and his sister. Then comes the temporal death of Ladislas, who is receiving Extreme
Unction. Above are the Virgin and two saints presumably mediating in favor of the king's
ascending soul. Above this in turn, as a horseman reborn in fame and eternity, Ladislas rides
forward. All this, and even the epitaph, says something that will prove true of Alfonso and
the Arch:

> Unrighteous death, alas, is ever unexpected in the affairs of men;
> Just as the magnanimous king bathes the world in hope,
> Lo, he dies: the noble king was roofed over by this stone
> While his soul, single and free, sought starry Olympus.[65]

The structure of politics and patronage during the early years of Alfonso's rule was consciously eclectic. There was the tribal capital with its polyglot empire, the wide-ranging taste of the king in objects, languages, bureaucrats, and intellectuals, the triumph with its varied contingents, and the Castel Nuovo itself, which summarized its functions in expressively differentiated architectural languages. A matching rhetorical use of style appeared in the ascending tableaux of Ladislas' tomb. All of these conceptions would reappear in Alfonso's own marble monument.

Chapter 3: TOWARD CLASSICISM, 1443–1451

HE CATHEDRAL ARCH, THE EQUESTRIAN TRADITION, AND THE BOYMANS DESIGN   I am assuming that the marble arch near the cathedral was actually begun at the time of the procession, though Panormita says that little of it was to be seen (Doc. 2). The miniature in Valla's *De rebus ferdinandi* (*fig. 9*) shows a curious structure that may represent, after a fashion, this planned arch. It has an entrance flanked by two Corinthian columns rising from pronged bases, with a lintel and corner pilaster. The flat surfaces are decorated with rectangular rinceau panels. Although there is no reason to think that this is anything but imaginary in design, its appearance in an illustration of Alfonso's procession adds weight to Panormita's and Vinyes's eyewitness declarations that the Arch was at least begun (Docs. 1 and 2).

The original cathedral site had a special significance in Neapolitan legend. Here from time immemorial had stood a colossal antique bronze horse, said to be the work of Virgil. The horse was held to be a symbol of Earth, and it was used to cure sick animals. In 1283, Conrad IV, celebrating his conquest of Naples, equipped the unharnessed effigy with reins, and the following distich was inscribed on it:

> Thus far unharnessed, now the horse
> Obeys his master's reins; the just Parthenopean king rules.[1]

In this manner did the animal symbolize the people, while the reins stood for royal rule stemming from Parthenope, first queen of the city. The body of this original horse was melted down in 1322 to make a bell for the cathedral,[2] but the two seggi adjacent to the site, the Capuana and the Nido, displayed versions of the horse on their arms.[3] Meanwhile the head and neck of the creature were preserved and ultimately entered the Aragonese collection. The equestrian symbol was repeated on coins, among them Aragonese issues that included Conrad's pun on *equus* and *aequus*.[4] The subsequent tradition of equestrian portraits of rulers in Naples—those of Charles himself, of Ladislas, and the 1487–94 statues of Ferrante and of Alfonso of Calabria over the western city gates—involved the same idea.[5] Alfonso I, as Conrad's and Ladislas's successor, and like them a triumphator now peaceably ruling his subjects, also had himself portrayed in this way on coins and elsewhere. It is therefore more than possible that the cathedral arch, under construction near the spot where Conrad's statue had originally stood, was also to include such a representation of the new king.

A few years after the triumph another heroic portal was designed, and this did indeed feature an equestrian image of Alfonso. The design is recorded in a drawing now in the Boymans Museum, Rotterdam, and it has been identified as a preliminary sketch for the Castel Nuovo Arch (*fig. 16*). While I shall show that this is unlikely, the drawing does warrant detailed discussion.[6] (I owe the suggestion for my new interpretation to Michael Baxandall.)

The structure in the Boymans sketch is about 12 centimeters wide by about 30 centimeters high. There is no scale. It is executed in pen, pencil, and a reddish wash on grayish-white paper. The ornaments are mostly left in white or heightened with white pigment, and the inscription at the bottom, *Bonanu de Ravena,* is brushed in in red. In typical Neapolitan fashion the design consists of two equally high arch compositions superimposed one above the other. The lower is in the International Style, but, filled with heraldic ornament, it is much more festive and secular than the upper part of Ladislas's tomb. The upper arch is classical, divided into two horizontal zones, and peopled with statues. Flanking the lower arch are twisted ribbony columns, in pairs, with elaborate Corinthian capitals and pronged bases, which support entablatures brought out en ressaut. The columns stand on wholly inadequate molded bases. The entablatures are handled curiously: at the bottom is an inverted corona, then a frieze, then a right-side-up corona, another frieze, and finally a very heavy corona with bead mold, dentil course, and leaf-carved torus. This corona is the only part of the lower entablatures that extends across the arch as a whole. Between the pairs of spiral columns is a molded equilateral pointed arch, rising on grouped shafts and opening into a rib-vaulted chamber. The room terminates on the far side with a polyfoiled tympanum over a round-headed opening. On its lateral walls figured relief panels are indicated. Flanking the pointed-arch opening are shields with the arms of Aragon *per saltire,* signed with crowns. Above, on conical brackets, stand putti holding an enormous wreath again containing the arms of Aragon, this time with helm and bat crest. Flanking the wreath, above the shoulders of the putti, are the arms of Alfonso I, again with bat crests. On the left-hand upper frieze is some vegetation, perhaps in honor of the Order of the Lily. On the right, in the corresponding place, is Alfonso's emblem of the open book. Beneath each of these is a three-faced putto possibly signifying Prudence.

The upper arch is even more curious. It is mounted on double receding plinths that follow the plan of the ressauts below. The lower frieze is blank and, with its cornice, runs across the whole structure to a base for the equestrian statue in the center. Above, on either side, are repetitions of this frieze and cornice, but they do not carry across. They support pairs of what I take to be Corinthian or Composite fluted pilasters which are very stubby and have round-headed, vegetation-sprouting niches between them. Above them a flat, continuous cornice, similar to the main one but without frieze or architrave, runs across, interrupted in the center by an enormous winged putto head. The round arch in the middle has a truly colossal bead-and-reel architrave springing from fluted, possibly Roman Doric pilasters, and the spandrels are filled with roundels of heads, on the left a profile of a man, apparently, and on the right, full-face, seemingly a woman. The equestrian figure rides directly forward, the horse charging, the warrior with plumed helmet and raised sword. The flanking figure on the left seems to be in legal or academic garb and the other may be a female warrior Virtue.

The niches across the top, framed by Gothic clustered shafts with foliage capitals, are arranged as follows: the outer ones, containing tall allegorical women, are pointed-arched, and the next pair, containing putti, are round-headed, as is the central arch with its seated female figure. One can see her civic crown and (in the original but not in the photograph) the tip of one of her wings. More winged putto heads decorate the spandrels. Above these is another heavy corona oddly penetrated by arched corbels. As an upper cresting, five Aragonese shields are separated by bifurcated lucarnes, all sprouting ornamental flames.

The low proportions of the upper arch, its stubby flanking pilasters and gigantic keystone ornament, the curious way in which the ressauts flatten into the upper facade, and the corbeled corona all bespeak a designer who was singularly ill-at-ease with the language of antique architecture, as well as that of Brunelle⸱⸱i and Alberti. Erected in this form the Boymans arch would have had, at best, the illiter⸱⸱⸱ *panache* of scene design. On the other hand its exploitation of two architectural styles, the plotting and shaping of the voids, and the deployment of the colossi argue an artist who was familiar with the tombs of Charles of Anjou and Ladislas (*fig. 15*) and with later Neapolitan monuments such as that of Gianni Caracciolo (*fig. 23*).

A more striking ancestor of the Boymans conception, however, and one at the time considered to be antique, is the Porta Romana, Capua, already mentioned (*fig. 17*).[7] Here we have a similar "classical" round arch with flanking heads in roundels (albeit on the ground story); a large roundel in the center, corresponding to the wreath in the Boymans drawing; a similar upper section, two stories high, the lower with a large niche flanked by smaller ones and separated by stubby pilasters; columns en ressaut; and finally a row of upper niches of which the central group is slightly smaller than those on the end. A seated central figure with pairs of attendants is also common to both. The difference between the two, in fact, lies mainly in the Boymans drawing's heavy cornices and wide pilasters—in its "classical" framing elements. The most curious detail of the Boymans design, meanwhile, that "double-corniced" main entablature, is found in another monument, Frederick II's portal of Castel del Monte in Apulia.

More orthodoxly antique remains supply other possible source material. The idea of superimposed arches could have come from Miletus, whose city gate also boasted columns, while in Athens, in an upper niche of the Arch of Hadrian, was a seated statue of the emperor. Both monuments had recently been visited by Ciriaco d'Ancona.[8] Alfonso would, I should think, have especially relished the latter as a prototype, since he called himself Duke of the Athenians. Nearer home was the city gate at Perugia, which had an upper seated *civitas* figure, paired pilasters, and similar spandrel portraits. The Arch of Germanicus at Spoleto had had an upper niche with a horseman in it, as did that at Ancona. Roman coins, those minted by Gallienus for the rebuilding of Byzia for example, show a gate with paired flanking columns and an upper row of niches; the so-called Arco di San Giorgio, Rome, may also have been similar. A great "Roman" palace that possessed superimposed arches with classical ornament was that of Theodoric, the palace of the exarchs at Ravenna.[9] Here too appears a lower entrance vestibule, as in the Boymans Arch. (One recalls the inscription at the base of the Boymans drawing, which can be read: "Bonanu de Ravena.")[10] Finally a similar arrangement of triumphal arches, sometimes with a surviving enthroned emperor statue, was to be found in the central bay of the *scaenae frons* of Roman theaters, including those at Verona, Lyon, and Orange (*fig. 18*), and, quite possibly, at Naples itself.[11] Thus the Boymans conception draws on a variety of classical precedents that link it almost equally firmly to palace and city entrances and to the stage.

THE CASTEL CAPUANO FESTIVAL   As to the purpose of the structure called for in the Boymans drawing, we must turn to Lorenzo Valla. In his attack on Bartolomeo Fazio, written in 1446–47, Valla describes occasions when, in competition with Fazio, Panormita, and others, he was asked to write inscriptions for various monuments in the kingdom. On one such occasion, he says,

> Giovanni Carafa,[12] the valiant Neapolitan councilor, when he was charged with hav-
> ing painted, in the Castel Capuano, an image of the king, armed and seated on a
> horse and with four Virtues, Justice, Charity or *Largitas,* Prudence, and Temperance or
> Fortitude (the picture is dark), came to me and asked me to write an appropriate number
> of verses, composing one for each placard that the images were individually holding.
> And he added that I must finish at least two of the verses within two days, so they
> could be inscribed on the upper figures, now just about finished.

Valla adds that after finishing not two but three of the verses, and in one day, they were duly inscribed and discussed by the many who came to look. But then Panormita arrived, criticized them, and contributed alternative lines of his own. Alfonso, called upon to judge between the two contributions, diplomatically decided not to have any inscriptions at all.[13]

On another occasion, Valla goes on, he and Panormita wrote lines for a recumbent marble statue of the sleeping Parthenope. Panormita's verse was:

> Parthenope, vexed with war for many years:
> "Now, reborn through Alfonso, I rest."

And Valla's:

> Parthenope, the maiden long disturbed by Mars:
> Martial Alfonso says: "Rest thyself."[14]

Valla's distich was chosen over Panormita's on the ground that in Panormita's lines the sleeping virgin was made to speak, which Alfonso thought "indecens."

Nonetheless Alfonso did not throw away Panormita's rejected distich with its speech by Parthenope. Instead, apparently, he commissioned, or utilized, an image to suit it and added this new image to the Castel Capuano group of his own equestrian portrait with four Virtues. Thus on 22 March 1446 he wrote to his old friend and fellow-campaigner, Cardinal Lodovico Trevisan, chamberlain to Eugenius IV, thanking him for sending certain works of art. He mentions a "primera ymagen e pinturas," and continues:

> And since everything should be told to a true friend, and to hear your opinion as to what I am doing, I give you my idea and design for the setting for the sketch that represents the statue of the city of Naples who, long torn by war and now having found peace, rests herself. I enclose the verses I've had written:
>
> > "I am that Parthenope, vexed with war for many years,
> > Now at last, reborn through Alfonso, I rest in peace."[15]

In other words, Panormita's distich for the painting had been revamped and applied to a proposed real statue sent from Rome.

If Cardinal Trevisan's Parthenope cannot have been the one for which the lines were originally composed (since the goddess is speaking); and if at the same time she *is* resting, we can perhaps conclude that the poet envisaged her sitting down. Also, Alfonso says he is sending the cardinal that sketch which *represents* the statue, not the statue itself. In other words, what happened was this: Alfonso had received from the cardinal a design for a proposed seated image of Parthenope. In return he sent his own, alternative "pensamiento e invencion" for the image's setting, along with an appropriate inscription that he happened to have on hand.

In my opinion the Boymans drawing is an elevation for a festival arch created for a specific occasion, or as a permanent scaenae frons, or both, in the Castel Capuano. It was here that such celebrations would have had to take place until the completion of the Sala dei Baroni in 1456. One notes, too, the deadline for completing the verses, and yet that, when Valla wrote, he implied that the portrait and virtues were still visible. The lower arch would function as the palace entrance. Above this would be set a classical triumphal arch with the king's equestrian portrait flanked as in Valla's description by four Virtues, two above and two below, much as in the *regia* of a classical scaenae frons. The original conception, described by Valla, would have called for Virtues and a horseman as we see them in the drawing, but without the three upper central figures. Under the changed conception—Alfonso's new "pensamiento e invencion" of March 1446—a seated Parthenope would have been added. Indeed the Boymans drawing could actually *be* the new design Alfonso sent the Cardinal; and in this case we would have for it the precise date of March 1446.[16]

Parthenope is an appropriate myth-figure for such an arch. Though more famous as a siren, she had another, not entirely distinct identity as a virgin queen, daughter of Eumelos and foundress of Naples, which in fact was originally called by her name.[17] Later on the inhabitants founded a new city, and though they called this Neapolis, Parthenope's tomb was erected in its center, and she became its patroness. Annual games were held in her honor.[18] Statius, in the *Sylvae*, describes Parthenope's tomb as a tall structure of marble with a special chamber for the statue of the queen, which was a seated crowned figure.[19] It is conceivable that the Castel Capuano scaenae frons was intended to recall this tomb.

In ancient art, indeed, Parthenope is depicted much as she appears in the Boymans drawing.[20] On Campanian and Sicilian coins she appears as a draped, seated female figure with wings and with either a staff or a bird in her hand. In other cases the queen is shown in the guise of Athena, accompanied by a winged naked ephebe presenting a cup[21] (and we note in the upper niches of the Boymans drawing the similar cup-bearing putti). There were a number of larger representations of Parthenope in Naples. Friedrich Karl von Duhn suggests that in the tympanum of the Temple of the Dioscuri (visible in the Quattrocento), there may have been a seated relief figure of her, flanked by the Dioscuri—and this, of course, is another possible interpretation of the two Boymans putti.[22] A colossal statue of Parthenope, of more indeterminate origin, at one time stood near Santo Stefano, and the famous "Capa Napuli," a gigantic marble Greco-Roman head, was located outside Sant' Eligio.[23] The historical site of Parthenope's tomb was thought to be near San Giovanni a Mare, not far from the Castel Nuovo. From several viewpoints, therefore, the Siren Queen was an ideal Neapolitan symbol for the composition of strife, a symbolism made explicit in Panormita's lines for her portrait.

Beneath Parthenope in the drawing is Alfonso; somewhat as in Conrad's inscription, he is reining in a horse. Perhaps more specifically he appears also as Parthenope's father, Eumelos,[24] a role suggested by Panormita's inscription: "opera Alphonsi parta." Appropriately enough, Eumelos was reputed to be the greatest horseman of antiquity, and some Neapolitan and Campanian Greek coins display his equestrian figure on the obverse, with a head sometimes taken to be Parthenope's on the reverse. The rearing horse, reined in by its rider, would stress the idea of the ruler as a *domator equi*.[25]

Thus would the upper half of the Boymans design constitute a euhemeristic tribute to the sources of Alfonso's power, while the lower half, more contemporary in feeling, would have served as the entrance for the actors.

Such an interpretation fits in not only with Alfonso's general policy but with the political and military situation in March 1446.[26] It was a period marked by peace after long war and by Alfonso's achievements as a papal *condottiere*. As a result of the Peace of Terracina, negotiated with Alfonso on the pope's behalf by Cardinal Trevisan, Alfonso, in return for papal recognition, had promised to drive Francesco Sforza and his armies from the Papal Marches. During the fall and winter of 1446 he had done just this, and thereby for the moment helped to secure his own realm as well as Eugenius's. Alfonso was now ready to negotiate a more general peace with Francesco's allies, the Venetians and the Florentines. Even the bellicose pope was happy with the prospect of an end to the fighting, and raised the hope of a *pax italiana*. Eugenius even urged Alfonso to get on with the settlement and sent Alfonso de Covarruvias, apostolic prothonotary, to Naples to ask the king to send ambassadors north to Siena to treat with the enemy. The pope, and more particularly Cardinal Trevisan, who had been Alfonso's military ally during the winter campaigns, thus now saw Naples as the source of peace. This is precisely the theme of the Boymans imagery and of Panormita's lines, and it would explain Trevisan's gift to Alfonso of designs for a Parthenope statue. Covarruvias arrived in Naples at the end of March 1446, and it could even have been for a masque of peace honoring his visit that the Castel Capuano scaenae frons was first put to use.[27] Unfortunately the *cedole di tesoreria* from 31 December 1444 to the end of August 1446 have always been missing, so there are no records of court expenditures for such an event.[28] Nonetheless the foregoing, I think, is a likely identification for the Boymans arch, and I would emphasize that, as a masque structure, the pavilion would almost certainly have involved the mingling of actors and courtiers with statuary. In this respect it is a particularly crucial forebear of the Castel Nuovo Arch.

PISANELLO The Boymans drawing has been linked to Pisanello,[29] who arrived in Naples in 1449.[30] That is too late for him to have designed or painted the Castel Capuano arch, but one notes that he had intended to go to Naples as early as about 1444, though he was not in the end able to do so.[31] Possibly in 1446 he sent instead an assistant, who made the Boymans design.[32] The artist's combination of International Gothic in painting and Roman revivalism in medallic sculpture would have appealed to Alfonso. Indeed, in the fresco of Saint George and the princess of 1433–38, in Sant'Anastasia, Verona, a diminutive, fully armed knight rides out toward us on an immense charger whose heavy body, solid harness, and slit nostrils are all again present in the Boymans artist's conception. Besides this, as noted earlier, there are sketches in the Codex Vallardi corresponding to details of the Boymans design, and this same sketchbook also contains drawings by Pisanello.[33] The upper cresting in the pavilion has been likened to the tall, spongy finials and lucarnes on folio 20, and the twisted columns to those on folio 216. There are also correspondences between the Boymans cornices and other drawings in the Paris collection.[34] In this context, and considering Pisanello's origins, the Arca of Can Grande I, Santa Maria Antica, Verona, comes to mind as well.

When Pisanello finally arrived in Naples he was assigned an income of 400 ducats a year, as we know from a *privilegium* dated 14 February 1449.[35] While he is praised as being one of the "viros ingenio excultoque preditos" that a ruler should have about him, and particularly acclaimed as a painter and sculptor in bronze, he is given no specific duties. He is, however, expected to produce sculptural "monumenta insignia" that will transmit Alfonso's fame and qualities to the future. Obviously great things were planned. The author of this document could hardly have been thinking only of the medals that Pisanello actually did make in Naples, or of such transient things as theatrical pavilions. I believe that what he had in mind was the transformation and removal to Castel Nuovo of the cathedral arch.

While we do not know what Pisanello planned for this arch, there is evidence that it would have been very different from what we see in the Boymans drawing. This evidence lies in the famous medals Pisanello made for members of the Aragonese court in the late 1440s, especially the one inscribed LIBERALITAS AUGUSTA, dated 1448 (*figs. 19, 20*). First, the heraldic setting, more normal hitherto in Alfonso's portrait iconography, has been bypassed. Instead of heraldry, on the king's helmet is the image of a sun shining on an open book inscribed VIR SAPIENS DOMINABITUR ASTRIS. The reference, of course, is to Alfonso's device of the open book, but the idea has been classicized. The inscription is in Roman majuscule. The sitter's head is solid and noble. The obverse of the medal is even more classical: a mighty eagle perches on a tree in the upper center, while below him the limp body of a wounded animal lies dead.[36] This design seems to be derived from an antique Agrigentine coin-type (*fig. 21*), but the eagle (with captive hare) is also a Hohenstaufen symbol, and stands for the Kingdom of Sicily as well.[37] Behind the eagle is a barren natural amphitheater. Below the main scene, almost like an audience, three lesser birds and a fourth, younger and smaller still, look on. Above is the motto LIBERALITAS AUGUSTA. *Liberalitas,* one of the prime moral virtues of the Renaissance, the attribute of princes, and even an economic and social policy, meant the intelligent and appropriate rewarding of one's relatives, clients, and allies, and the wise distribution of power. Its symbol was the eagle, which shares its prey with other birds. For Pontano, who wrote an essay on the subject, one great instance of Liberalitas was the occasion in 1435, mentioned above, when Filippo Maria Visconti gave Alfonso his freedom during the latter's imprisonment in Milan. Similarly Filarete explains the eagle in his nest as an omen of fertility for the city of Sforzinda.[38]

In my opinion Pisanello's medal refers to a similar act of generosity on the part of Alfonso: his policy of distributing parts of his empire among members of his family.[39] We have noted that Henry was made King of Navarre (and Infante of Aragon); that Giovanni was from 1432 Viceroy of Sicily, and that Pietro, the third brother, who died in 1438, had been governor of Naples between 1423 and 1433 while Alfonso was out of Italy. To this we must add that in 1443 Ferrante had been designated heir to the Italian mainland kingdom, and in 1448—the year commemorated in the medal—he was made Duke of Calabria, the official heir apparent of Naples. Under my interpretation Alfonso is the central eagle, conqueror of an empire (the dead prey), who is now liberally offering this spoil to his three brothers and his son—Ferrante being the smaller of the four watching birds. The scene would also imply that Alfonso was a Hohenstaufen successor. It would even constitute a sort of heroic reissue of an antique coin type. More important, Pisanello's medal would reflect, perhaps even announce, the king's post-1448 policy of concentrating on his own personal rule in South Italy. It would present the new policy, finally, in a new artistic guise: as a direct

revival of antiquity. Far from being the designer of the polyglot Boymans pavilion, Pisanello's role in Naples was to create the earliest completely classicizing "Roman" work of art
commissioned by Alfonso.[40]

THE BRANCACCI AND CARACCIOLO TOMBS   Alfonso's celebration of Romanness and Italianism in the LIBERALITAS medal may have been his own first use of a pure
and exclusive classical language, but there were already in his capital two outstandingly
famous tombs more or less in the new style. The first of them is early, that of Cardinal Rinaldo
Brancacci in the family chapel of Sant'Angelo a Nilo (fig. 22). The work of Donatello and
Michelozzo (mainly Michelozzo), this tomb was carved in their shop in Pisa and dates from
1427–30. Thus it is coeval with the tomb of Ladislas.[41]

The Brancacci tomb consists of a single elegant arch rising from narrow Composite
columns with stopped flutes into an upper arch paralleling the porch of the Pazzi Chapel.
In arranging his figural population Michelozzo (if he was, as I assume, the designer) created
a far greater dramatic sense than is present in the tomb of Ladislas. Where the latter seems
to have sprung from the heads and bodies of its bearers, here the caryatids actually carry
the sarcophagus on their shoulders. The arch no longer enshrines them, they stand freely
within it and seem to move through it.

The relief on the front of the sarcophagus focuses this effect of dramatic anticipation. It
represents the prototype of the Christian soul's heavenward journey: the Assumption of the
Virgin. Probably Donatello's only contribution, the relief summarizes the meaning of
Michelozzo's vertical progression behind it, making the sarcophagus less the repository of
mortality than a vehicle of spiritual progress, the theater of divine action. Donatello's Assumption constitutes a possible prototype for the two lateral reliefs in the Aragonese Arch,
which also embody the idea of a heavenly ascent from a saracophagus.

In addition to this horizontal, naturalistic procession of sarcophagus and bearers there
is a vertical progression—a far more dramatic one than that of Ladislas's tomb. We anticipate
the momentary fall of the curtains, which I think stand for mortal life, when the angels will
have let them close in front of the effigy; and it is only during this moment, when the curtains
are raised, that we see beyond the angel of death to the more remote machinery of salvation,
where the Virgin is accompanied by the infant Christ and by praying saints. The goal of the
upward procession is then presented to us in the tympanum, where a Byzantine and sacerdo-
tal God blesses in his flame-rimmed tabernacle.

The stylistic juxtapositions that express similar ideas in Ladislas's tomb are here replaced
by dramatic juxtapositions: the confrontation between the withered, naturalistic face of the
cardinal and the angel's countenance, full of noble, animated grief, is an example. Here and
elsewhere relationships are established between individuals. As will be the case with the
Arch of Alfonso, the Brancacci tomb is concerned with a precise moment, with definite
persons, and with a specific relationship to the viewer.

A second Florentine tomb in Naples takes us forward to Alfonso's actual reign (*fig. 23*). This is the monument to Gianni Caracciolo in the octagonal chapel that is entered through the lower opening of the tomb of Ladislas in San Giovanni a Carbonara.[42] The tomb is a kind of inner pendant to an outer royal gate, possibly executed by one of the artists involved in that gate, and it is thus again comparable to the arches of Alfonso and Ferrante in the Castel Nuovo. The date is not 1433, as in the inscription, but 1441.[43] Like the tomb of Ladislas this may include work by Andrea da Firenze. It stands on immense Gothic pedestals that could bear the weight of the nave piers of a church. From these rise guardian atlantes, three bright-eyed warriors in Roman armor. The middle one is bearded, holding a club, and is perhaps Hercules. A Herculean reference may also be intended in the right-hand figure with his decapitated monster—the hydra's body?—and axe. The sarcophagus is treated as a kind of attic with projecting corner niches. In the center, floating angels present a wreath with a rampant lion in it, this scene being flanked by standing warriors. In the outer, projecting niches, are the crowned Madonna and Child on the left and, on the right, a thurifer. Above is an inscribed pedestal for the statue of the tomb's inhabitant. Gianni himself is flanked by a pair of heraldic lions in crested helmets (*mascherati*), gazing up at him. Piers of superimposed niches rise at the four corners of this space, martyrs in the lower pair and Annunciation figures above them. The piers culminate in feathery flame; but it may be that originally an arch or canopy was intended to form an upper chamber. Valla's inscription, classical in style and without Christian reference, supports the Herculean allusions of the statuary below. Gianni says in the inscription: NIL MIHI NI TITULUS SUMMO DE CULMINE DERAT. He also has a pagan and classical air, though he appears in modern surcoat and armor.

The small relief thrust forward from the sarcophagus, the advancing caryatids, and the use of classical moldings all probably derive from the Brancacci tomb. The niched piers, the style of the classical figures, and the idea of the effigy's being resurrected and appearing as a warrior, seem to have been adapted from the adjacent tomb of Ladislas. The rigid military formalism of this result, its sense of watchful confrontation, and its Herculean imagery all serve to bring the tomb close in spirit to Alfonso's Arch.

It is clear that a current of antiquarian classicism ran side by side with the Gothic current in Naples in the years preceding the construction of the Arch. To match the Christian-medieval triumph and the Angevin precedents in art and patronage, there were the Virgilian horse, Parthenope, and the tombs of Rainaldo Brancacci and Gianni Caracciolo. In the Boymans pavilion of 1446 the two currents reached equilibrium. Then, in 1448, when Pisanello created his much more purely antique statement of Alfonso's "Neapolitan" policy, classicism became dominant. It was from this classicism, and from earlier classical precedents in the Brancacci and Caracciolo tombs, that the definitive conception of the Aragonese Arch was achieved.

Chapter 4: THE LOWER ARCH, 1453–1457, 1465

ORE CLASSICISM   In the years following the events of the last chapter there were further signs of Roman revivalism in Alfonso's court. One was the king's collection of Roman coins and medals, a collection that would, of course, have complemented his patronage of Pisanello. Alfonso is said to have kept antique portraits of Caesar in an ivory chest, like relics.[1] Eileen Driscoll has claimed that the king saw himself as a latter-day Trajan, and she has identified the left-hand pedestal profile on the Arch as a portrait of that emperor (*fig. 42*).[2] In 1458 Alfonso did in fact erect busts of Trajan and Hadrian, two emperors of Spanish birth, on the newel posts of the courtyard stairs.[3]

Another indicator of the king's interest in things Roman is Panormita's famous statement that Alfonso used Vitruvius as a bible for reconstructing the Castel Nuovo;[4] and undeniably the diamond-cut masonry on one of the tower scarps and even the round towers themselves are the sort of thing the Roman author advised.[5] Alfonso may even have intended the Largo del Castello as a kind of forum. Vitruvius says that in seaports these should be near the harbor (*De Architectura* 1. 7), and in October 1450 Alfonso was planning to line this square with colonnaded buildings,[6] which would have given it a Roman look. Even the idea of the triumphal-arch vestibule itself may be a realization of Vitruvius's prescription for "vestibula regalia" as the entrances to princely houses (*De Arch.* 6. 5). Nor is there any difficulty in imagining that Alfonso saw the Arch's two-story elevation as correctly Roman. In connection with the Boymans drawing I mentioned a number of antique two-story gates that could have been drawn on as models, and most of those examples apply equally well here. Many ancient gates, in fact, were set between round towers; the Porta Romana at Capua is a good example. I have found nothing in Vitruvius to imply that a two-story format is actually improper.[7]

At the same time, *pace* Bernich and Driscoll, there does seem to have been little direct influence from Alberti in Alfonso's Romanism. So far as I know, there was no copy of the *De re aedificatoria* in the Aragonese library.[8] In speaking of triumphal arches, furthermore, Alberti prescribes a form quite different from that adopted at Naples: an arch one story high and based on that of Constantine. He adds that ancient triumphal arches were built into the walls of cities (rather than being palace entrances), and that they became freestanding monuments only when the city walls were moved outward (*De re aedificatoria* 8. 6). In contrast to this, Alfonso's arch was swallowed rather than isolated by the outward expansion of the Castel Nuovo walls. Above all Alberti emphasized triumphal arches as symbols of military conquest—just the reverse of Il Magnanimo's message of peace and clemency.[9]

Nevertheless there is one aspect of Alfonso's Romanness in these years that may have to do indirectly with Alberti. We noted that in 1442–43 Alfonso had allied himself with the papacy and made friends with Eugenius IV. More particularly, Cardinal Trevisan, who had supplied the Parthenope design, was like Alfonso a builder, and in charge of reconstructing parts of Eugenius's capital. His work on the Ponte Sant'Angelo included two chapels for which in 1451 the cardinal employed the young Paolo Romano; two years later, Paolo became one of the Arch sculptors. By this time Nicholas V was pope, and he is said to have commissioned a grandiose plan from Alberti for rebuilding the Borgo Leonino. There was to be a "porta cum fornice triumphali" flanked by towers forming a gate to the pope's palace. This could well have involved something along the lines of the Castel Nuovo arch. There was also to be a large colonnaded square,[10] a feature we have seen Alfonso was planning in Naples. These suppositions, if well founded, give Alberti a certain background connection with the Arch, if only through Trevisan.

A final "Roman" element at the time was the sculptural style practiced by Paolo Romano, Isaia da Pisa, and other artists in Rome who were called to work on the Arch. Under the domination first of Filarete and then of Giovanni Dalmata, their school had developed a rigidly classical manner, sometimes almost Early Christian in effect. Their style is close to that of the Caracciolo tomb, so it had been introduced in Naples before the arrival of Alfonso's artists. But a similar archaizing "Roman" manner set the prevailing tone of the Arch sculpture.

ONOFRIO DI GIORDANO, PIETRO DA MILANO, FRANCESCO LAURANA   In 1451 Sagrera's tenure as protomagister was interrupted, and he turned his attention exclusively to the Sala dei Baroni. His replacements were Onofrio di Giordano, Pertello de Marino, Coluza di Stasio, and Carolo de Marino, all natives of the Campanian town of Cava dei Tirreni. On 19 April 1451 they signed a contract under which they agreed to finish the Castel Nuovo in thirty months, beginning on the last day of April in that year—that is, the work was to be done by October 1453 (Doc. 5).[11] The budget was 41,000 ducats. This provided for all materials, except that the court was to supply certain decorative marbles, food and drink for the workers, and artillery carriages for transporting stone.

While the walls and towers were to be completed as they had been begun under the Catalans, the Italians were to make the ravelins and ditches in a new manner, according to the court's designs. They also received plans for outer defenses and a barbican, and for the gate towers. These too were to be finished "secondo la nostra divisata per la corte" and linked by a transverse piperno arch.[12] The type of *bastuni* used by Sagrera on the Torre San Giorgio were not to be built. Presumably these variations were in part intended to accommodate the ornamental entrance gate, but the contract's stipulations primarily involve the "modern" lower defenses.

At the same time, however, the new Italian contingent was explicitly exempted from building either the Arch or the "marbles or figures and foliage, or the woodwork of the doors, windows, floor, or seating," in the rest of the castle, which the Catalans continued to carve. Despite Alfonso's increasingly classical taste and his new "Neapolitan" policy, each tribe continued to bring its own style to its job within the whole.

The advent of the Italians meant not only "modern" ravelins but a further element of architectural classicism. Here the main figure is Onofrio di Giordano, one of the *capomaestri* of the 1451 Italian group. He had built for Queen Giovanna, who called him "optimus architectorum," and he later worked in Ragusa (Dubrovnik) as chief architect of the republic. From 1436–42 he reconstructed the Dalmatian city's hydraulic system and was responsible for a number of architectural works. As state architect Onofrio was succeeded by Giorgio da Sebenico and ultimately by Michelozzo, so he was a productive builder in an important succession.[13] Later, under Alfonso, he served in important financial capacities as well as being an architect. Among the extant structures in Dubrovnik that contain his work are the Palazzo dei Rettori (1436 ff.), the domed Fontana d'Onofrio (ca. 1440), and a fountain in the Piazza San Biagio. The arcade of the Palazzo dei Rettori has stubby columns with rich capitals, several of them storiated, by various hands, and the San Biagio fountain is classical in style, with wide steps supporting an octagonal basin composed of panels decorated with sculptured ephebes (*fig. 24*). Rising from the center is a short twisted column above which putti squat, supporting a figured dish with spouting mascheroni.

But in conception, if not in form, the Fontana d'Onofrio is the most significant of Onofrio's structures in Dubrovnik. It is a great polygon on a stepped base articulated with sixteen freestanding Corinthian columns en ressaut. According to report it was originally two stories high, with orders and a full entablature on each, and the dome had a lantern. This would have constituted an almost unheard-of elaborateness for provincial architecture in the early Quattrocento. Unfortunately the fountain is now very different—topped with a small saucer dome on a stepped base dating from 1667. Carlo Ragghianti has suggested that the original fountain is one of the earliest central-plan structures of the Renaissance derived from a Roman prototype, and he boldly adds that it may have influenced Alberti's planned rotunda for the Tempio Malatestiano in Rimini.[14] In any case, a possible prototype for the Dubrovnik fountain is a mausoleum at Capua Vecchia, of which Giuliano da Sangallo has recorded the main features in his Vatican *Libro* (fol. 8r). This was round rather than polygonal and possessed a full entablature like the fountain, but it had no exterior dome, only a stepped-back pilastered second story covered with a conical roof. A similar structure in the countryside near Naples was the mausoleum at Gaeta, also recorded in Sangallo's book (fol. 7v). Thus when Onofrio appeared in Naples in 1451, he was (so far as we know) the first person there who could be called a Renaissance architect, in the sense in that he had designed an adaptation from the antique containing classical orders.

In my opinion it was Onofrio among the new protomagistri who was in charge of preparing the two-towered piperno matrix for the lower arch. Avena notes that this part of the monument, in its foundations and tufa backing, is excellently and solidly built (in contrast to the upper half, which is later).[15] Onofrio, the most distinguished architect on the site, was like Pisanello before him one of the king's familiars. And he no doubt also had a say in the design of the Arch. With his background he would never have approved of a repetition of the thin Gothic shapes of the Boymans arch. His desire would have been for another piece of Roman classicism adapted from some existing antiquity.

And, whatever Onofrio's actual role, that was the chosen course. Where Dalmatia had been given a Neapolitan antiquity, Naples was given a Dalmatian one: the famous Augustan arch at Pula in Istria.[16] Like the Dubrovnik fountain, this too boasted Roman Corinthian columns en ressaut. The appearances of such columns in Dubrovnik and Naples are among the earliest in any Renaissance building (and the Dubrovnik specimens are awfully medieval-looking). The Castel Nuovo Arch also carries a full complement of dolphins, genietti, mascheroni, and so forth—such as had been lavished on Onofrio's smaller fountain in Dubrovnik.

The sculptor in charge of this new arch in Naples had also been working in Dubrovnik, and for that very parish of San Biagio that had built the smaller fountain. In all probability, therefore, he had been one of Onofrio's assistants. Indeed this sculptor, Pietro da Milano,[17] had been summoned from Dubrovnik by Alfonso and told to bring his family and effects with him to Naples just after Onofrio and the Neapolitan masters took over (Docs. 6a, 6b, 8). After a delay and a second summons he arrived; and in July 1453, along with a young, previously unheard-of sculptor also from Dalmatia, Francesco Laurana; and with Paolo Romano and Pere Joan, the two travelers were paid 346-odd ducats for work done through May of that year on the "arch di triumph" (Doc. 9). This is the first hint of a separate contract for the Arch to come to light. There were thirty-three assistants involved. Some of the work perhaps consisted of transporting and rough-cutting the marble for the lower half of the entrance. It is probable that this was stone originally delivered for the arcivescovado arch of 1443; and it is at least possible that, as Summonte says, Pietro da Milano had been involved with that original monument and was now returning after ten years to continue work at the new location.[18]

In Naples Pietro became one of the leaders of the local school of classical "Roman" sculptors that dominated Neapolitan tomb manufacture for the rest of the century.[19] His penchant for heavy, proto-High Renaissance architecture appears in the inner arch (*fig. 51*). His figures, by contrast, tend to be wispy, graceful, nervously immobile, like the putto in figure 24, while his heads are curious weighted knobs (*fig. 54*). Pietro may well have been, with Onofrio Giordano, responsible for the choice of the arch at Pula as a model, and also for Spalato-like qualities we will see in the Arch's details.

Francesco Laurana probably came over as Pietro's assistant. While Pietro was married, had a family, and was in fact famous—Alfonso mentions his "known skill" (Doc. 8)—Laurana appears here in his first documented artistic role. But he too, on the Dalmatian coast, would have absorbed the lessons of Giorgio da Sebenico, and in his later work he, like Pietro, could alternate between heavy classicism and a limp, sweetish version of the International Style. Like Pietro too he divided his activities between various parts of the Aragonese–Angevin world, traveling north to Provence and south to Sicily, and stopping off at Naples.

The third sculptor of 1453, Paolo Romano, was also young and without much reputation. He had worked for Trevisan, and I presume he later became one of that clerical condottiere's favorite artists, since in 1467 he made his tomb. In 1453, besides working on the Ponte Sant'Angelo chapels, he had made windows for the old Senatorial Palace on the Campidoglio.

The fourth sculptor, Pere Joan, was a man of sixty or so with a long record of achievement behind him. He had created sculptures for the Casa del Consejo Municipal, Barcelona, including the Saint George on the courtyard balcony (1415–18), and had begun an impressive reredos for the High Altar at Tarragona, on which he worked from 1426 until 1436. His also is the alabaster reredos of the cathedral at Saragossa (1441–45). Pere Joan could create a teeming graceful swarm of figures, clad in almost Art Nouveau robes and fronds (*fig. 25*). The womens' heads are pure ovals, the men's, grotesque and bulldog-jawed. In Naples Pere Joan and his assistants apparently produced many works in this outré style; but now only disappointing fragments remain, for example, the two roundels with antique profile heads over the Porta del Trionfo in the Sala dei Baroni. The only piece of figure sculpture on the Arch that seems to be theirs is the rather feline Saint Michael (*fig. 112*). Pere Joan is mentioned as "mestre de fer ymatges" for the whole of the Castel Nuovo (7 October 1453);[20] but by this time his name had completely disappeared from the documents for the Arch proper.

In 1453, then, this was the disposition of talents: Onofrio di Giordano with Pietro da Milano set the new conception of a bona fide classical copy for the lower arch. Pietro then carried out the work, assisted by Laurana and Paolo Romano. In addition there was an experienced sculptor from Catalonia in charge of figure carving for the whole of the Castel Nuovo, and he worked with these three during the early stage before the Arch shop was fully independent.

Immediately subsequent documents and sources for work on the lower arch are lacking. But two years later, on 28 July 1455, an anonymous observer in Naples wrote to Francesco Maria Visconti that "[Alfonso] is making a sculptural marble arch for the portal, worked in the antique manner, with sumptuous and marvelous architecture. The foundations are already laid, and the marble workers are working with eagerness and special diligence" (Doc. 11). This supports our assumption that the emphasis so far was on architecture, while the sculptors' role was primarily to produce antique ornament. And Fazio, also writing in the mid-1450s, says that Alfonso "built an impressive triumphal arch from whitest marble," and (elsewhere) that he "restored Castel Nuovo with a triumphal arch of magnificent structure and workmanship, second to nothing in the world" (Docs. 12, 13). Shortly after this, on 4 December 1456, there was an earthquake, and the king was relieved to know that the two chief works then in hand at the Castel Nuovo, the Sala dei Baroni and the Arch, were unharmed.[21] By this time, therefore, the Arch had been to a considerable extent erected. This is confirmed in turn by a ruined relief in the Sala dei Baroni, completed about 1456, which showed the lower half of the Arch, without the triumph frieze, in place between the two portal towers.[22]

The choice of the arch at Pula (*fig. 26*) had several possible motives. First, like so many Roman arches in their Quattrocento state, it functioned as a portal. At the same time, with its paired columns en ressaut, its single-arched opening, and its tall plinths, it was not unlike the upper arch in the Boymans drawing. It therefore fitted in with that most recent contribution to the Neapolitan tradition of two-story pavilions. Finally, the arch at Pula had been joined to a medieval inner gateway. Thus it possessed the inner room or vestibule we also see in the Castel Nuovo.[23] But modifications were necessary to adapt the Pula arch to its new setting: the level of the archway itself had to be dropped to accommodate the enormous Aragonese shield and griffins, the frieze had to be heightened for the long inscription, and the arch itself was jacked up on sub-pedestals to make it higher.

THE ARCHITECTURE AND THE RELIEFS   As an antique trophy, the lower arch symbolizes preparation for the kingship of Naples; it is a vestibule not only to the Castel Nuovo but to the upper arch (*fig. 27*). A pair of stepped piperno plinths flank the opening, from which rise a fillet, then an inverted corona (as in the Boymans arch), and then two superimposed friezes. These are separated at the bottom by a corona, in the middle by a torus, and at the top by another corona. From this almost over-ample supporting complex rise the slender, fluted Corinthian columns, their shafts rising approximately 9½ diameters from double-torused bases. Above, en ressaut, the order continues with a triple fascia as architrave, a sculptured frieze, and a full modillioned cornice. The capitals are apparently adapted from a model in San Lorenzo fuori le Mura, Rome (*figs. 28, 29*)[24] rather than from the Pula arch (*fig. 30*). The plane behind the columns contains the actual opening. The pedestals jog around and into this opening, but the upper pedestal frieze is interrupted by the lower of the two superimposed pilaster panels supporting the molded archivolt. These panels are carved with foliage arabesques by four different hands, the upper pair being thicker and deeper, the lower more dainty, and that on the left consisting of broad, flat leafage and thong-like stems. The spandrel griffins (*fig. 31*), which may relate to a detail from the Codex Vallardi (fol. 6; *fig. 32*), the cornucopias, and the arms of Aragon—the latter signed with Alfonso's crown—are carved with ebullient force.

The ideals of the Order of the Lily are symbolized not only in these griffins but throughout the Arch. The amphorae that appear on the outer pedestal frieze (*fig. 40*) probably refer to it, as do the similar vessels filled with lilies held by one of the Victories on the upper arch (*figs. 89, 91*) and the upper griffins (*fig. 93*). In the triumph frieze Alfonso wears the Order's necklace (*fig. 75*).[25]

The narrative reliefs on the lower arch front are Herculean in subject-matter. On the front of the left-hand ressaut, between the loops of the putti-borne garlands, more putti carry a sacred fire, while a female centaur on the right helps a putto mounted on her back to carry a sail (*fig. 33*). On the return two cloaked figures appear on the left, one supporting the other, who is fainting or dying. To their right a bearded man, again with his cloak flying behind him, approaches with an infant in his right arm. This, I believe, is the incident when Hercules's wife Deianira confronts her father, Oeneus, after Hercules has killed one of Oeneus's relatives. The bearded man on the right would be Hercules with his and Deianira's son, Hyllus, about to flee with Deianira as a result of the crime.

In the center of the arch, on the neck of the left-hand cornucopia, are Hercules and Deianira again, with Chiron—a later scene from the story of Hercules' travels. On the right-hand cornucopia is a more abstract incident: a group of putti in a bacchic procession. Next, on the front of the right-hand ressaut, is another procession, of music-making putti. The return on this side is decorated with the seated, bearded figure of a man, his cloak flying back from his body, who reaches after a woman to his right, with her back to us. She grasps a club as she seeks to escape. This is the next episode in the tale, Hercules lusting after Phaedra.[26] In the central part of the main frieze occurs still another processional or travel motif: as in the arch at Pula, little wagons are being drawn by pairs of putti-driven horses, dashing toward each other on either side of the inscription. In sum, the outer plane of small-scale ornamental sculpture on the lower arch introduces the twin themes of Alfonso's knightly virtues and a Herculean voyage.[27]

The chief works of sculpture in the lower arch are the two inner lateral reliefs (*figs. 35, 37*). Functionally they are not unlike the rectangular central panels on the sarcophagi of the Brancacci and Caracciolo tombs, but their basic derivation is of course Roman, for instance from the similarly placed reliefs on the arches of Titus and Constantine in Rome, and of Trajan at Benevento. The inner western Trajanic relief from the Arch of Constantine, now inscribed FUNDATORI QUIETIS, bears a close compositional relationship (*fig. 36*). The emperor, who would of course have been identified as Constantine in Alfonso's day, stands on the left, flanked by allegorical assistants, while in the background his troops are arrayed at a higher level.[28] A floating allegorical figure (probably Roma or Virtus), dressed in thick supple draperies, places a crown on the emperor's head. He stands gracefully and freely as he turns to an Amazon on his left, as with the confidence of one who knows that justice and victory go hand in hand.

Something similar could be said of the Arch's inner reliefs.[29] On each side a central hero stands in a pose reminiscent of that of the emperor. In both cases the hero is flanked by a pair of attendants carrying attributes or symbols. In the left-hand relief (*fig. 35*), the right-hand knight is quite close in pose to the Roma or Virtus. The troops in the background, facing at right-angles to the main group and disposed in ranks of profiles, as well as the arrangement of spears above, may equally derive from the Roman work. One can add, as a literary parallel, that in Porcellio's *Parthenope capta* (fol. 190, 1.3), the king is given this same epithet, *fundator quietis.*

However, as in the LIBERALITAS medal, this Roman background is enlivened with what might be called "naturalistic" heraldry—heraldic symbols in an existentially rationalized setting. Just as, in the medal, the eagle and wounded prey have been removed from their blazons and placed in a landscape, so here Alfonso's heritage is expressed not by complex bearings on a single shield but by warriors each carrying a shield that is differently inscribed. In the right-hand relief (*figs. 39, 41*) the main figure rests his arm on a shield bearing the cross of Calabria. Just behind him, to the right, stands a man with an Aragonese shield. Further right is another youth grasping a shield with Aragon per saltire in chief and base, and in the flanks an eagle displayed sable: the arms of the Aragonese Kingdom of Sicily. In the opposite relief (*figs. 35, 38*), the figure on the far left of the observer carries a *schiacciato* shield on which a winged figure in a streaming chlamydon carries a wreath enclosing the Aragonese arms. Next to him is a man, now headless, who has a shield with Sicily per saltire with Aragon, and a scene of Daphne turning into a laurel tree.

The central figure in the right-hand relief resembles Alfonso, with his beaked nose and battered mien (*fig. 39*). The attendant on his right, his head wreathed in a garland of camellias, and holding an Aragonese shield, would symbolize Alfonso's Spanish paternity, and the one even farther to the right would represent Aragonese rule in Italy, that is, the Kingdom of Sicily (*fig. 40*).

In the other relief, on the left, the central figure is the young Ferrante, whose massive, pendulous face is easily recognizable (*figs. 37, 38*). The event must have to do with his having been acclaimed heir on 26 February 1443.[30] Here too the Aragonese–Sicilian theme appears, not only in the two shields but on the surcoat of the elderly man on the far left, which bears a siege perilous: this individual could in fact be Ferdinand I of Aragon, Ferrante's namesake and the forebear most closely identified with the device. But the use of the siege perilous would also refer to Ferrante's right—in some dispute due to his bastard status—to succeed his father on the throne of Naples. The bearded men in both scenes may be Spaniards, and if so they and the black man in the left-hand panel, just to the right of Ferrante, could allude to Naples's current system of alliances.[31] In any case, as in the LIBERALITAS medal, the lower arch, within an imperial context, presents Ferrante as Alfonso's successor in the kingdom of Naples. And it does so, again like the medal, by means of antique borrowings in which heraldic symbols are naturalistically presented.

In their doll-like proportions and military stiffness the figures in both scenes are related to the sculpture of the tomb of Gianni Caracciolo (*fig. 23*). The heavy, rotund armor with its thick joints, the fixity of gaze, and the littleness and solidity of the figures, are all to the point. But more important is the carryover of Herculean emblems. In the right-hand relief is a club-bearer (like the right-hand atlante on the Caracciolo tomb) and at the extreme ends a man with a chained lion[32] and another man with a dog. The lion could be the one slain by Hercules on Mount Cithaeron to free Thebes, and the dog either Orthros or Cerberus, the dog that Hercules bound. A muzzled dog, possibly again Cerberus, also appears at Ferrante's feet in the opposite relief, while his attendant, in Herculean fashion, wears a lion's head on his helmet.[33]

Hercules is connected, in Neapolitan mythology, with an aspect of Parthenope not yet discussed—not with Eumelos's daughter the virgin queen but with the siren Parthenope, Ulysses' temptress. In this story Parthenope is the daughter of the horned river god Acheloos. Hercules fought Acheloos, who during the fight transformed himself into various kinds of sea-snakes and monsters. Eventually the hero was able to break off the river god's horns, which then turned into cornucopias. Parthenope and her sisters Ligea and Leucosia were born of the blood that flowed.[34] Afterward, in place of his horns, Acheloos grew a pair of asses' ears. Hercules thus established the atmosphere of abundance in which it was possible to build Naples. Indirectly he brought Parthenope into the world. According to G. A. Summonte he actually refounded the city, so that his voyage from Calydon to Naples (like Aeneas's voyage from Troy to Rome) was that of a predestined city-builder.[35] All of this, of course, unites the lower reliefs to the outer figural reliefs of Hercules' voyage from Calydon, giving it a climax; and it also anticipates the triumph frieze. Hercules, that is, is the mythical ancestor and forerunner of the Aragonese voyager who appeared in 1442. Meanwhile, a procession entering the Castel Nuovo would be watched by spectators comprising the king's own *regale prosapia*, the *fundatores quietis* of Parthenope's kingdom.

Unlike their Roman prototype, the Arch scenes take place in interiors. On the right is the inside of a chamber with three arched openings along the back and one on each side, and a coffered ceiling. Two exiguous columns screen the front. On the other side the room has only one arch, at the back, and flat-headed openings along the sides. Putti playfully blow trumpets and display Aragonese shields in little windows left and right, while the arms of Aragon occupy a large central hexagonal panel in the ceiling. Both reliefs, as noted in the first chapter, are miniatures rather than perspectives. Yet they do continue the arch's space, anticipating the real volume of the vestibule directly ahead. Within this real volume, in turn, above the inner portal, will appear in 1465 a third miniature scene continuing the tableaux of the two lateral panels: Ferrante's coronation. This, as we shall see, was the culmination of the whole interior (*figs. 53, 54*).

The decoration in which the lateral reliefs are set elaborates the theme of the struggle between Hercules and Acheloos. On the left, below, putti display thick garlands of nuts, vegetables, and flowers, while a head of the vanquished Acheloos, with his asses' ears (*fig. 43*), and a crude winged female head, possibly Medusa, possibly Parthenope, stare forth.[36] Above them a heavy torus carved with oak leaves and acorns forms a spongy support for Hercules-Ferrante and his entourage. In a thin horizontal strip across the top, and matching the dainty colonnettes of the sides, is a recessed frieze in which gamboling *genietti* tumble

and pipe music (*fig. 35*). They are composed into three groups divided by the four Aragonese symbols, the knot, the siege perilous, the open book, and (now destroyed) the hill of
diamonds. Above this, in turn, is a wider frieze in which at either end river mouths (perhaps
again referring to Acheloos) loose a flow of water filled with sea monsters ridden by putti
or naiads. These monsters may reflect the forms taken by Acheloos in his struggle with
Hercules. On the left is a Proteus-triton with a lion's head, and then a putto on a two-headed
dolphin. In the center a lion's mask gushes with more water, and to the right are a putto
riding a goat-headed triton, and another bearded triton, with lyre, who is bestridden by a
nude woman. Possibly she is again the siren Parthenope.[37] Some of these creatures could
also refer to the islands of the Bay of Naples, which, like those at the mouth of the River
Acheloos in Greece, calm the waves; the goat-headed triton would be Capri. On the other
hand the lyre-player and his companion, as Riccardo Filangieri suggests, may be Phorcys and
Keto, who calm the waves with music.[38] The figures recall drawings on a sheet now in the
Boymans Museum (I-523; *fig. 34*). On the outer left-hand pedestal, above, is a medallion
of Caesar (*fig. 42*).[39] Below this, the head and torso of the infant Hercules, who is over-
powering two snakes, emerge from acanthus leaves.

On the opposite side the outer plinth begins with the amphorae of the lower panel.[40]
Then come the putti bearing a vegetable garland, with the head of a river god on the return.
Beneath the main relief in the semicircles formed by garlands, are (on the left) a chariot-
borne putto driving a pair of sea-monsters (*fig. 45*) and (on the right) an infant triton
with bow and arrow who heads toward the snakes, carrying a nereid on his back (*fig. 44*).
These may be episodes in the struggle between Hercules and Acheloos. Again, too, the details are adapted from sarcophagi, and the "lid" above the relief shows more river mouths
and sporting dolphins ridden by genietti who dive beneath the waves to the music of tibia
and syrinx. Thus one might say that the historical figures of Alfonso and Ferrante rise as
sons of Hercules and of Aragon and Sicily, from a lower layer of myth. This layer takes the
form of sarcophagi whose lids are raised to permit the human inhabitants' resurrection.

Above the zone formed by these scenes, on either side, are two pairs of empty niches
(*fig. 46*) divided by pilasters with stopped flutes and elaborate capitals. I assume they were
once filled, or intended to be filled, with Virtues, perhaps the same four—Prudence, Justice,
Temperance, and Largitas—that seem to have decorated the equestrian portrait of Alfonso
in the Castel Capuano. Similar statues now stand in colossal form at the summit of the
Arch (*fig. 87*). Above the niches is the vault, divided into octagonal coffers that display,
alternately, six-winged seraphim and stylized flowers and fruit, set into acanthus rosettes.
In the center two, putti hold the arms of Calabria (*fig. 47*), signed with a crown and surrounded by the four family symbols. The vault thus becomes a stone lattice through which
symbols of abundance are pressed.[41] It rounds off the upward procession from myth, through
history and then abstract virtue, to a heaven climaxing with the shield of Calabria, whose
dukedom was the route to the throne.

THE INNER ARCH   The inner arch was executed in 1465[42] by Pietro da Milano and Laurana. It is a monument not to Alfonso I but to Ferrante. The first payment from Ferrante to "Mestre Pere Marmoraro en accoriment de son salari," 50 ducats, appears for 8 June 1465. In the following months Pietro received 300 ducats more. The work lasted through 30 September 1465 (Docs. 21, 22, 23, 25–31).

Psychologically, in proceeding from the outer to the inner arch we go from antiquity to the Renaissance. Otherwise, too, there is considerable stylistic contrast, from the lean and elegant to the broad and chunky. And yet this second arch is also the complement of the outer, forming its inner wall. At the bottom two stubby Composite columns, with shafts only about six diameters high, flank a rather low, wide arch. The columns rise through a full entablature to a heavy cornice. The entablature is broken in the center to allow for a rectangular panel containing two large, smiling putti grasping an inclined shield, and still containing remnants of its bearings: the arms of Aragon quartered with those of the Durazzo (*fig. 52*), a further attempt to link Ferrante with his predecessors on the throne of Sicily.

Above this is a second, much smaller arch flanked by exceedingly narrow niches (*fig. 48*), the arch being carved in forced perspective with a coffered vault (*fig. 51*). In it are the remains of a scene of procession and coronation in which Ferrante sat between two bishops who placed the crown on his head (*figs. 53, 54, 55*).[43] Courtiers are gathered on either side. Above, in the lunette, two grotesque heads peer down as in the left-hand lateral relief in the outer arch. Above this in turn is a triangular pediment topped with a small drum and dome. The inner arch may even have been intended as forced perspective, that is to be seen as a distant repetition of the outer structure. Such an effect is still achieved, from a distance, and when the vestibule has enough light in it.

But if the inner arch is a repetition it is also a simplification. There is, for example, only one inscription beneath the coronation relief: SUCCESSI REGNO PATRIO CUNCTISQUE PRO-BATUS / ET TRABEAM ET REGNI SACRUM DIADEMA RECEPI. (I succeeded to my father's kingdom having been thoroughly tested / and received the robe and holy crown of the realm)[44]—again the idea of preparation. Another simplification is the use of single rather than paired columns, these being engaged and not freestanding. The row of niches has been eliminated, and there has even been a certain telescoping, in that the arms-bearing putti break through the main cornice, as it were carrying further the implied action of the griffins of the outer arch. We might thus think of the inner arch as a kind of synopsis of the other.

Finally, the proportions of some features of the inner gate may be described as Albertian. The wide, abstract membering is significant in this regard, and the broken main entablature could even derive from Sant'Andrea, Mantua, only begun in 1459. At the same time the idea of the arched field for the attic relief could come from such antique prototypes as the so-called Arch of Domitian in Rome, later recorded by Giuliano da Sangallo (*fig. 50*). Otherwise the ornament consists mostly of nondescript vegetable spirals, in the spandrels of the lower arch, for example, and elaborate S-volutes, also with vegetation, on the niches above.

Though the capitals are fanciful, bristling with monsters and heads, and decorated with flower-filled amphorae, on the whole the decorative array is limited, and the spare surfaces of the architecture predominate. But if this later structure lacks the poetic elaboration of the outer arch, it does parallel the factuality of the triumph frieze.

THE BRONZE DOORS   Historical fact is again the main emphasis in the bronze doors that complete this inner wall. They are signed by a mysterious artist named Guglielmo Lo Monaco, said to have come from Paris but actually an Umbrian.[45] In six panels (*figs. 57–63*) they celebrate Ferrante's victory over the rebellious barons at Troia, Apulia, on 18 August 1462, a battle which effectively crushed the hopes of Ferrante's Angevin rival, Jean d'Anjou, for the throne. The panels were probably made in 1474–77.[46]

The scenes are each equipped with a Latin distich, and they have been described by Fazio, who was probably the author of the program. The upper left panel (*fig. 58*) shows Ferrante's meeting at Calvi, near Capua, with his great enemy Marino Marzano, Duke of Sessa. It is inscribed: PRINCEPS CUM JACOBO CUM DIOFEBO QUE DOLOSO / UT REGEM PER[I]MANT COLLOQUIUM SIMULANT (The prince with Jacopo and the deceitful Deifobo; they simulate a conference so that the king may be slain). Four horsemen are in colloquy in the foreground, the mushroomy forms of their horses' caparisons matching the nearby trees. Beyond are a tree-rimmed hill and the tall flat towers of Calvi. Next to this (*fig. 59*) is the actual attempt on Ferrante's life, the king defending himself with his sword from Marino while Deifobo and the king's attendant also fight, more compactly, on the right. The background is similar to that in the first panel. The verses read: HOS REX MARTI POTENS ANIMOSIOR HECTORE CLARO / SENSIT UT INSIDIAS ENSE MICANTE FUGAT (The Mars-mighty king, more spirited than famous Hector, probed with his shining blade, that the plot might perish).

The next scene is at the bottom, on the left (*fig. 60*), and shows the Angevin retreat from Accadia, a town on the Gulf of Manfredonia. The verses are: HINC TROJAM VERSUS, MAGNO CONCUSSA TIMORE / CASTRA MOVENT HOSTES NE SUBITO PEREANT (having been struck with terror, the enemy move their camp away, toward Troia, lest they immediately perish). A clamorous crowd in procession winds back and forth across the panel in three loops. Tents are struck, goods are packed up, oxen haul wagons, trumpeters lead the way. By a stroke of irony a later cannonball destroyed the part of the panel depicting the walls of Calvi.

Next to this, on the right (*fig. 61*), we see the subsequent entry into Accadia by the Aragonese. A funnel of soldiers flows into the center background: where before the enemy was seen in a layered procession without receding distance, the Aragonese now appear in perspective. Here the verses read: AQUA DIAM FORTEM CEPIT REX FORTIOR URBEM ANDEGAVOS PELLENS VIRIBUS EXIMIIS (The stronger king took the strong city of Accadia, striking down the Angevins with his excellent troops).

The climactic scenes are in the two middle panels. On the right is the Battle of Troia (*fig. 62*), with the verses: HOSTEM TROJANUS FERDINANDUS VICIT IN ARVIS SICUT POMPEIUM CESAR IN AHACTIS [OECHALIIS] (The Trojan Ferrante conquered the enemy in the field, as Caesar conquered Pompey at Oechalia). Ferrante's square standards punctuate a scene of strife that, no doubt fortuitously, in some ways anticipates Leonardo's *Battle of Anghiari*. In the middle ground, beyond an arched bridge, the Angevins are chased from the picture by orderly ranks of Aragonese. Beyond that, in a sort of coda, three horsemen in unison pursue a refugee to a distant grove.

Finally, on the left, just beneath the first scene, is the siege and surrender of Troia (*fig. 63*), with the lines TROIA DEDIT NOSTRO REQUIEM FINEMQUE LABORI / IN QUA HOSTEM EUDI [FUDI] FORTITER AC PEPULI (Troia gave rest to our side, and an end to the labor, in which place the enemy shed much blood and was routed). Here the Aragonese knights enter the city's pedimented gate while some fighting continues in the foreground.

These scenes are more interesting for their use of kinetic order than for their beauty. The eye's route through the sequence is first a zigzag, then a spiral that ends near the beginning. The first two scenes are cinematic in that they give the impression of moving figures on a static background. The other four can also be seen in this way: first there is a self-enclosed zigzag (the Angevin retreat from Accadia, *fig. 60*), and then a helical motion to the right and upward. Thus the complete action consists of a large funnel of men plunging into the depths of the scene (*fig. 61*), then a widening and swaying of the funnel—almost broken by the bridge (*fig. 62*)—and finally the new equilibrium in the last scene where the last bits of the funnel are swallowed by the gate. The frames of the scenes of continuous pursuit and victory are a focusing device. They thus parallel the use of pavilions in the triumph frieze (*fig. 64*). The effect is a corollary to the sense of voyaging and procession throughout the Arch.

Around the six scenes are wide borders punctuated at the corners with medallions bearing the heraldic images of the dynasty. At the lower left-hand corner of the left-hand valve is a portrait of the artist inscribed GUILLELMUS MONACUS ME FECIT, and on the other valve, in a corresponding corner medallion, is an unknown man with long hair and a round face—possibly Fazio. Formerly, at the top of the doors, there were similar portraits of Ferrante and his first queen, Isabella del Balzo. The foliage decoration winding between these medallions is in the same flat, leathery style as the foliage of the inner arch's marble carving.

In individual composition the panels reflect contemporary manuscript illustrations. The handling of the groups of horsemen and the streams of warriors also owes a clear debt to the two relief panels of about 1456 in the Sala dei Baroni. More generally, of course, the doors are influenced by Ghiberti; or, at least, there is the same desire for landscape depth, figure recession, and dramatic action. One also senses the impact of Filarete's bronze doors for Saint Peter's of 1440–45: there are similarities of composition, for example, in the use of inscriptions, while Gothic and antique rigidities are similarly mixed, and the foliated frames have a scale and function like his. Nonetheless these earlier works all give a self-conscious dignity and individuality to each figure. In typical Florentine fashion they exploit static, stately encounters between individuals, an effect lacking in Guglielmo's scenes, which concentrate not on isolated tableaux but on continuous teeming action. One is not surprised to learn that Guglielmo was an armaments expert.[47] Indeed, the Neapolitan doors are really more "antique" than the others mentioned. They more clearly evoke the columns of Marcus Aurelius and Trajan. They also reflect that habitual Aragonese concern for sculpture that records specific moments of current history. As the main narrative element in the lower part of the inner arch, the doors form a prelude, decked out with epic conventions, to the more ceremonial coronation, detailing the "test" Ferrante was subjected to before he was crowned.

THE ATTRIBUTION OF THE SCULPTURE   Most of the sculpture of the lower part of the Arch of Alfonso (as distinct from that of Ferrante's inner arch), was completed by early 1457. The artists involved were mainly Pietro da Milano, Paolo Romano, and Francesco Laurana. Pere Joan, we have seen, probably worked only briefly with these artists of such different outlook, and Isaia da Pisa and Andrea dell'Aquila, who had recently arrived in Naples, were to concentrate on the next phase of the monument, the triumph frieze. This must be the basis for identifying the sculptural contributors to the lower arch; but here and throughout our study we will not be able to make specific attributions as with Florentine work. The Arch workshop was organized in a Roman fashion, with a large force of semi-anonymous sculptors working rapidly. Each stone was, or could be, the work of more than one artist, and the fact that a given person received payment for certain work does not mean that he performed it all by himself.

Nonetheless some conclusions can be drawn about various hands. The figure style of Pietro da Milano must appear in the coronation relief, since he was in charge of making it. Looking at it we see quite plainly two hands and two hands only: the group on the left (*figs. 53, 55*) is flattened, almost concave, the figures standing on divergent axes. A wrinkled plane of drapery blankets their legs and arms. Their cheeks are high and bony and they have pronounced eye-sockets. The group on the right (*fig. 54*) is different: its members are aligned on vertical axes, and the bodies on their legs are like pods on slender stalks. There are no cross-currents over a continuous surface plane, as in the left-hand group. The heads are round and full, the chins are cupped by the conical necks, the skulls by the hair. (These figures, by the way, are not at all "soulless and phlegmatic" as Valentiner says.)[48] The upper coffered vault, with its thick floral ornament, is in convincing forced perspective. The recessed spaces within which the courtiers stand, on the contrary, have coffers that are mere rhomboids with no illusion of depth.

The left-hand lateral relief (*fig. 35*), though more Donatellesque, could have been partly executed by the author of the right-hand group in the coronation scene. There is the same convincing perspective in the coffers, which are carved with similar floral ornaments. There are even similar little windows. The figures have the same nodding, globular heads and alert, straight bodies. Both groups are therefore likely to be the work of Pietro da Milano.[49] The way Pietro forms the body, with its long torso fitted out with pads of flesh, can also be equated with the weathered panels on the Fontana San Biagio (*fig. 24*).

The other lateral relief, on the right (*fig. 37*), is in a style not unlike that of the left-hand group in the coronation scene (*figs. 53, 55*). There is the same effect of a convex plane covering the bodies, even though considerable individuation is attempted. There are the same divergent axes, the rear figures craning their necks over the shoulders of those in the first rank, and the same ridgy facial features. The ceiling coffers, handled with the same rote perspective as the horizontal ceiling strips in the arch of Ferrante, contain similar papery rosettes. If we glance at a documented relief by Laurana, Christ Carrying the Cross (1479–81), now in St.-Didier, Avignon, we see these characteristics again. The group of women on the left is particularly relevant to the coronation courtiers (*fig. 56*).

The hands of Pietro da Milano and Francesco Laurana are discernible elsewhere in the lower arch. It is possible, for example, that Laurana made the arms-bearing putti for the inner arch (*fig. 52*), for these figures have characteristic lackadaisical stances and grimaces, and are analogous to some of the Avignon figures. But as to the rest of the lower arch, we should allow for other artists. Close inspection shows every sign of a numerous body of carvers, and we have seen that Pietro da Milano, Pere Joan, Paolo Romano, and Francesco Laurana had no less than thirty-three assistants, several of whom could have been figure sculptors.

To sum up: Alfonso's Italian policy of the early 1450s was matched by a turn to the art of Rome, that of the caesars and that of the current popes. The king maintained the tribal administration of the Castel Nuovo shops, but added a group of Italians. One of these new Italian masters, Onofrio di Giordano, an expert in Roman antiquities, probably dictated the basic form of the lower arch. Pietro da Milano (who had assisted Onofrio in Dubrovnik), Francesco Laurana, and Paolo Romano began carving this lower arch in 1453. This part of the monument affirms Ferrante's claim to the throne. It is, to use Vitruvius's phrase, a "vestibulum regalium," and in two senses: from sarcophagus–like pedestals on either side, carved with tributes to the foundation of Naples, rise figures of Ferrante and Alfonso supported by groups who mingle the attributes of Hercules with the heraldry of the House of Trastámare. Above bends a heaven of abundance. The vestibule was completed, and made into a kind of room—the second sense in which it is a vestibulum—by the inner coronation arch of Ferrante, which dates from 1465. This too is chiefly the work of Pietro and Laurana. The bronze doors by Guglielmo Lo Monaco, of ten and more years later, carry on the account of Ferrante's preparation by chronicling his greatest victory. They lead in turn to the inscription—again emphasizing Ferrante's preparation—to the coronation scene. That scene becomes an inner parallel to the triumph frieze of Alfonso I, which we must next consider.

Chapter 5: THE TRIUMPH FRIEZE AND THE UPPER ARCH, 1455–1458, 1465

HE ARTISTS AND THE DESIGN OF THE FRIEZE   The triumph frieze (*fig. 64*) is no mere episode. It is the key to the interpretation of the entire monument. There are three documents that I interpret as being related to it. One reveals merely that Isaia da Pisa worked from May 1455 to May 1456 as a "mestre de fer ymatges de pedra marbre" at the rate of 25 ducats per month (Doc. 15). The second tells us that in January 1456 Isaia and Andrea dell'Aquila worked at the Castel Nuovo for an unspecified time on an unspecified job, for 30 ducats each (Doc. 14). Then, when Isaia had finished his one-year contract, in May 1456 we have a record that Andrea worked for two months and twenty-eight days at about half Isaia's salary. Andrea was paid for "the work he has done on the marble blocks [*pedres*] of the triumph of the Castel Nuovo portal" (Doc. 16).[1] I will assume that Isaia had been carving the triumph frieze during this fourteen-month period, and that Andrea's work included setting it in place and perhaps completing it after it was erected. According to these records a total of 356 ducats was paid to the two artists.

Isaia da Pisa, Filarete's successor as one of the leading sculptors in Rome, had completed the tomb of Cardinal Chiaves in the Lateran in 1447, and he is said to have carved the tomb of Eugenius IV now in San Salvatore in Lauro (mentioned by Porcellio). In 1450–51 he is recorded in Orvieto, where he made a design for the cathedral facade. His style is abstract, his figures grave. He is the most oriental and "Early Christian" of these sculptors (*fig. 76*).

A notion as to other work Isaia may have contributed to the Arch, and his standing among the other sculptors in Naples, is given in certain verses written in about 1455, possibly before the frieze was begun and quite probably before it was erected. These are by Porcellio, who was in Naples at the time:

> The marvelous monument of Eugenius's tomb will be witness [to Isaia's talent]
>   And the royal arch of Alfonso;
> That man of triumphal virtue and strong arms,
>   At Naples chose [Isaia] from a large group [of competitors].[2]

These lines could be interpreted to mean that Isaia carved a Virtue, or even several Virtues, and some of the Arch's heraldic ornament. By this the upper colossi might be meant, or the missing Virtues for the inner niches. Similarly the spandrel griffins with their Aragonese shield (*fig. 31*) could conceivably be the "fortibus armis."[3]

Andrea dell'Aquila, who was one of Isaia's assistants, seems to have brought very different qualities with him. Nothing known of his work or experience permits us to see him

46

as an antiquarian like Isaia or Pietro da Milano. Andrea's importance is that he is the first Florentine-trained artist to work on the Arch. In 1458 Niccolo Severino, the Sienese ambassador at Naples, wrote to the architect of the Siena cathedral, Cristoforo Felici, recommending Andrea in the highest terms both as painter and sculptor, calling him a disciple of Donatello's and a protégé of Cosimo's, and adding: "at present he has made a part of the king's triumphal arch, which is a very noble work, praised by everyone beyond all the other [parts of the arch done] by other masters, so that he is much envied by these others." This probably refers to the lower griffins, which would have been newly set in place in 1458.

Isaia and Andrea are new to the scene. But their preferences in prototypes run to the antique as with the other sculptors. Aside from such obvious examples as the lateral interior reliefs of the Arch of Titus there are others, now destroyed or transformed, such as the so-called Arco di Malborghetto, twelve miles distant from Rome on the Via Flaminia (*fig. 66*). Here is a tripartite attic triumphal scene roughly to the same scale as that in Naples.[4] On the other hand, the two end pavilions and the very high attic in the Castel Nuovo Arch could derive from Alfonso's 1420 trip to North Africa, where he may have admired the Arch of Caracalla, Cuicul (Djemila), Algeria (*fig. 67*).[5]

Such classical reminiscences were only employed, however, to eternalize a recent actuality. Thus the end pavilions, with their arched openings and with what I take as Parthenope busts in their tympana, probably stand for the seggi, at each of whose headquarters the 1443 procession had paused.[6] The frieze would accordingly commemorate the new king traveling through the city to receive the mandate of each district. The group in the left-hand pavilion, probably representing the Seggio del Popolo, is modeled with sharp rigidity on some Roman scene on the order of the so-called Forum Reliefs. Next, before a backing of pilasters and tympana tied together with a heavy entablature, are several other distinct groups: the ambassador from Tunisia and his suite; the barons and officials following the royal chariot;[7] the carriage itself, with three men bearing the poles of the baldaquin; the seated king; then the four white horses led by a female genius (a group probably taken from the Palazzo Conservatori relief of the triumph of Marcus Aurelius);[8] and finally the band, full of noise and gaiety in contrast to the solemnity of the others. They are all proceeding toward the next seggio en route.

Isaia and his assistants have omitted the allegorical floats, but within the procession the royal group itself embodies certain allegorical meanings. The chariot is a kind of sarcophagus, its bucrania clearly expressing mortality.[9] Like the heroes of the inner lateral reliefs, therefore, Alfonso the triumphator is a resurrection figure. As in the actual procession René's robe is draped across the back of the siege perilous. The throne is also, of course, the curule chair of classical triumphs. Alfonso carries the orb of empire, and originally he held a scepter in his other hand: he is thus ALFONSUS INVICTUS. He wears the collar and probably also the gown of his Order of the Lily: ALFONSUS PIUS. Banderoles with the arms of Calabria, Sicily, Aragon, and his own arms make a fringe for the baldaquin: ALPHONSUS

HISPANUS SICULUS ITALICUS. The frieze thus represents the qualities of the king, and the main tribal elements of the capital: the people, the barons, the Florentine enclave, and the court. In line with the "Neapolitan" policy, perhaps, the Catalans and the arms of Catalonia are omitted, while the moral policy of the reign is displayed in another omission, that of the bound prisoners who were de rigueur in such processions: indeed there is no military element whatever in the frieze. It is the triumph of peace: ALFONSUS CLEMENS.[10]

THE ATTRIBUTIONS   If we examine the division of blocks in the frieze (*fig. 65*) we can easily distinguish different hands. Of the seventy-two pieces marked out by Avena only eighteen carry figure sculpture. The most important are the female head in the left tympanum (1), the group of People (2, 3, 4, and 5), the ambassadors and barons (6 and 7), Alfonso (8), the two forward baldaquin bearers (9), the Parthenope bust above the horse (10), the horses and Victory (11), the marching bandsmen (12), the female head in the tympanum over the equestrian musicians (13), and the mounted bandsmen (14, 15, 16, 17).

The People are clearly meant to look "classical" or Parthenopean (*figs. 68, 69*). The immobile figures in the front row wear *cotes-hardies* of Late Antique stiffness, which with the sponginess of their faces and hair makes them reminiscent of Isaia da Pisa (compare *fig. 76*, the viol-playing angel). But a few of the sensitive, eager faces in the second row with their rough facets reflect the style of Laurana. Nor are the bearded and turbaned Moors on blocks 6 and 21 (*figs. 70, 71*) dissimilar. Their hands are held like heavy objects, and they have long trunks, stocky legs, and large heads. Their rippled drapery and Gothic sweetness anticipate Laurana's work in Avignon.

The barons on block 7 are more finely and sharply detailed (*figs. 72–74*). They walk in a quiet, swaying manner, though with nervous urgency. They possess a variety of facial types. Some are clearly by Pietro da Milano and others (*figs. 73, 74*) are by a more Florentine hand—perhaps Andrea dell'Aquila.

The king (block 8) has been attributed to Isaia da Pisa, and this effigy surely does belong to his world of oblate forms and spherical segments (*fig. 75*). A comparison with Isaia's Grotte Vaticane Madonna (*fig. 76*) is particularly revealing, but as usual the comparison cannot provide assurance that only Isaia's hand was involved in the two pieces. Block 9, with the two remaining baldaquin bearers (*figs. 77, 79*) has been ascribed to Mino da Fiesole, who was in Naples at about this time, though he is not documented as having been in royal employ.[11] It is possible that the heads—and these only—are by Mino, for they have some of the qualities that we find in Mino's known work (*fig. 78*).

Block 11, the horses and genius (*fig. 80*), is usually attributed to Paolo Romano, and I see no reason why he should not be given responsibility for it. The dryness, hollowness, and antiquarianism of the figures is Roman but lacks Isaia's orientalism. The head of the genius seems shrunk around the base of her nose, the eyelids are stringy, and there is an elastic pull of the lower part of the body to its right, features visible in many of Paolo's statues—the Sant'Andrea at Ponte Milvio (1463) for example.

The musicians on block 12 make up one of the few groups about which scholars agree (*figs. 81, 82*): they assign it to Domenico Gagini, who, they presume, was familiar with Donatello's work and with Luca della Robbia's cantoria. Although Gagini is not documented in Naples until the beginning of 1458, this elegance and gaiety, this cursive rhythm, is unmistakably Gagini. The artist who carved the mounted musicians on the return attempted a similar effect and was not wholly unsuccessful. Finally come other musicians, more grotesquely comic (*fig. 83*). This artist too was influenced by Florentine precedent, but probably only by local examples such as the trumpet-playing putti on the Brancacci tomb. It is at least conceivable that Vallardi drawings 2296 and 2619 are preparatory sketches for these figures, and they have been published as such.[12]

The noble female heads on blocks 1, 10, and 13 may represent Parthenope (*figs. 84, 85, 86*). Their eyes consist of interlocked spherical fragments, the jaws are strong and sharply angled, terminating in slight bulbs for the chin. The two outer heads (*figs. 84, 86*) reflect Isaia's style.

I conclude that while the division of labor stood as the documents suggest, the three masters of the lower arch and other, unnamed artists aided Isaia and Andrea in carving the frieze. Despite the difficulty of making individual attributions, some consideration seems to have been given to the sculptors' different backgrounds or specialties in parceling out the groups within the procession. Thus the "classical" Parthenopean People were done under Isaia's direction, as was the hieratic king; the exotic ambassadors went to the Slav, Laurana, the Roman genius to Paolo Romano, and the Florentine bandsmen were executed in Florentine style by Gagini and assistants. Though according to this description Andrea dell'Aquila seems to have played a minor role, I think that he, Donatello's pupil, may have been the executant of the Donatellesque griffins.[13] He would have had assistance—for example on the wings of the right-hand creature—but Andrea's one known previous employment had been in Florence in 1446 as a heraldic painter, and it may well have been fame in this department that brought him to Alfonso's notice. Certainly these are among the most heroic griffins of the Renaissance, and they would well justify Niccolo Severino's words: "una cosa molto eletta."

THE UPPER ARCH   On 31 January 1458, a new contract was signed according to which Isaia, Pietro, Francesco Laurana, and Paolo Romano were paid 200 ducats as part of a total of 3,800 "to carve completely the figures of the triumphal arch of the said Castel Nuovo" (Doc. 17). These four artists were joined by a Domenico Lombardo and a certain Antoni de Pisa. The latter is now generally identified as Antonio Chellino or Chellini, and the former as Domenico Gagini. The agreement almost certainly involved the nine colossal statues of the upper arch. On 28 February the same group of six sculptors received another

200 ducats (Doc. 18). No payments are recorded for the next three months; from the beginning of June 1458 to the end of April 1460 the cedole have always been missing; and
for the years 1460–64 no payments for work of any sort are mentioned—thus out of 3,800
ducats we only have indications that 400 were actually paid. This suggests a budget cutback
of up to 90 percent. The lack of further payment records squares with the fact that a number of the colossi were never put in place, while only two of those that now exist are of
good quality.[14]

On the other hand, the architectural part of the upper arch was probably under execution
or even complete by the beginning of 1458. Given the wording of Documents 17 and 18,
this was doubtless the subject of a separate (lost) contract. Structurally, this part of the Arch
departs from the lower half. It is not keyed into the flanking towers, and on the whole, says
Avena, it is an amateurish building job[15]—such as one might expect from a sculptor. In
design, too, Pietro departs from the earlier precedent. He is no longer a simple copyist,
though he may have been influenced by the upper half of the Boymans design (*figs. 16, 87*).
If this is the case, he reduced the number of niches from five to four, and made the attic more
directly a niche-sarcophagus.[16] He also removed the flanking lower niches and brought the
paired lower columns out en ressaut, replacing the heraldic cresting with a more classical
Venetian-style tympanum. The upper corona, without architrave or frieze, is not at first
glance "correct," though it does have a classical precedent in a monument already mentioned
—the attic pavilions of the Arch of Caracalla, Djemila (*fig. 67*).

Otherwise; however, the design of the upper arch is governed by the lower. The palmettes
and other floral carving of the antae, the vault with its deep coffers filled with heads and
emblems, the putti carrying the arms of Aragon in the center of that vault, and the Composite order—all are suggested below. Indeed, the more normal elements of the lower arch
that had been "removed" to make room for the great griffins—the spandrel Victories with
their putti—appear here instead. The source of these Victories is probably Benevento (or
it could be Pula), while the griffin frieze in the upper entablature (*fig. 93*) can be likened
to various Roman friezes, including that on the Temple of Antoninus and Faustina, as well as
to innumerable sarcophagi.[17] But, as one expects with work designed by Pietro, the closest
Roman parallel is again in Dalmatia, in the familiar wingless griffins in the frieze of the
Temple of Jupiter, Split.

Because the attic story is handled as a niche-sarcophagus and finished with a heavy corona,
the segmental pediment above seems extra. But it serves, of course, to raise the whole structure in relation to the towers, and to re-echo, like the arch-voids but more gently, the towers'
outward swelling. Aside from Venetian and Dalmatian examples, the source of this tympanum could well have been the arch at Fano (a town, by the way, in which Vitruvius was
known to have built). This arch (*fig. 88*) is recorded with a triangular pediment filled with
just such river gods. Also interestingly, the gate is flanked by round towers treated in part
with diamond-point facing as in the scarps of the Castel Nuovo. However, the Sangallo

Vatican *Libro* drawing I use for documentation has an air of anachronistic fantasy that raises suspicions. As to other features in the upper arch, the oddly chokered Ionic capitals with their anthemiated necks (*fig. 94*) are untraceable to Roman sources—unless the artist copied some pastiche of a Corinthian lower section with a pair of Ionic volutes stuck on it.

The quality of the relief carving throughout is high, in places exquisite. Only an inspection from scaffolding, however, proves this. The perfection of every tiny element, even of fillets and blank spaces, and the sharp precision of all moldings, shows that the carving carried out under the architectural contract of 1458 was as careful as the earlier. Only the soffit of the upper vault is somewhat coarse in execution.

THE FIGURE RELIEFS AND COLOSSAL STATUES   Of the two new artists who joined the group, Antonio Chellino had been an assistant of Donatello's, working on the Gattamelata monument and on the Santo altar at Padua. But it is not possible to single out any work unquestionably by him before his arrival in Naples, though we are told he executed a bronze angel and one of the Evangelist symbols on the Padua altar.[18]

Domenico Gagini, like Pietro da Milano a Lombard, came from a well-known family of sculptors connected mainly with Genoa. Filarete identifies as a pupil of Brunelleschi's a certain Domenico del Lago di Lughano, who may be our Domenico (see below). Gagini had been working on the facade of the Chapel of San Giovanni Battista in the cathedral at Genoa, and in 1455 he was assigned the decorations of the chapel of San Girolamo del Rozo, Genoa (now destroyed), and may also have executed the existing baptistry facade of this church. Gagini, like Isaia da Pisa and Paolo Romano, was thus trained in the operation of the large sculptural workshop whose final product had a certain anonymity. His style had something in common with Laurana's but is more rounded and vigorous (compare *figs. 106, 108*). I have just discussed his musicians in the triumph frieze (*figs. 81, 82*), and he appears to have executed the central soffit panel of the upper vault in a somewhat softened version of this manner (*fig. 99*), but also imitating the figure style of antique sarcophagi (*fig. 100*).

The team of sculptors as fully assembled in Naples bore strong resemblance to the ideal team Filarete (MS Magl. 44v) brought together for the construction of the triumphal portals of the castle at Sforzinda. These portals were carved with Francesco Sforza's victories (and reverses). The members of this group are identified as Antonio da Pisa, Isaia da Pisa, Domenico del Lago di Lugano, "a Slav who was a good master" (Laurana?) and "a Catalan," either Pere Joan or Sagrera. Pietro da Milano, Paolo Romano, and Andrea dell'Aquila are thus left out. But Filarete, writing in the 1460s, seems to have heard about the Neapolitan shop and its project. That shop's, or tribe's, near-industrial methods would have appealed strongly to Filarete, who after all was writing about a city that was to be constructed in only ten days!

As to the various roles taken by individuals in this group, it is difficult to see a recognizable hand in the Victories of the upper arch (*figs. 89, 90, 91, 92*). But I would suggest as a pos-

sibility the artist responsible for the barons in figures 73 and 74, in all likelihood Andrea
dell'Aquila. These Victories possess the same loose-limbed elegance and deep eyes, similar
faceted lips and cheeks, done more nervously than with Laurana, and the same two manners
of handling drapery—the one clinging and diaphanous (on the putti, *figs. 90, 92*) and the
other thick and heavy-hemmed.

I have already noted the relationship of the tympanum river gods (*fig. 96*) to those on
the arch at Fano. They could represent the Sebeto and the Acheloos, or else the two branches
of the Sebeto.[19] Their present appearance is due to their having been smashed and then crudely
reinforced with clamps. The tympanum that supports them is backed with well-squared
tufa (instead of rubble as in the rest of the upper arch). Avena thinks this means a third
period of construction;[20] but it may simply reflect that the tympanum was free-standing while
the arch below was buttressed by the towers. In any case the gods are beautifully carved (*fig.
97*). They and the mascheroni that serve as antefixes belong to a single shop. There is in
both a pleasing yet rather forbidding delicacy, a handsome cowl of hair, and deep-plunged
eyes, and yet there is still Gothicism in both river gods' legs—the legs of muscular old men
with sharp tendons behind the knee. One of the heads may be derived from the Jupiter on the
Porta Romana, Capua (*fig. 98*), while a drawing in Berlin (*fig. 95*) may be a preparatory
sketch for the right-hand figure.

The colossi are a different story. The statue on the left of the nicchione, with its wreathed
head, cuirass, and toga (*figs. 101, 102*) may be one of the pair sent from Rome in 1447
(Doc. 4), in which case its mate would have been intended to stand on the right. In any
event the present statue does not seem to belong to any one of the Arch sculptors.[21]

The four Virtues vary in quality, and at least two of them show evidence of having been
adapted from other purposes. The first on the left, Justice (*figs. 103, 104*), displays the
drapery, pose, and facial treatment we now expect of Pietro da Milano. There is the heavy
jaw, the conical neck, the swaying stance, the attempt at heavy liquid folds of cloth, that
we get in the coronation relief and in the courtiers in figure 54. But the feet of Justice float,
even though every intention has been toward solidity (her balance and sword have been
removed). As was frequently the case with the non-Florentine sculptors in Naples, the figure
is to an extent modeled on local Florentine precedents, in this case the caryatids of the
Ladislas and Brancacci tombs.

The next figure, Temperance, reveals a greater mastery (*figs. 106, 107*). The drapery
falls in solid heaviness around the gently inclined body. The head is thrust forward, and the
balance of the body is echoed in the position of the hands. The head is sculptured with shell-
like eyes and melting conical planes that were to become characteristic of Gagini. The
Temperance was thus made by the most accomplished of the newcomers, showing a mastery
of colossal scale until then absent from the Castel Nuovo workshops. Both Justice and
Temperance are of a solemn classical type also recalled by one of the artists involved with
the Codex Escurialensis (*fig. 105*).

The other two statues are less happy. The Fortitude (*fig. 108*) may have been destined for another location, since it is too short for its niche and has had to be bolstered with a sub-pedestal. The head is an old replacement, so battered as to be without diagnostic value. The thickly fluted drapery, the cocked feet, and the stiff, uncertain axis, relate it a little to the female genius in the frieze; but it would be foolhardy to attribute it on this slight basis.

The last statue, Prudence (*fig. 109*), is even smaller and more unabashedly Gothic in style, with a large head and a pronounced *hanchement*. That it might have been made for another purpose is suggested by the finished surfaces across the back. The treatment of the head, with its great-lidded eyes, tall forehead, upswept, swirling hair, and soft, short nose, suggest the youthful Laurana; it anticipates his standing Madonnas, too, in the wrinkled plane of the drapery.

Turning to the upper tympanum statues (*figs. 110, 111, 112*), the Saint Anthony Abbot (*fig. 110*) reflects the style of the Tunisian ambassadors in the frieze (*figs. 70, 71*), and is therefore possibly also attributable to Laurana. The Saint Michael (*fig. 112*) I have already attributed to Pere Joan or his school; it is comparable to a Saint George figure in the Museo Provincial, Lérida (*fig. 113*), possibly by Pere Joan himself. These three figures, including the fragmentary Saint George (*fig. 111*)[22] and quite possibly Laurana's Temperance and the Fortitude, could have been made before 1458, that is, before the arrival of Gagini, who was so obviously superior to the other sculptors on the site.

THE PLANNED EQUESTRIAN GROUP   Such a scheme of attributions leaves nothing for Donatello's pupil, Antonio Chellino. We have noted that he was with Donatello during at least part of the time the Gattamelata statue was being planned and made, and that he was a worker in bronze. My proposal is that he was brought in to assemble, chase, and erect a colossal bronze equestrian portrait of Alfonso, to be created by Donatello for the upper niche. The tradition of the knightly Neapolitan ruler on a horse and the precedent of the Boymans pavilion support my contention, but there is other evidence as well.[23]

On 12 July 1471 Diomede Carafa wrote to Lorenzo de' Medici thanking him for sending a "testa del cavallo" which he has placed in his house (Doc. 32). Diomede says nothing about its size, material, or provenience. However, the colossal horse's head now in the Museo Nazionale, thought to be part of the old bronze Virgilian horse that once stood before the cathedral, was at one time in Diomede's collection and is probably the same object (*fig. 115*).[24] Sarnelli's 1697 guidebook illustrates this head standing in the courtyard of Diomede's palace along with a small equestrian figure, now lost, said to have been adapted from the larger piece.[25] A number of writers have even gone so far as to suggest that Diomede's possession had no relation to the cathedral horse, but that it, and perhaps also the small statue, were made by Donatello or his assistants in preparation for an equestrian portrait of Alfonso.[26] This idea stems from a passage in the Codex Magliabecchiana: "Donatello made a head and neck of a very large horse, a very worthy work, which he began and was going to complete with the rest of the horse. On it was to have been the image of King Alfonso of Aragon; it is in Naples today, in the house of Count Maddaloni di Carafa" (Doc. 20).[27]

Even more convincing evidence for a planned contribution by Donatello, as Juan Ainaud de Lasarte has recently shown, takes the form of two letters written by Alfonso, one to Doge Francesco Foscari and the other to the Venetian ambassador in Naples, both dated 26 May 1452. The letter to the Doge reads in part: "When we heard about the skill and subtlety of mind of Master Donatello in making statues of bronze and marble, we had a great desire to have him near us and in our service for a time" (Doc. 7). Alfonso goes on to mention "that bronze Gattamelata statue just now made by him."[28] One can therefore conclude that Alfonso did intend having Donatello make a version of the Gattamelata for Naples. It almost goes without saying that this would have depicted Alfonso himself and would have stood in the Arch's upper niche, which was being planned and begun at that moment.

It is possible that in forming this conception Alfonso was thinking of a passage in Statius which describes another colossal bronze equestrian figure, loftily placed in the context of a "nova palatia." In his poem on a statue of Domitian, Statius describes the reins as being pulled sharply back, with the emperor's face expressing power for peace or war, and then declares: "O lofty head enclosed within pure bronze, thou wilt see to look forth upon temples shining, while the new palace rises from despised fire, more beautiful" (*Sylvae* I, 11. 32–35).[29] One also thinks of Filarete's conception of a palace entrance (*fig. 114*).

But is the Nazionale piece actually a relic of this proposed statue? Such an idea conflicts with the well-attested tradition that the head is antique. But it does seem possible that an antique original, symbolizing Naples and owned by Alfonso, could have been sent north in 1452 as a model for Donatello. The Nazionale sculpture would have been an ideal prototype not only because of its history but because, with its massively thick neck, swelling veins, and ridging around mouth and jaw, it is similar to the Gattamelata animal (*fig. 116*).[30] The piece we see today in the Museo Nazionale would thus be a remodeling of the old head, literally conflating its two contradictory proveniences. It would have been made at Lorenzo's behest as a gift for Diomede, who had not only been Alfonso's friend and minister but who was known as a collector of antiques.

Assuming the truth of these speculations, the sequence of events would have been this: Chellino, the bronze expert, arrived in Naples to supervise the erection of a nicchione group that Donatello was producing. But in June 1458, a few months after he arrived, the king died. Nothing except perhaps a bozzetto had been made for the equestrian statue, and in the following years Ferrante was excluded from his capital, which resulted in further inaction. When the new king returned in 1465, plans for finishing the Arch were drastically cut back, with Ferrante concentrating mostly on his own part of the monument. Any remaining idea of completing the equestrian group would have been given up with Donatello's death in 1466. In this same year, in fact, Ferrante commissioned a different, humbler object for the upper niche, "a great vessel of gilded copper, seamed with silver . . . in the form of a heart, to contain the embalmed heart of the most glorious Lord King Don Alfonso of immortal memory" (Docs. 24, 26).[31] Finally, in 1471, Lorenzo sent the prototype, the Virgilian head, now reworked by some Florentine artist so as to make a suitable gift, back to Naples for Diomede's collection.

As to the rest of the upper group, it is likely that the standing military figure on the left of the nicchione (fig. 101) was intended as one of a pair representing Peace and War.[32] Also, it is at least conceivable that below the horseman was to have been Parthenope's sarcophagus and, lying on it, Alfonso's antique recumbent statue of her. One notes in this connection that Diomede's collection contained a "mulier nuda dormiens."[33] Thus would a third relic of the project for Alfonso's group have found its way to Diomede's palace. Such a hypothesis also fits in with Valla's inscription—"Parthenope, the maiden long disturbed by Mars: martial Alfonso says, 'rest thyself' "[34]—words that imply the presence both of a resting siren-queen and of a condottiere gesturing pacifically toward her. The group's situation, on axis with Mont'Echia and Virgil's tomb, would also have been appropriate: the poet would be lying in sight of a replica of his most famous work of sculpture (cf. also fig. 5).

To conclude briefly, the attic frieze of the lower arch was designed by Isaia da Pisa and executed between May 1455 and July 1456. It reports the facts of the triumphal procession of 1443, each socio-political element being the work of a different and in most cases appropriate artist. The upper arch was erected during the rest of 1456 and all of 1457, probably under the supervision of Pietro da Milano. It was intended to house a marble and bronze group consisting of an equestrian portrait of the king, Parthenope on her tomb, and flanking statues of Peace and War.

The conception behind the upper arch was a fascinating and ambitious one—a climactic restatement of the ideas of the lower interior reliefs. But in this planned upper group Alfonso was probably to appear as Eumelos, rather than Hercules; and he was also the immemorial Neapolitan ruler riding forth on his funeral monument. The monument was perhaps intended as well to house Alfonso's legendary ancestress, recreating her early, unforgotten shrine. In this context the upper attic becomes more literally a sarcophagus, whose lid is formed by the river gods in their tympanum. Finally, as figures in a yet higher and nobler resurrection, the saints carry the Arch's ascending procession into the sky.

Chapter 6: THE INFLUENCE OF THE ARCH

SCULPTURE   I have already suggested in a general way some of the influences that emanated from the Arch of Alfonso. Eileen Driscoll claims that its sculptural classicism—she is speaking only of the use of motifs from antiquity—was created out of Alfonso's own desires and had an insignificant effect on the later careers of the artists involved.[1] But we have seen that the Arch's classical style, at least in the more general sense, already existed in Naples, and that Pietro da Milano remained there after 1465 to continue teaching it to a number of local younger sculptors, of whom the most prolific was Jacopo della Pila.[2] Surely the example of the greatest of the Neapolitan sculptural monuments had its effect in this widespread development.

Neapolitan classicism, however, now settled into a rigid and repetitious mold, and the grace that sometimes inhabits the arch figures becomes, even in close adaptations of them, an abstraction of linear ridges and generalized solids. Innumerable tombs of noblemen in San Domenico Maggiore, San Paolo Maggiore, and other churches in Naples and the provinces bear witness to this. There are exceptions, it is true: the monument of Francesco Carafa, San Domenico Maggiore (1470), has reliefs more in the manner of Laurana than of Pietro, and the same is true of the Miroballo tomb in San Giovanni a Carbonara with its rich program of carvings: a generous triumphal arch with deep reveals from whose bases lions emerge, the center filled with a sculptured altar whose frontal is formed by a schiacciato Resurrection. There are lateral reliefs in forced perspective as in the Arch, and a central relief with a vault also in forced perspective, statues of Virtues, and so forth. Again, the tomb is full of more personal reflections—not all of them second-rate—of Laurana, while the Prudence is one of many such copies of Gagini's original. More distantly, the upper arch's griffins reappear at the base of the tomb of Galeazzo Pandone in San Domenico Maggiore (ca. 1520) by Giantommaso Malvito. But by now they have elegant Mannerist legs and a catlike grace completely missing from the prototypes.

Other details from the Arch appear in Neapolitan architecture. The curious capitals of the upper nicchione are repeated in the reredos of the altar in the chapel of Saint John the Baptist (sixteenth-century) in Sant'Agostino della Zecca; and the Palazzo Santangelo has a heavy torus between friezes, a device imitated from the Palazzo Carafa, and probably thence from the pedestals of the lower arch. The stubby fluted Corinthian columns that decorate Ferrante's inner monument seem to have influenced those on the Malizia Carafa tomb and also that in the courtyard of the Palazzo Carafa; all of which suggests that Pietro da Milano's shop produced architectural ornament for houses as well as tombs.[3]

One can also trace hints of influence from the triumph frieze. An example is the stiff, processional Adoration of the Magi relief from the ciborium of Cardinal d'Estouteville (1474), now in Santa Maria Maggiore, Rome.[4] This is the work of Mino da Fiesole (at the

56

time immersed in Roman classicism) and assistants. Such obvious features as the pilastered architectural backing, the uniformly serried horses, and the schiacciato background figures to the right are in all probability reflections of Mino's experience of the Naples frieze. Yet the Neapolitan monument is not sufficiently unique to make the possibility certain.

There are a number of less sophisticated echoes of the Arch. One is a doorway in the Cenacolo dello Santo Spirito, Florence,[5] from a house in Sassano Teggiano (Salerno), dated 1471. It consists of a Catalan stilted segmental arch with broad smooth archivolt whose outer side is decorated with a cable molding and a simple torus and fillet. Above this simple Gothic opening, in the narrow spandrels formed by the archivolt's gentle curve, mascheroni lean forth among leaves. They are quite obviously taken from the heads in the vault coffers of the lower arch. The frieze itself is flanked by family arms, within which are griffins and trophies derived from those in the upper arch's frieze.

The Arch seems to have been used as a source for tombs as much in France as in Italy. The agents of this influence could have been Laurana and Pietro da Milano, both of whom later traveled to France, or else figures from the end of the century such as Guido Mazzoni, who worked for a period in Naples before going north with Charles VIII. One instance is the tomb of Louis de Brézé, husband of Diane de Poitiers. This is a black-and-white marble structure in Rouen cathedral dating from 1535–44 (fig. 117). It is clearly a variant on the Neapolitan conception, complete with equestrian figure. The most important artist involved seems to have been Jean Goujon, but he probably made only the design.[6] Actually the tomb can best be seen as a mingling of several different Neapolitan conceptions, including not only the Castel Nuovo Arch but the Boymans pavilion (in the upper seated figure of Virtue) and even possibly Mazzoni's celebrated terra-cotta Lamentation in the Church of Monteoliveto—this being reflected in the gisant and his accompanying mourners (at one time more numerous than now). The canephoras, representing Virtues, would be a Frenchified way of avoiding the niche-zone of the Neapolitan arch, while the profile equestrian statue imitates, with additional grandeur, the portraits of Ferrante and Alfonso of Calabria that were placed on the eastern gates of Naples in the 1480s.

Turning once again to the question raised by Driscoll—the effect of the Arch on the later careers of its artists—we have noted that Pietro da Milano's destiny was tied up almost entirely with Naples. He seems to have been away from that city only from about 1461 to about 1465. During this period he utilized the design of the inner arch coronation scene (fig. 48) for a medal for René and Jeanne de Laval (fig. 49). Nevertheless it is difficult nowadays to find in Naples a work of sculpture clearly by Pietro, despite numerous documents as to his activity there[7]—which suggests that he became more of an administrator than practical carver. This consummation was perhaps foreshadowed by the industrial methods used by the Arch sculptors in 1453–58.

Laurana, on the contrary, was an indefatigable traveler. Though he too returned to Naples, he never stayed. Laurana made several trips to France,[8] and settled down from 1467–71 or so in Sicily. More importantly, where Pietro had already mastered the existing, rather anonymous style of the Neapolitan shops by the time he arrived in Naples in 1452, Francesco seems to have learned a great deal working on the Arch, and yet to have developed a personal style quite different from the prevailing Neapolitan mode. Surely, for example, the round soft faces of his famous Madonnas owe more than a little to Pere Joan, to knowledge gained from equivalents, made in Naples, to the Tarragona altar (*fig. 25*). The method of composition in the latter and in Francesco's Avignon relief is as similar as the figure style (*fig. 56*): there is the same cascading descent of figures toward the front, the same smallness of body, with smooth heads and upthrust brows. At the same time Gagini, already a master of the colossal statue, embodied the corrective classicizing force that superseded Pere Joan's influence with Laurana, contributing to yet another aspect of the famous Madonnas of the next few decades. In a different way Laurana's putti on the column bases in the Mastrantonio chapel in San Francesco, Palermo, and those on the base of the bust in Washington of Isabella of Aragon, are comparable to the putti of the lower arch. Francesco's interest in architecture first appears in the chapel at Marseilles, which owes something to Gagini's Chapel of Saint John the Baptist in Genoa and almost nothing to the Arch, except perhaps for the drum and dome arrangement over the tabernacle, which echoes Ferrante's portal.

Domenico Gagini's fate was more like Pietro's than Laurana's. Gagini was a finished master when he arrived in Naples in 1457–58, and there is not, as I have noted, the slightest faltering in his magnificent Temperance, except perhaps a slight swollen awkwardness in the flex of the right wrist. Nor, in fact, is there any dramatic development or improvement in the series of elegant Madonnas that follows, though some, for instance that in the sacristy of Santa Barbara, are more abstract. But Gagini's later work in Naples and Sicily simply refines what he had been able to do before he came south. The only unaccountable thing about him is that, like Antonello da Messina, he should have remained in the provinces rather than making the capital his headquarters. This is all the more surprising in view of the fact that his Temperance was such a favorite Neapolitan model for later statues of that Virtue.[9]

Paolo Romano, chiefly a humble ornament-carver insofar as the Arch was concerned, gained broader recognition when he returned to Rome. One sees his more developed hand in the large statues of Saints Peter and Paul now in the vestibule of Radio Vaticana (1461), while his architectural experience would have counted in the benedictional pulpit he helped to make for Pius II in 1463–64. His masterpiece is the statue of Saint Paul now on the Ponte Sant'Angelo. Paolo's (and his large shop's) ability to turn out colossal statues at a rapid pace may reflect methods learned in Naples in 1458,[10] and it was perhaps also their Neapolitan experience that brought Paolo and Isaia da Pisa together in later Roman projects involving these same industrial methods, the Tabernacle of Sant'Andrea in Saint Peter's for example, and the coeval benedictional pulpit just mentioned.

Andrea dell'Aquila and Antonio Chellino are more obscure. Valentiner has made Andrea responsible for the tabernacle in the Church of the Madonna del Soccorso, Aquila, as well as for a number of paintings.[11] If the Santa Barbara tympanum is his, then he too was an influence on the young Laurana, and Laurana's exquisite Madonna above this tympanum (1474) would be a return tribute. But Andrea is still an equation with too many unknowns in it. Chellino, the most obscure of all the Arch sculptors, we have noted, is described by Filarete so as to imply that he was still living in 1460–64 (see above, p. 59). But more we do not know.[12]

On the whole, then, the peculiar formula of the Castel Nuovo Arch was only occasionally imitated in later tombs, though various details and programmatic devices reappear with more frequency, especially in Naples. The style of the figure sculpture reinforced the classicizing currents already present in the city, currents that continued to flow until the revolutionary impact in the 1480s of Antonio Rossellino's and Benedetto da Maiano's two chapels in Monteoliveto. The organization of the shop and the anonymity of the style that resulted were re-echoed in the later careers of Paolo Romano, Isaia da Pisa, and Pietro da Milano, while Laurana—a more gifted and individual artist—drew several elements of his personal style from his first Neapolitan experience.

ARCHITECTURE   In architecture there is a different story to tell. If it is difficult to find later reflections of the Arch's sculpture, it is easy, perhaps too easy, to trace the influence of its architectural form. One example would be the tomb of Louis de Brézé in Rouen (*fig. 117*), just mentioned. I have discussed the Arch's impact on the Italian scene in the first chapter of my study of Alfonso II, so here I will merely sketch in a few additional details. These primarily concern the development of the Renaissance frontispiece.

After the construction of Alfonso's arch, and not before, the motif of two superimposed triumphal arches, the upper functioning as a sort of window of appearances, was quite common as an entrance feature. Often these entrances-cum-belvederes contained monumental sculptural groups or processional friezes. Sometimes, too, flanking towers existed, often more fully integrated than at Naples into the frontispiece design. But ultimately the towers disappeared as the military aspect of the palace was deemphasized. Again as in Naples, festival decorations could play a role in transmitting the formula: thus a drawing now in the Cabinet Rothschild in the Louvre (no. 1424) depicts what I take to be two street decorations (*fig. 118*), that in the foreground being an integrated towers-and-arch composition and the more distant one being very nearly a direct quotation of the upper half of the Castel Nuovo Arch.

The most frequently noted collateral relative of the Castel Nuovo Arch is not actually an entrance but the well-known tower-flanked belvedere of the Ducal Palace at Urbino. Its architect was either the mysterious Luciano Laurana, who worked in Naples as an artillery maker in the 1470s[13] or, alternatively, Francesco di Giorgio. But one notes that Francesco did not visit Naples until 1490, while Luciano actually saw the Castel Nuovo at the time the Urbino palace was being erected. However the relationship between the belvedere in Urbino and the Arch in Naples, while worth mentioning, is not overwhelmingly close.

A related development is Alberti's experiments with upper niches, or else with temple-fronts set on three-part triumphal-arch bases, like those at the Tempio Malatestiano, Rimini, and at Santa Maria Novella, Florence. This parallel is also interesting because, as at the Castel Nuovo, it was a question of juxtaposing Gothic buildings and revived Roman frontispieces. The fact that tombs were included in the outer walls of the Tempio and that a statue of Sigis-mondo was planned for the upper niche also recalls the Arch program. But since some of these features in the Tempio may have been planned as early as about 1446, the influence may have traveled from Rimini to Naples rather than vice versa.

The double-arched palace frontispiece had a longer and richer life in the North than in Italy, though here I shall not attempt to do more than suggest a few of the variations. One of the most striking now stands in the courtyard of the Ecole des Beaux-Arts in Paris. This is the frontispiece from Anet, by Philibert de l'Orme, begun in 1548 (*fig. 119*).[14] This has a more knowingly "classical" Roman Doric basement order of the sixteenth century, paired columns en ressaut with an inscription between, Ionic paired columns on pedestals flanking a large rectangular window, and then a burst of richness at the top in the form of paired Corinthian columns with sculptured lower drums, again on pedestals. These flank an arch in whose spandrels Fontainebleau-like Victories recline. The Victories are the work of Jean Goujon, as is one of the reliefs of Roman deities between the columns. Below is a sculptured frieze forming a pedestal for the missing statue of Louis de Brézé, who stood, armed cap-à-pie like Gianni Caracciolo, grasping the emblems of the Grand Seneschal of Normandy. Above are ciphered trophies and another pedestal on which Louis's arms were displayed.

Two destroyed frontispieces of great châteaux echoed these same ideas—Fontainebleau with its three superimposed arches forming a freestanding gate, and the portico of the foun-tain court at Ecouen (*fig. 120*), which repeated the Anet system but with further simplifica-tions and with an equestrian statue rearing in its upper niche. There were less similar royal or equestrian portraits over monumental portals at Verger (Anjou) and Madrid (Neuilly-sur-Seine), both now destroyed. From here one traces the frontispiece in French church architecture, at the Versailles cathedral (1752–54) for example, by Hardouin-Mansart de Sagonne, or in the familiar pattern of the Louvre pavilions (*fig. 121*). But by this time the device is so thoroughly integrated into French classicism that one hardly feels a particular resonance from Naples.

In England the Arch-derived frontispiece made a number of appearances. So far as I know the earliest was at Caius College, Cambridge. Here in 1559–73 a series of "moral" arches, the Gates of Humility, Virtue, and Honor, were erected at the behest of Dr. John Caius[15] who had traveled to Padua, Rome, Florence, and Bologna but not, apparently, Naples. The plan of the college, and therefore possibly the idea of the gates, derives, as Pevsner points out, from Anet.[16] We see similar structures also at Kirby Hall, Northamptonshire (1572), at Burghley House, in the same county (1585), and at Hatfield House, Hertfordshire (1611)—the last derived from the 1577–85 gate of Somerset House, London. In these Elizabethan gates, that of Hatfield House (*fig. 122*), for example, there is a great richness of garlands and trophies, while in the upper space the scale of the royal arms recalls the Boymans drawing.

The final touch will be Antonio Niccolini's strange design for rebuilding the docks of Naples (*fig. 123*), already cited as an illustration of the Arch's renewed prestige under Neoclassicism.[17] Niccolini planned a kind of Neoclassical "correction" of the Castel Nuovo, based on Castel del Monte (*fig. 11*) though with casemated towers. The Arch, unchanged, was to be preserved as its frontispiece. Niccolini's conception incorporates "improvements" such as a post-Renaissance academic critic might suggest, improvements which in fact had already appeared in the Arch's immediate successors and cousins: an intervening bay between towers and arch as at Urbino, greater relative height for the frontispiece, as had been planned for the Tempio, and the exploitation of this height in the form of a dramatic skyline, as in the French and British examples. In a way that seldom happens in the history of architecture, indeed, Niccolini's scheme resets a prototype in a context that makes use of later refinements on that prototype.

The Castel Nuovo Arch had a long period of gestation, beginning life in 1443 as a marble monument offered by the seggi to their new king. At this time Alfonso's policy was to administer the various political tribes of his capital and empire in a manner that preserved their identity. The king's own taste appropriately ran to eclectic sumptuousness. Stylistically, the procession of 1443 was polyglot, and similar expressive juxtapositions of the Catalan, the "Aragonese," the Italian, and the antique appear in the Castel Nuovo. Even the Arch itself partakes of this spirit and owes much to prototypes like the tomb of Ladislas, which prefigure its general form, its use of different styles, and its sense of processional movement.

But beginning with the arcivescovado arch of 1443 we can also detect a tendency to classicism in Alfonso's taste. This was partly dictated by his new "Neapolitan" policy of the late 1440s, with its emphasis on local traditions. Thus a replica or adaptation of the Virgilian horse may have been intended for the arcivescovado arch of 1442, and such a replica, with royal rider, was certainly included in the Castel Capuano scaenae frons three years later. The appearance of Parthenope and her two attendants in this design is another step in the same direction. Alfonso's increasingly classical taste manifests itself again, now stylistically and not just iconographically, in Pisanello's medals; at monumental scale, the tombs of Rinaldo Brancacci and Gianni Caracciolo point down the same road. But in spite of this increasing classical overlay, the idea of artists and styles as role-players in an eclectic whole can still be discerned in the Arch, especially in its lower half.

Against this background the Arch itself appears as a device designed to join together the ceremonies at the Castel Nuovo, the image of the triumph, and, quite possibly, the metaphor of Alfonso as Parthenope's father and savior. The lower part of the Arch is accordingly a hymn to the preparation for kingship, both iconologically and architecturally forming a pedestal for the upper. Within it, the city's origins are depicted in a layer of mythical monsters and classical sarcophagi. Then, risen from these stone containers, Alfonso and Ferrante appear as Hercules-figures accompanied by their Aragonese progenitors. Here they would watch as their larger, living selves entered the Arch. Meanwhile, above, the triumph frieze with its various contingents repeats the greatest of Alfonso's processions. Finally in the upper arch we find a more unified rhetoric expanded to godlike scale. This upper arch, in my view intended as Parthenope's tomb, is the setting for Alfonso's humanist transfiguration. Present, past, and future were thus embodied in a continuous many-directional procession in which style and scale changed expressively. The conception, I believe, was one of the great imaginative acts of the Renaissance.

Appendix 1. EXTRACTS FROM THE DOCUMENTS AND SOURCES

I. A DESCRIPTION OF THE TRIUMPH

28 February 1443
Antonio Vinyes to the *Conselleres* of Barcelona

Ihesus. Molt honorables . . . : Per tant com és cert que per innada e fael naturalesa vostres coratges se són alegrats, e s'alegren de les grans victòrias, per lo molt alt e molt excellent princep e poderós senyor, lo senyor rey, triumfalment, en a per temor e migà de la sua spasa obtengudes.

És donchs pertinent que vostres grans savieses sien avisades de la grandissima e triunfal festa e solemnitat, feta al dit senyor en la entrada que de present ha feta en la sua ciutat de Nàpols, la qual bellicosament en lo present any, segons a tot lo món es notori ha entrada, e a ses mans subjugada. La dita festa e solemnitat tant com n'e pogut compendre és sots la forma següent: Lo senyor rey aprés hach a sa mà, segons dit és, e conquistada la dita ciutat de Nàpols, discorrent e cobrant ab sa mà poderosa les ciutats, viles e castells sotsmesos al domani de Nàpols, axi en les parts de Abruço e de Puylla, com de altres parts, e aquelles a sa reyal mà sotsmeses, és retornat en la dita ciutat de Nàpols, la qual lo ha recebut altament com a lur rey e seynor.

E dissapte que's comptave xxiii del mes de febrer lo dit senyor vench en lo monastir de Sent Anthoni, qui és assats prop la dita ciutat, e aturant aqui los digmenge e dilluns prop següents, les grans dances e alegria se comencen per los setges e altres parts de la ciutat.

E aprés lo dimarts demati vers viiiiº hores, que's comptave xxvi del dit mes de febrer, lo dit senyor volent entrar en la dita ciutat, per la part de la plaça del Mercat vers lo Portal del monastir del Carme, los ciutedins e ministres de aquesta ciutat de Nàpols hagueren fet derrocar aquí gran troç de mur, e al encontra del dit senyor ans que fos entrat, li fonch presentat un gran carro molt magnifich de iiii rodes, ab gran bastiment dessús dites rodes fet a manera de cadafal. Lo dit carro e rodes dalt a baix ere deurat, e dalt havie una molt rica cadira cuberta de brocat d'or e dos coxins del dit brocat, lo i per seure, l'altre per los peus, e lo siti perillós. E lo dit senyor venint en caballs, vestit de roba carmesí roceguant folrada de martes, ab cara molt ardent, clara e alegra, descavalcant de son cavall, pujà sobre lo dit carro, e sech en la dita cadira, e prestament li fonch posat dessús per los pus magnífichs homens de la ciutat, un molt rich pali de brocat d'or qui tenie xxii bordons, lo qual coste mil cccc ducats. E axí lo dit carro tirat per iiii molt bells cavalls blanchs en dos, ab cordons de seda e ab sengles coxinets de carmesí, vench fins al mur tranchat. E aquí aturat li vench un molt poxant entremés ab gran cadafal, fet per los mercaders cathalans, sobre lo qual entremés eren les iiii Virtuts, e lo siti perillós que lo dit senyor fa per sa divisa o empresa. E la una de les dites Virtuts ab alta veu significà e parlà al dit senyor que la dita empresa del dit siti perillós, per la benaventurada conquesta havie son obtente, com algun altre rey, príncep ne senyor no ere stat digne de seure sobre aquell siti, sinó lo dit senyor qui havie supeditat e obtengut lo dit rey-[al]me. E discorregut lo dit entremés ab moltes naturas de jochs que hi feren, vench altre entremés fet per los mercaders florentins, e sobre un cadafal hagueren posat un home armat de ernés, com qui stave de peus sobre un pom gros, en designació del món, estant devant lo dit senyor ab alta veu li dix en substància semblants peraules: *Re Alfonso, re de pau, Déus te mantengue en ta prosperitat, e la bella Florença en sa libertat. E no't vulles altificar de tanta glòria, car béns són de fortuna, e lo món és qui rode.*

E dites aquestes o semblants paraules, artificialment feren rodar lo dit gran pom, fet a manera de món. E discorreguts. . . .

Lo comte de Sant Valentino, lo comte de Mareri, lo comte de Lauria, lo comte de Bochu, lo comte de Calatanoxeta, lo comte de Aderno, lo comte de Calataballota, lo compte de Olivito, lo comte de Mirabella, lo comte Gilabert, Romeo Caldora, Iacobo de Lagonisa, Carbo di Campobaixo, lo almirall de Cicília, lo almirall de Aragò, lo mestre justier de Cicília, lo conservador de Cicília, lo mestre portalà de Cici-lia, los embaxadors de Florença, lo embaxador de Jénova, los embaxadors de l'Àguila, mestre Iacobo Gayatano, Francisco de Montragono, e molts altres homes generosos e magnats.

E axi altament, lo dit senyor, entrant e passant per la dita plaça del Mercat ont ere començat lo arch triumfal que fan per memòria de la dita entrada, tirà la via dels Cambis o Banchs, e tots los carrés empaliats, tirà la via del Setgia de la Porta Nova, e aquell setgia altament empaliat e acompanyat de damas molt poxantment e ricosa vestides de carmasins e altres draps de seda, e lurs manyoses fornides de perles e fermalls e molts ministrés. Per mostrar la gran festa al dit senyor les dites dames dançaven. E axí discorrent lo dit senyor los setgias de Porto, e de Nido, e de Capuana, que aximateix eren empaliats e fornits de damas e ministrés, e continuant les grans dançes, lo dit senyor, molt alegrement, entrà en lo Castell de Capuana, ont havic aximateix de g[r]ans entremeses, dances e alegries. E aquella nit mateixa lo Castell de Sent Elm, lo Castell Nou, e lo Castell del Ou, e encara tota la ciutat han fetes grans luminàries e alimares.

Aprés, mossenyors molt honorables, aquella nit matexa, vengueren al dit senyor los dits prínceps, duchs, comtes e barons, e suplicarenlo que fos de sa mercè que, aprés son óbit, volgués proveyir e heretar don Ferrando de Aragó, del reyalme de Nàpols; e aquell en lo dit cars, los donàs per rey e senyor, car ells se offerien decontinent ferli homenatge, la qual cosa, lo dit senyor, molt liberalment atorguà.

Aprés, inmediadament, los dessús dits prínceps, comtes, duchs e barons, feren al dit senyor altre suplicació, que attès que lo papa e lo dit senyor no's podien concordar, que fos de sa mercè darlos licència que ells poguessen trametre o scriure al dit papa, que's concordàs ab lo dit senyor. En altra manera ells li significarien que no podien viure axí, e d'aquí avant lo papa los hagués per excusats, etc. E feta aquesta suplicació lo dit senyor molt benignament, la admeté, e ho atorguà segons ere demanat. De les altres cosas que per avant occorreran jo n'avisaré vostres grans savìeses, qui ordonen de mi tot lo que plasent vos sia.

Scrita en la ciutat de Nàpols, a XXVIII de ffebrer, any M.CCCC.XXXXIII.

[R. Filangieri, "Rassegna critica delle fonti per la storia di Castel Nuovo," ASPN, 63 (1938), 330–32; and José Maria Madurell Marimón, Mensajeros barceloneses en la corte de Nápoles de Alfonso V de Aragón, 1435–1458 (Barcelona, 1963), no. 164.]

2. THE ARCH OF 1443

Jamque Alphonsus per media sui triumphalis Arcus fundamenta coepta jam iter faciebat, monumenta que rerum suarum paululum conspicatus.

[Antonio Panormita, De dictis et factis Alphonsi regis Aragonum et Neapolis, in Janus Gruterus, Lampas, sive fax artium liberalium . . . , 2 (Florence, 1737), 39.]

3. THE ARCH OF 1443

Parve agli Eletti della Città far qualche memorabil dimostrazione di questo celebre, e segnalato Trionfo; e perciò eressero a communi spese un'Arco marmoreo, rappresentandolo a' Posteri; e fatto perciò venire quantità di bianchissimi marmi, condussero con buono stipendio da Milano Pietro di Martino, eccellentissimo Scultore di quei tempi, dal quale con mirabile artificio fu costrutto, e con bellissime statue compito; e volendolo porre avanti le scale della porta picciola dell' Arcivescovato, Cola Maria Bozzuto, il quale avea Servito al Re in quella guerra, ando a dolersi, che l'impediva il lume della sua casa: il Re ridendo dell'inconsiderata richiesta, disse che avea ragione; e ringraziando gli

Eletti, gli richiese si contentassero, che quello si erigesse nel Castello nuovo, ove fino a' nostri tempi si scorge nell' entrar dell' ultima porta.

[G. A. Summonte, *Historia della Città e Regno di Napoli* (1596 ff.), 4 (Naples, 1749), 16.]

4. THE TWO STATUES FROM ROME

28 September 1447

E nello stesso giorno con una saettia [Alfonso] fa transportare da Roma alla città di Napoli due statue di marmo con ordine di consegnarle ad Arnaldo Sanz castellano di Castelnuovo.

[Paraphrased in Camillo Minieri-Riccio, "Alcuni fatti di Alfonso I. d'Aragona," *ASPN*, 6 (1881), 254.]

5. EXCERPTS FROM THE CONTRACT FOR FINISHING THE CASTEL NUOVO

19 April and 21 May 1451

. . . Capitoli concordati et firmati fra la Maesta de lo S. Re da una parte et Honofrio de Iordano, Pertello de Marino, Coluza de Stasio et Carolo de Marino, maistri moraturi della Cava da l'altra parte. . . .

Item formeranno lle tre torri, cioè la torre di sancto Giorgio et li due torri dinante la porta dello castello tutte de fori in basolato di peperino et de dintro ali cantuni delle porte et finestre scalune et grade, dove bisognara et cholle iorlande como ordinara la corte a la grandeza de la torre dello Ovo. Et più formeranno alli doe torri de la porta lo poio et lo grado et tutte lle altre cose, che fra lle dette doe turri seranno besogno excepto lle marmore et pavimente . . .

Item formeranno de petra de piperno ad filo tutte lle scarpe delle turri et mura de lo castello, cioè de la torre de Beverello sino alla torre dello Ovo sequendo llo ja commenzato e nelle doe torri de la porta secondo la nostra divisata per la corte et faranno le copate alle doe turri de la porta secondo la corte divisara, salvo che non siano tanti bastuni, come ave fatto mastro Guillermo a la torre de Sancto Giorgio. Et ancora faranno la copatella di tutte lle scarpe et parapetti et mergoli ad tutto lo vaglyo et faranno la sporta de lo ponte fra lle doe turri de la porta secondo se pretende et lo arco et lo pilone de lo ponte de vasoli de piperno, seconda e divisato. . . .

. . . Ma li detti maestri non voleno essere tenuti ad laborare marmore ne figure e fogliagi ne alo lignyame de porte, finestre, ni de solaro e banchi. . . .

[H. W. Schülz, *Denkmäler der Kunst des Mittelalters in Unteritalien*, 4 (Dresden, 1860), 186–87.]

6. PIETRO DA MILANO IS RELEASED FROM HIS WORK AT SAN BIAGIO AND DEPARTS FROM RAGUSA

a. 3 May 1452

Prima pars est de dando libertatem dno R[ectori]. et eius parvo Consilio ad contemplationem Majestatis dni Regis Aragonum de liberando familiam et avere et raubas [roba] Magri petri lacipide de Mediolano quod possint libere ire et portare ubi voluerint.

b. 2 June 1452

Prima pars est de franchando plegios Magri petri lacipide de Mediolano occasione laborerij quod ipse promiserat facere communi nostro seu procuratoribus sancti blasii, et occasione denarorum habitorum pro quibus ipsi plegii [*sic*] promiserat pro tempo [*sic*].

[C. von Fabriczy, "Pietro da Martino da Milano in Ragusa," *Repertorium für Kunstwissenschaft, 28* (1905), 192–93.]

7. THE EQUESTRIAN GROUP

26 May 1452
Alfonso (at Pozzuoli) to Francesco Foscari, Doge of Venice

Illustrissimo Francisco Foscari Venetiarum duci amico nostro carissimo.

Illustrissime Dux, amice noster carissime, cum audiverimus ingeni solertiam atque subtilitatem magistri Donatelli in statuis tam eneis quam marmoreis fabricandis, magna nobis voluntas recessit eundem penes nos et in nostris serviciis per aliquod tempus habere. non enim, ut arbitramur, vos latet quam nos in huiuscemodi statuis et operibus et eneis et marmoreis delectemur, quam ob rem vos precamur et rogamus vehementer ut contemplatione nostri eidem magistro Donatello quod ad servitia nostra se conferre possit, libenti animo licentiam concedere velitis, et quia, ut accepimus, ab isto illu- strissimo Domino nondum ei satisfactum est de eo quod sibi debetur de quadam statua enea Gattamelate quondam per eum facta, integre sibi satisfieri nostri potissimum intuitu curretis, ut commodius iter non versus carpere possit, in quo agendo quamplurimum nobis complacebitis. super hoc enim plenius vos nostra nomine alloquetur venerabilis et religiosus magnificusque et dilectus consiliarius et orator noster frater Ledovicus Dezpuig claverius Montesie cui ut in eo fidem tamquam nobis adhibere vobis placeat iterum vos rogamus, datum Puteolis die xxvi. maii anno a nativitate Domini M.CCCC.LII. rex Alfonsus.

[This and a very similar letter, to the Venetian ambassador in Naples, Zaccaria Vallareso, are published in Jordi Rubió, "Alfons 'el Magnánim' rei de Nápols, i Daniel Florentino, Leonardo da Bisuccio i Donatello," *Miscel·lània Puig i Cadafalch, 1* (Barcelona, 1947–51), 25–35.]

8. ALFONSO TO THE RECTORS OF RAGUSA

3 June 1452

Rex aragonum etc.

Spectabiles et magnifici viri amici nostri carissimi: aliis nostris cum literis scripsisse vobis me- minimus vos quam maxime deprecantes ut Petro de Mediolano sculptori lapideo a vobis certo salario conducto quem ob eis in sua arte ingenium singulare nobiscum aliquamdiu habere cuperemus licentiam prestaretis ad nos cum uxore et omne eius familia et rebus veniendi et apud nos essendi dum eius opera in aliquibus fabriciis nostris uteremur.

[C. von Fabriczy, "Neues Zum Triumphbogen Alphonsos I.," *Jahrbuch der preussischen Kunstsamm- lungen, 23* (1902), 3–16.]

9. THE LOWER ARCH

17 July 1453

Item lo dit jorn doni an Jacme Gil de mon ofici, havent carrech dela obra del Castell nou, por manament del S. Rey, ab cedula maridada dada lo dit XIIII jorn, CCCXXXXVI d. II t. XVI gr. por paguar a Pere Johan, Pere de Milana, Paulo de Mariano e a mestre Francisco da Zara, ab lurs formulors que por tots son XXXIII, del quel es degut fins per tot maig p. passat.

[R. Filangieri, "Rassegna critica," *ASPN, 63* (1938), 336–37.]

10. PERE JOAN

7 October 1453

Pere Joan is described as "mestre d'obres" for the court.

[Paraphrased by R. Filangieri, "Rassegna critica," *ASPN, 62* (1937), 315, n. 2.]

At this point occurred a lacuna in the cedole, from November 1453 to June 1455.

11. THE ANONYMOUS LETTER TO FRANCESCO SFORZA

28 July 1455

. . . dala Porta fa un arco de marmori scorpidi et lavoradi a l'antica con una architetura somptuosa et mirabele. Sono già gitadi li fondamenti, et lavorasse per li marmorarii con studio et singular diligentia.

[R. Filangieri, "Rassegna critica," *ASPN, 62* (1937), 267.]

12. FAZIO PRAISES THE ARCH

Arcem instauravit [Alphonsus] cum arcu triumphali magnificentia, structura, opere nulli omnium in orbe terrarum secundam.

[Bartolommeo Fazio, *De viris illustribus* (1454–55) (Florence, 1745), p. 78.]

13. FAZIO PRAISES THE ARCH AGAIN

Inter turrim mediam et angularem ad occasum vergentes, portam cum ingenti arcu triumphali, ex marmore candidissimo, constituit [Alphonsus].

[Bartolommeo Fazio, *De rebus gestis Alphonsi Aragonum* (1451–55), in Gravier, *Raccolta, 9, 255.*]

14. THE TRIUMPH FRIEZE: ISAIA DA PISA

31 January 1456

A mestre Ysayes mestre marmorar qui lauora en lo Castell nou de Napols en paga per rata del salari que deu haver per lo lauor que fa en lo dit Castell nou de Napols . . . XXXd.

A mestre Andria del Aguila axi mateix mestre marmorar qui lauora en lo dit Castell nou de Napols per la predita raho . . . XXXd.

[C. von Fabriczy, "Der Triumphbogen Alphonsos I am Castelnuovo zu Neapel," *Jahrbuch der königlichen preussischen Kunstsammlungen, 20* (1899), doc. 3.]

15. FURTHER PAYMENTS TO ISAIA DA PISA

May 1455–May 1456

A mestre Ysayes mestre de fer ymatges de pedra marbre qui lavora vuy en la fabrica del Castell nou de Napols a compliment de CCLXXXVII d. IIt. Xg que li eren deguts per los treballs per ell sustenguts lavorant en la dita fabrica del Castell nou de Napols per temps de—XI mesos—XV jorns que finiren lo derrer dia del propassat mes de Abril a raho de—XXV d. que li mana pagar lo dit senyor per castun mes. Car veritat es ques los—CXXXVIII d. li son stats ja pagats per mj dels quals li fac exida co es dels—CVIII d. en lo meu quart libre ordinarj en c [carta] CCCCXXXXVIIII e dels—XXX d. atras en c. CLXXXXV . . . CXXXXVIIII d. IIt. X gr.

[Ibid., doc. 4.]

16. ANDREA DELL'AQUILA WORKS ON THE TRIUMPH FRIEZE

31 August 1456

Item donj mestre Andria maestre marmorar—VIIII d. IIIIt. VI½ gr. los quals li eren deguts ab albara de scriua de racio scrit en la Torre d'Ottauo lo derrer dia del present mes de Agost per resta de—XXXVIIII d. IIII t. VI½gr. que devia haver per lo lavor que ha fet en les pedres marbres del Trihumfo del portal del Castell nou dela ciutat de Napols es a saber: per temps de dos mesos e—XXVIII dies comptant del III.ᶻᵒ dia del mes de Juny propassat fins per tut lo dit present mes de Agost arazo de—XII duc. lo mes co es lo hun mes e XXVIII dies, e laltre mes arazo de—XVI duc. III t. VI g. mj prech segons en lo dit albara se conte que cobre. Car veritat es que los—XXX d. li foren accorreguts per mj segons apar en la exida que mi fac en lo meu—VI.ᵉʳ libre ordinarj en c.— . . . VIIII d. IIII t. VI½.

[Ibid., doc. 8.]

There was no mention of the Arch in the cedole for the first semester of 1457. The cedole for the second semester have always been lacking.

17. THE COLOSSI

31 January 1458

Item doni a mestre Ysayes de Pisa, Anthoni de Pisa, Pere de Milana, Domjnico Lombardo, Francisco Adzara e Paulo Romano mestres marmorars CC d. los quals los acorregui en la ciutat de Napols por mans de mosser Loys Sarcola havent carrech de pagar les despeses ques fan por causa de la fabrica del Castell nou de Napols ab albara de scriua de racio scrit en Atella lo derrer dia del present mes de Janer en accoriment e paga pro rata de aquells III.ᵃ DCCC duc. por los quals han pres a stall de acabar integrament les figures del arc triumfal del dit Castell nou segons en lo dit albara se conte que cobre . . . CC duc.

[Ibid. doc. 9.]

18. FURTHER PAYMENT FOR THE COLOSSI

28 February 1458

Item doni a mestre Ysayes de Pisa, Antonj de Pisa, Pere de Milana, Domjnico Lombardo, Francesco

Atzara e Paulo Romano mestres de fer figures de pedra marbre—CC d. los quals los acorreguj en la ciutat de Napols per mans de mosser Loys Sarcola ab albara de scriua de racio scrit en Troya lo derrer dia del present mes de febrer en acoriment e paga pro rata de III.ª DCCC d. per los quals han pres a stall e se son convenguts ab la cort de acabar les figures del arch triumfal que fa fer lo S.ᵒʳ Rey sobre lo portal del Castell nou de Napols segons en lo dit albara se conte que cobre . . . CC d.

[Ibid., doc. 11.]

The volumes of cedole were lacking from June 1458 to the end of April 1460. Then from 1460 through 1464 there was no mention of the Arch.

19. ANDREA DELL'AQUILA

3 June 1458
Nicola Severino to Cristoforo Felici

. . . Qui si trova uno Andrea, o vero maestro Andrea da l'Aquilla, che veramente si puo chiamare maestro: el quale fu discepolo di Donatello, che costì si trova, et a lui e notissimo et alevossi molti anni in Fiorenza in casa di Cosmo. Costui e singolare pictore et anco maestro di scoltura, et al presente ha fatto una parte de l'arco triumphale del re, che è una cosa molto eletta et da ciascuno laudata oltre a tutte le altre de gl'altri maestri: il perchè e dagli altri molto invidiato: et anco la conditione de la terra si de la moria, et si de la suspitione per la malattia del re lo induce e conforta a partirsi.

[N. F. Faraglia, "Le Memorie degli artisti napoletani . . . ," *ASPN, 8* (1883), 277.]

20. THE BRONZE EQUESTRIAN STATUE

[Donatello] Fece una testa et il collo d'un cavallo di molta grandezza, opera assai degna, la quale comincio et fece per finire il restante del cavallo; sul quale a essere aveva l'immagine del re Alfonso d'Aragona; la quale hoggi è in Napoli in casa il Conte de Matalona de Caraffi.

[From Codice Gaddiano, XVII.17, Biblioteca Nazionale, Florence, fol. 66. Published by Antonio Filangieri, "La colossale Testa di cavallo in bronzo del Museo Nazionale di Napoli," *Arte e Storia,* anno 20 (15 October 1901), pp. 127–28. See also the passage in the Codex Magliabecchiano published in G. Milanesi, *Catalogo delle opere di Donatello e bibliografia degli autori che ne hanno scritto* (Florence, 1887), s.v., and that in the Codex Strozziano, published by Hans Semper, *Donatello, seine Zeit und Schule, vol. 9, Quellenschriften für Kunstgeschichte* (Vienna, 1875) pp. 306–09. These latter two are essentially the same.]

21. THE INNER ARCH

8 June 1465

E mes donj al dit en Pere Bernart (regent la regia Thesaureria) per misa del banch de Antonio de Gayeta cinquanta duc. per donar a maestre Pere marmolar en accorriment de DCCCV duc. deu haver per la fabrica del arch triumphal del Castell nou ha pres astall . . . L d.

[Fabriczy, "Der Triumphbogen," doc. 13.]

22. PAYMENT TO PIETRO DA MILANO

4 July 1465

A mestre Pere marmorar en accorriment dela fabrica del arch triumphal . . . L d.

[Ibid., doc. 14.]

23. MORE PAYMENTS TO PIETRO DA MILANO

30 September 1465

Item donj de manament del S. R. per ma den Johan de Guares a mestre Pere dal Mila picapedrer les quantitats deius scrites les quals lo dit S.ᵒʳ lj mana donar, e son en paga e prorata de DCCCL duc. que li eren deguts per causa dela obra de pedra marbra ha feta en lo arch triumphal sobre la porta del Castell nou los quals li donj en les jornades seguents ço es

a VIII de Juny passat—L d.
a IIII de Juhol   —L d.
a XIII d'Agost   —L d.
a VIIII de Setembre —L d.
a XII del dit   —L d.
a XXVIII del dit   —C d.
             CCCL d.

[Ibid., doc. 15.]

24. THE HEART CONTAINER

2 April 1466

Item lo dit jorn donj de manament del S.ᵒʳ R. a mestre Andria Gallardo argenter VIII duc. los quals lo dit S.ᵒʳ li mana donar, e son prorata del preu de hun cor de aram que deu fer per metre lo cor del S.ᵒʳ R. don Alfonso de gloriosa recordacio en lo Castell nou present Andreu Ferrer.

[Ibid., doc. 16.]

25. THE INNER ARCH

31 May 1466

Item donj de manament del S.ᵒʳ R. per ma den Johan de Guares (scriua dela sua tresoreria lo qual ha carrech de pagar la fabrica del Castell nou) a mestre Pere de Mila pedrapiquere e cap mestre de totes les obres de pedra del Castell nou les quantitats de peccunja deius scrites les quals lo dit S.ᵒʳ les li mana donar e son a compliment de DCCCL d. que li eren deguts per causa dela obra de pedra marbre que havie feta en lo arch triumphal sobre la porta del dit castell les quals li donj en les jornades seguents co es

a XVI de Octubre de l' any passat—C d.
a XVIIII del dit   —C d.
a II de Noembre   —C d.
a VII de Decembre   —L d.

a XXIII del dit	—L d.
a XVII de Marc del present any	—L d.
a VIIII del present mes de Maig	—L d.
	D d.

com per mi e per part mja per lo dit en Johan de Guares son stades reyalment pagades les sobredictes quantitats al dit mestre Pere en paga e satisfactio dela dita obra en scomplir e finjr lo sobredit arch a tota sa despesa.

[Ibid., doc. 17.]

26. THE HEART CONTAINER

30 June 1466

Item donj de manament del S.ᵒʳ R. a mestre Andria Galasso argenter dela present ciutat de Napols XIII duc IIII tarens los quals son a compliment de XXXIII duc. II tar. X grans li eren deguts ab albara de offici de scriua de racio scrit en Capua a XXIIII dies del mes de Maig propassat per lo compir de hun gran vaxell de aram daurat e soldat de argent que ha fet aforma de cor per tenjr en a quell conservat lo cor del gloriosissimo S.ᵒʳ R. don Alfonso de immortal memoria lo qual deu star pengiat en l'arch triumphal del Castell nou de la dita ciutat lo qual es stat consignat al mag.ᶜʰ moss. Pasqual Diaz Garlon . . . XIII d. IIII t.

[Ibid., doc. 18.]

27. THE INNER ARCH

14 October 1467

A mestre Pere marmorar en accorriment del que deura hauer per la obra del portal del Castell nou . . . L d.

[Ibid., doc. 19.]

28. ANGELILLO ARCUCCIO PAINTS THE CORONATION RELIEF

4 May 1468

A mestre Angerillo Artuzzo pintor II duc. en accorriment o per camprar or per daurar lo pom e la corona dela ymatge de marmora dela M.ᵗᵃ del dit S.ᵒʳ [Ferrante] qui sta en lo portal del Castell nou de Napols . . . II d.

[Ibid., doc. 20.]

29. PAYMENTS FOR THE INNER ARCH

16 July 1468

A mestre Pere marmorar en accorriment del que deura haver per la obra del portall del Castell nou dela dita ciutat . . . X d.

[Ibid., doc. 21.]

30. MORE PAYMENTS FOR THE INNER ARCH

16 November 1471

A mestre Pere marmorar en accorriment de la obra del portal del Castell nou . . . xv d.

[Ibid., doc. 24.]

31. THE CORONATION RELIEF

27 November 1471

A mestre Joan Remolo argenter en accorriment de aco que deura hauer per lo pintar e daurar de hun ceptre ha de tenir la ymatge del S. R. [Ferrante] sta en lo portal del Castell nou . . . II d.

[Ibid., doc. 25.]

32. THE EQUESTRIAN GROUP

12 July 1471
Diomede Carafa, Count of Maddaloni, in Naples, to Lorenzo de' Medici in Florence

Magnifice domine et fili col^me. Ho ricevuto la testa del cavallo la S. V. se digniata mandareme, de che ne resto tanto contento quanto de cosa havesse desiderato et ringracione V. S. infinite volte si per essere stato dono digno como per haverlo da la S. V. Avisandola llo ben locato in la mia casa che se vede da omne canto; certificandove che non solo de V. S. ad me ne starà memoria, ma ad mei fillioli, in quali de continuo haveranno la S. V. in observancia et serannoli obligati extimando l'amore qu'ella ha mostrato in volere comparere con tale dono et ornamento alla dicta casa. Si ho da servire la S. V. son parato et pregola me vollia operare che volintiero sarà da me et de bona vollia servita et recommandome alla S. V.

[G. Filangieri, "La Testa di cavallo in bronzo già di casa Maddaloni," *ASPN*, 7 (1882), 416.]

Appendix 2. BIOGRAPHICAL DATA ON THE ARTISTS

The bibliography in this appendix is centered on the artists' Arch contributions. It is limited to documents and attributions. Other works may be found in the Bibliography.

ANDREA DELL'AQUILA

Nothing is known of Andrea's birth (except that it was probably in L'Aquila). He is said to have studied under Cosimo's patronage and to have been a pupil of Donatello (Doc. 19). In 1446 he lodged a complaint with Florentine authorities against the parish of Modigliana, which owed him 20 florins for painting coats of arms (Valentiner).

In January 1456 Andrea joined the group of sculptors working on the Arch at the rate of 12 ducats per month (Docs. 14, 16). He probably left Naples in the summer of 1458 along with the other sculptors. No other documents have so far come to light.

Valentiner has made a number of attributions, including the marble relief of the Madonna and Child in the Ospedale San Giacomo, Rome, which is signed "opus Andriae," the tabernacle in the Church of the Madonna del Soccorso, Aquila, and—quite wrongly—the inner left-hand lateral relief of the Arch. Even more boldly he suggests that Andrea may have been a painter, too, and identical with the Master of the Castello Nativity.

Valentiner, W. R. "Andrea dell'Aquila, Painter and Sculptor." *Art Bulletin, 19* (1937), 503–36.

———. "Andrea dell'Aquila in Urbino," *Art Quarterly, 1* (1938), 275–88.

CHELLINO, ANTONIO

Antonio [di] Chellino, or Chellini, also known as Antonio de Pisa and possibly also as Antonio de Lugano, was probably born about 1400. In February 1446 and apparently until 12 May 1449 he worked in Padua as an assistant of Donatello (Janson). He is said to have created one of the bronze relief evangelist symbols and an angel on the Santo altar (Valentiner). On 12 May 1449 he received 82 lire for mouldings and large blocks (*priede grande*) for the altar in Padua (Janson).

We find him in Naples in January and February 1458 (Docs. 17, 18). After this there is a gap in the records. In 1460 an oration given in Ferrara by Lodovico Carbone mentions a certain Antonio Pisano, goldsmith and painter. Zippel wonders if this could have been Antonio, but probably Pisanello was meant. Filarete, in the *Trattato* (composed in the early or mid-1460s) seems to describe Chellino as still living, though of course he could have been mistaken.

On purely stylistic grounds Fabriczy assigns to Antonio two terra-cotta reliefs of the Madonna and Child which in 1906 were at Piazzola (near Padua) and Costozza (near Vicenza, now called Barzello), dating from the Paduan period, 1447–54; a Madonna in the Via Pietrapiana, Florence, which he dates ca. 1454; and other work in Siena. See also Rolfs. On the Arch, Valentiner assigns to him the upper Victories and vault, and the lunette over the Chapel of Saint Barbara.

Fabriczy, C. von. "Antonio di Chellino da Pisa." *L'Arte, 9* (1906), 442–45.

Filarete, Antonio. *Treatise on Architecture,* Book 6.

Janson, H. W. *The Sculpture of Donatello.* Princeton, 1957. 2, 163–66.

Rolfs, W. *Franz Laurana.* Berlin, 1907. 2, 202, n. 1.

Valentiner, W. R. "Andrea dell'Aquila, Painter and Sculptor." *Art Bulletin, 19* (1937), 514–21.

Zippel, G. "Artisti alla corte degli Estensi nel Quattrocento." *L'Arte, 5* (1902), 405–07.

GAGINI, DOMENICO

Domenico Gagini, also known as Domenico Lombardo (Fabriczy), Domenico dal Lagho di Logano, and Domenico de Bisono (i.e. Bissone), was a member of a well-known family of Genoese sculptors. He was probably born about 1425.

On 5 April 1448 "Domenico Petrus de Bisono intagliator marmorum" was working in Genoa on the facade of the Chapel of San Giovanni Battista in the cathedral. The project lasted until 1465, but Domenico himself did not remain (Cervetto), for in 1455 he was assigned the decorations of the Chapel of San Girolamo del Rozo, Genoa, now destroyed. The baptistry facade of this church, which does exist, has been given to Gagini and assistants on stylistic grounds (Thieme-Becker).

In early 1458, Gagini was among the workers in Naples (Docs. 17, 18).

In 1460–62 Domenico was in Palermo, where he made signed repairs in the mosaics in the Cappella Palatina. Notarial archives in Palermo indicate that on 8 January 1463 he had settled in the city. From 1464 there is a signed font in the cathedral at Salemi, and from 1463 the signed tomb of Pietro Speciale in San Francesco, Palermo, now destroyed (Di Marzo and Mauceri). Documents from 1468 indicate that Domenico was gambling in merchandise. In 1472 there is record of a claim for payments for the work on the Cappella Palatina, and in 1475 Domenico decorated the magnificent chapel of Santa Cristina in the Palermo cathedral, now destroyed (Di Marzo and Mauceri). Bottari assigns to him the 1469 bust of Pietro Speciale now in the Galleria Nazionale, Palermo—though the portrait is in many ways Lauranesque—and a bust in San Domenico, Andria, of Francesco II del Balzo.

From 1480 there is a signed Madonna in the Church of San Mauro, Castelverde (Di Marzo and Mauceri), and in 1482 a signed sarcophagus for San Gandolfo, in the Polizzi cathedral (partially destroyed). In 1484 Domenico and his shop made figurated capitals in Santa Annunziata, Palermo (Di Marzo and Mauceri). Gagini is less believably credited with two statues of the Virgin in the Hospital de la Sang, Palma de Mallorca (Ainaud de Lasarte). These could be the work of assistants, however; perhaps they are two of the three such statues that on 14 May 1483 Domenico consigned to a certain Lorenzo di Faenza to be sold in Catalonia (Di Marzo and Mauceri).

Next, there is a document dated 10 January 1486 that charges "Honorabilis magister dominicus de gagini marmorarius civis panormi" with "faciendum et laborandum bene et magistraliter columpnas marmoreas quatuordecim cum eorum capitellis . . . et capitelli debent esse formata et sculpta [sic] secundum modum et formam quemadmodum sunt isti qui etiam sunt in dicto conventu Sancti Francisci . . . panormi." These columns for the Franciscan convent in Messina are now destroyed. The payment was 10 tarì, 8 grani (Mauceri). Di Marzo and Mauceri attribute parts of the side door of Sant'Agostino, Palermo, to Domenico, as well as the sarcophagus of Giovanni Montaperto (1485) in the cathedral at Mazzara, the Madonna dell'Udienza in the Carmine, Palermo, and that in San Salvatore in the same city.

Domenico Gagini died on 29 or 30 September 1492 (Di Marzo).

Accàscina, Mana. "Inediti di Scultura del Rinascimento in Sicilia." *Mitteilungen des Kunsthistorischen Instituts in Florenz, 14* (1970), 251–96.

Ainaud de Lasarte, Juan. *Alfonso el Magnànimo y las artes plàsticas de su tiempo.* Palma de Mallorca, 1955. P. 19.

Bottari, Stefano. "Per Domenico Gagini." *Rivista d'arte, 17* (1935), 77–85.

Cervetto, L. A. *I Gaggini da Bissone. Loro Opere in Genoa ed altrove.* Genoa, 1903. Pp. 35–50.

Di Marzo, G. *I Gagini e la Scultura in Sicilia nei secoli XV e XVI.* Palermo, 1880–83. *I,* 68–101.

Di Marzo, G., and E. Mauceri. "L'Opera di Domenico Gagini in Sicilia." *L'Arte, 6* (1903), 147–58.

Fabriczy, C. von. "Domenico Gaggini in Neapel." *Repertorium für Kunstwissenschaft, 28* (1905), 193–95.

Kruft, Hanno-Walter. "Die Madonna von Trapani und ihre Kopien. Studien zur Madonnentypologie und zum Begriff der Kopie in der Sizilianischen Skulptur des Quattrocento." *Mitteilungen des Kunst-historisches Instituts in Florenz, 14* (1969–70), 297–322.

Mauceri, E. "Nuovi Documenti intorno a Domenico Gagini." *Rassegna bibliografica dell'arte italiana,* 6 (1903), 170–74.

Thieme-Becker (1920), s.v. (B. C. Kreplin).

ISAIA DA PISA

Isaia da Pisa, sometimes listed as the son of Pippo Ghanti and sometimes as the son of the Pippo di Giovanni da Pisa who had assisted Donatello on the Santo altar, was born in Pisa in about 1410. In 1431 he was employed in the Vatican, and in 1447 he was apparently asked to complete Filarete's tomb for Cardinal Antonio Chiaves, now in the Lateran in changed form (Ciaccio). In this same year Isaia worked on the tomb of Eugenius IV, now also greatly changed, in San Salvatore in Lauro, Rome. Porcellio credits him with this and with the effigy of Santa Monica in Sant'Agostino, Rome. According to Seymour he was in Rimini in 1448. Isaia is recorded in Orvieto in 1450–51, where he made a design for a gable on the Duomo.

In 1456 ff. we find him in charge of the triumph frieze of Alfonso's arch, and he remains in Naples until 1458 (Docs. 14, 15, 17, 18).

On 11 July 1460 Paolo Romano and assistants were paid 10 ducats for work on the "prima porta in tinello" in the Vatican, and it is possible that Isaia was among these unspecified co-workers, for the two did subsequently work together. Thus on 8 March 1463, 100 ducats go to Isaia and Paolo for work on the tabernacle of Sant'Andrea, now in the Grotte Vaticane (Bertolotti, Ciaccio). In 1463–64 documents for the benedictional pulpit of Pius II mention Isaia as well as Paolo (Bertolotti), and payments to the former are recorded through 29 August 1464 (Bertolotti).

Porcellio corroborates some of these facts in his poem in praise of Isaia and also attributes to him statues made for Porcellio himself of Nero and Poppaea riding on animals, and a Madonna and Child (probably one now in the Grotte). The tomb slab of Maffeo Vegio, Sant'Agostino, Rome, is given to Isaia by Ciaccio, who also attributes two fragments in Viterbo, in the Museo Civico and in Santa Trinità. Burger attributes to him various pieces in the Grotte Vaticane, and the tomb slab of Fra Angelico, Santa Maria sopra Minerva.

Battaglini, Angelo. "Memoria sopra uno sconosciuto egregio scultore del secolo XV e sopra alcune sue opere." *Dissertazioni [Atti] dell'Accademia romana di archaeologia, 1* (1821), 115–32. [For Porcellio]

Bertolotti, A. "Urkundliche Beiträge zur Biographie des Bildhauers Paolo di Mariano." *Repertorium für Kunstwissenschaft, 4* (1881), 426–42.

Burger, Fritz. "Isaia da Pisas plastische Werke in Rom." *Jahrbuch der preussischen Kunstsammlungen,* 27 (1906), 228–44.

Ciaccio, Lisetta. "Scultura romana del rinascimento." *L'Arte, 9* (1906), 165–84.

Seymour, Charles, Jr. *Sculpture in Italy: 1400–1500.* Harmondsworth, Mddx., 1967. P. 134.

Thieme-Becker (1926), s.v. (R. Semrau).

LAURANA, FRANCESCO

Francesco Laurana, or Laurano, or Lovranna, or adZara, or Azzara, or Schiavone, was probably born at Vrana, the village just inland from Biograd, on the coast not far from Zara, i.e. Zadar (Requin). This town used to be known as Laurana (Jackson). I presume that Laurana was born about 1430–35 and that he came from the same artistic culture as Giorgio da Sebenico. L. Venturi has suggested that the artist executed certain small heads on the exterior of the apse of Sibenik cathedral, much of the architectural ornament in the ducal palace at Urbino, and the shield-bearing putti in San Francesco,

Rimini. A. Dudan claims he executed a relief of Sant'Anastasia for the cathedral in Zadar, now no. 257 in the Museum. The idea is unconvincing. Rolfs suggests Laurana may have worked with Domenico Gagini on the chapel of San Giovanni Battista in the Duomo at Genoa between 1448 and 1453. Finally, Valentiner has assigned him various sculptured portraits.

The earliest document referring to Laurana that I know of is the one that introduces him to Naples along with Pietro da Milano, Pere Joan, and Paolo Romano (Doc. 9; 17 July 1453). He continued to work on the Arch (Docs. 17, 18) through 28 February 1458. Burger suggests that Laurana then made the decorative surround for the niche containing Gagini's statue of the Madonna and Child in the sacristy of the chapel of Santa Barbara, Castel Nuovo, while R. Filangieri adds that Laurana may have made the triumph portal relief facing the Gran Sala.

There is a gap in Laurana's history until 1461–66, when we find him in France, probably with Pietro da Milano, making medals signed "Franciscus Laurana" for René of Anjou. In 1464 according to some sources he designed a fountain (now destroyed) in the village of Le Puy-Saint-Réparade, near Aix (Requin). I have supposed a return to Naples in 1465, and that Laurana then helped Pietro da Milano with the inner arch (see above, pp. 44–45).

In 1467 Laurana is known to have been in Sicily, working on commissions in Partanna, Sciacca, Noto, and elsewhere. On 3 June 1468, there is a contract specifying that "Magister Petrus de Bonitate et Magister Franciscus de Laurana, scultores, habitatores Panormi" are to build a chapel in the church of San Francesco, Palermo, with a sarcophagus supported on columns and an altar, for Antonio de Magistro Antonio (Mastrantonio), with a life-size Virgin and an outer arch with figures specified by Mastrantonio, for 200 gold *onzi* (Burger, pp. 171–72). This chapel still exists.

On 16 August 1469 another document records that "Franciscus Laurana . . . habitator . . . urbis Panormi et civitatis Venetiarum" had made for Paolo de Gammicchia, archpriest of Monte San Giuliano, a life-size image of the Virgin, in marble, modeled on one by Nino Pisano in Santa Maria Annunziata, Trapani, for 25 gold onzi. This had been intended for a church in Monte San Giuliano but the Palermo officials would not permit the statue to leave the city. So now Francesco is to make another, similar work for the original patron, paid for—oddly enough—in advance (Burger, pp. 172–74). The statue of the Madonna della Neve in the church at Noto is inscribed "Franciscus Laurana me fecit 1471."

In 1474 Laurana was again in Naples, for there are records that he was paid for a Madonna and Child over the entrance to the chapel of Santa Barbara in Castel Nuovo (Barone; Fabriczy).

Laurana returned to the north in 1477 and with Tommaso Malvito executed the Chapel of Saint-Lazare in the Old Cathedral, Marseilles, completed in 1481. In the years 1479–81, apparently alone, Laurana also carved the relief of Christ carrying the Cross for the church of the Celestines, Avignon. It is now in the Church of St.-Didier in that city. Quite probably also during these years he made the tomb of Charles, Count of Maine (d. 1473), in Le Mans cathedral.

According to my own inferences Laurana then returned for a third time to Naples (René died in 1480) and began the famous series of portrait busts of the female relatives of Alfonso of Calabria (later Alfonso II). There are seven of these, one of his sister Beatrice (private collection, New York), three of his daughter Isabella (Louvre; Musée Jacquemart-André; Galleria Nazionale, Palermo), and three of his wife Ippolita Sforza (formerly Kaiser-Friedrich Museum; Frick Collection; National Gallery, Washington). An eighth such bust of a relative of Alfonso of Calabria, resembling Ippolita, is now in the Kunsthistorisches Museum, Vienna. Finally there is in the Bargello a Laurana bust of Battista Sforza. My research indicates that the Neapolitan works, which I repeat are not documented, were made in the years 1487–89, which differs from Valentiner's dating.

In 1495 Laurana presumably followed his abdicated patron Alfonso II to Sicily, where the ex-king died in that same year and Laurana made the tomb slab of Cecilia Aprilis now in the Galleria Nazionale, Palermo. The bust of Pietro Speciale from the Palazzo Rafadali, Palermo (now in the Galleria Nazionale) is also a possible work of Laurana's from this period. The attribution of two male portrait busts in a private collection, recently published by Middeldorf and Kruft, is unconvincing.

Laurana made a final visit to France and is mentioned in Marseilles on 10 November 1500. On 12 March 1502 he died in Avignon.

Babic, L. "Luciano e Francesco Laurana." *Actes du XIXe Congrès international d'histoire de l'art*. Paris, 1959. Pp. 231–34.

Barone, N. "Le Cedole di tesoreria dell'archivio di stato. . . ." *ASPN*, 9 (1884), 397.

Burger, Fritz. *Francesco Laurana*. (Strasbourg, 1907). P. 38.

Causa, R. "Sagrera, Laurana e l'Arco di Castelnuovo." *Paragone* 55 (1954), 3–23.

D'Elia, M. "Appunti per la ricostruzione dell'attività di Francesco Laurana." *Annali*, Facoltà di Letters, Università di Bari, 5 (1959), 1–23.

Dudan, Alessandro. *La Dalmazia nell'arte italiana*. Milan, 1921. *1*, 166–77.

Fabriczy, C. von. "Toscanische und oberitalienische Künstler in Diensten der Aragonesen zu Neapel." *Repertorium für Kunstwissenschaft*, 20 (1897), 117–20.

Filangieri, R. "La gran Sala di Castel Nuovo." *Dedalo*, 9 (1928–29), 168–69.

Hersey, G. L. *Alfonso II and the Artistic Renewal of Naples*. New Haven, 1969. Pp. 30–43. Cf. the review of this work by H. W. Kruft, *Kunstchronik*, 23 (1970), 151–66.

Jackson, T. G. *Dalmatia, the Quarnero and Istria. . . .* Oxford, 1887. *1*, 363.

Middeldorf, Ulrich, and Hanno-Walter Kruft. "Three Male Portrait Busts by Francesco Laurana." *Burlington Magazine*, 113 (1971), 264–67.

Requin, H. "Documents inédits sur le sculpteur François Laurana." *Réunion des sociétés des beaux-arts des départements*, 25 (Paris, 1901), 498–508.

Rolfs, Wilhelm. *Franz Laurana*. Berlin, 1907. *1*, 31–45.

Trabaud, P. "Le Retable de Saint-Didier à Avignon." *Gazette des beaux-arts*, ser. 2, 23 (1881), 175–80.

Valentiner, W. R. "Laurana's Portrait Busts of Women." *Art Quarterly*, 5 (1942), 273–98.

———. "A Portrait Bust of Alphonso I of Naples." *Art Quarterly*, 1 (1938), 61–88.

Venturi, L. "Studi sul palazzo ducale di Urbino." *L'Arte*, 17 (1914), 420–41.

The literature listed under Gagini should also be consulted.

LO MONACO, GUGLIELMO

Guglielmo Lo Monaco de Parisio, earlier thought to have come from Paris, seems actually to have been Umbrian by birth; "Parisio" is "Perusia" not "Parigi" (Müntz). On 31 December 1451 Alfonso welcomed him into his service with a privilegium comparable to that written for Pisanello (Filangieri; Schülz). He is described as a maker of clocks and "aliasque res artificiosas" and is given an annual salary of 400 ducats—the same as Pisanello's.

On 13 April 1453 Guglielmo received 47 ducats, 4 tarì for placing metal bombards on the shore, and exactly three years later there is a record of his making a large bell for the Castel Nuovo. On 12 June 1456 has was given 52 quintals and 99 rotoli of bronze for making more bombards. On 31 January 1458 Guglielmo was paid 60 ducats on account of 1,117 owed for making a great clock for the Castel Nuovo. The following 28 March he received 100 ducats for gilding the roof of a fountain in the castle garden (all G. Filangieri). On 28 June 1458, just after Alfonso's death, Ferrante issued another privilegium confirming Guglielmo's position in the court and his 400-ducat salary (Schülz). On 31 May 1460 Ferrante paid Guglielmo 50 ducats to make powder for spingards and bombards and equipment for *trabucchi*—all types of cannon—while on 13 March 1469 Guglielmo's name is invoked in connection with a financial matter (all G. Filangieri).

According to R. Filangieri the bronze doors of the inner portal were probably made between mid-1474 and the end of 1475.

Filangieri, G. *Documenti per la storia le arti e le industrie delle provincie napoletane.* Vol. 6 Naples, 1891. s.v.

Filangieri, R. "Rassegna critica delle fonti per la storia di Castel Nuovo." *ASPN*, 62 (1937), 332, and n. 2.

Müntz, E. *Histoire de l'art pendant la Renaissance.* Paris, 1889. *1,* 114, 579.

Schülz, H. W. *Denkmäler der Kunst des Mittelalters in Unteritalien.* Dresden, 1860. *4,* 188–89, 195–96.

ONOFRIO DI GIORDANO

The documents for Onofrio di Giordano della Cava have been analyzed by Dudan. Onofrio was a native of Cava dei Tirreni and worked for Queen Giovanna, who called him "optimus architectorum." He arrived in Ragusa in 1436 as chief architect of the state and officiated at the reconstruction of the rector's palace, beginning 17 October 1437. He was also in charge of rebuilding aqueducts, and he constructed the Fontana d'Onofrio and another fountain at the Church of San Biagio, called the Fontana della Cava (Dudan). The contract for the Fontana d'Onofrio calls for its completion by 7 February 1438, but neither fountain, according to Dudan, was finished until ca. 1440. Another work in Ragusa was the Palazzo Onofrio (Dudan).

We next hear of Onofrio when he receives a passport from the rectors to return to Naples (4 November 1450; Fabriczy). In Naples he then signed the contracts of 19 April and 21 May 1451 for finishing the Castel Nuovo, working in concert with several of his countrymen (Doc. 5). Another document in the Archivo de la Corona de Aragón, Barcelona, mentions a "magistri Honofris de Jordano de Civitate Cave," who on 17 November 1451 was welcomed among Alfonso's courtiers and given the job of making certain purchases for the king.

On 9 July 1455 Alfonso received a request from the rectors of Ragusa for Onofrio to return to Dalmatia to help with the defense of the city against the Turks (Fabriczy). However Rolfs supposes, I think correctly, that Onofrio remained in Naples, where he apparently died in 1456.

Barcelona. Archivo de la Corona de Aragón. Privilegiorum. Cancellariae Neapolis, registro 2915, fols. 80r–87v.

Dudan, Alessandro. *La Dalmazia nell'arte italiana.* Milan, 1921. *1,* 171–75.

Fabriczy, C. von. "Onofrio Giordano della Cava." *Repertorium für Kunstwissenschaft,* 28 (1905), 188–90.

Rolfs, Wilhelm. *Franz Laurana.* Berlin, 1907. *1,* 48, n. 2.

The literature under Laurana should also be consulted.

PAOLO ROMANO

Paolo Romano was also called Paolo di Mariano da Sezze, Paolo di Santuccio Taccone da Sezze, Paolo de Urbe, and by various combinations of these names. His family, formerly well off, had lost its fortune. Paolo was born in Sezze, near Rome, about 1415–20. On 1 January 1451 he began to receive payments for work on three windows for the Palazzo dei Senatori on the Campidoglio, under the patronage of Nicholas V. On 3 March 1451 his father, Mariano di Tuccio da Sezze (who was also a sculptor), Paolo, and Pietro d'Albino da Castiglioni were working on two chapels on the Ponte Sant'Angelo. These are all the documents I know of before Paolo's arrival in Naples, where records of payments to him begin on 14 July 1453 (Docs. 9, 17, 18).

Paolo was back in Rome, but still working in humble capacities, in 1460. On 11 July 1460, along with unnamed co-workers, he was paid by Pius II for making the architrave "a la prima porta va in tinello, coll' armi di N. S. et per horo et colori et argento." This may still exist (Leonardi). Other sources show that at this time Paolo and one companion were living in quarters provided by the pope.

He was also now a Serviens Armorum, a member of an honorary college of forty persons founded in 1458 by Nicholas V.

Filarete (Book 9) mentions a Paolo de Roma who is a goldsmith, and Vasari identifies this man (2, 649) with a Paolo who with Niccolò della Guardia and Pietro Paolo da Todi made the twelve silver statues of apostles which had been in Saint Peter's, in the Chapel of Saint Andrew, from the time of the Sack of Rome. If this is indeed our Paolo, the statues might have something to do with the similar group that Pontano tells us Alfonso commissioned (De mag. 13).

On 10 November 1460 Paolo was working with Isaia da Pisa, making stone balls for bombards; indeed he was now part of a very large shop that may also have counted Isaia among its members. The shop's output for the period 1461–64 included nine colossal marble statues plus other major works— a vast accomplishment as regards quantity. On 11 March 1461, 30 ducats were paid to Paolo for statues of Saints Peter and Paul, made for the steps of Saint Peter's and now in the vestibule of Radio Vaticana. On 3 April 1461 another payment was made for *spiritelli* holding the arms of the pope— probably those on the bases of these Radio Vaticana statues. Paolo next received 25 ducats for another project, two marble heads of girls (thereafter sent to Pienza) on 13 July 1461, and on 3 May 1462, 8 florins went to him for two effigies of Sigismondo Malatesta to be publicly burned in Rome. On 25 January 1463 he received 30 florins to make a trip to Carrara in connection with statues in Saint Peter's and a head of Pius II to be placed over the door to the Vatican Palace. The latter may be the bust of Pius II now in the Borgia apartments.

On 8 March 1463 Paolo was working on a major commission with Isaia, the tabernacle of Sant'Andrea, for which payments continue until 29 August 1464. On 5 July 1463 the artist was commissioned to make a benediction pulpit to stand at the head of the steps of Saint Peter's. Meanwhile from 12 July 1463 through 1464 more payments were made for the statue of Saint Paul for the steps of the basilica, a work now to be seen on the Ponte Sant'Angelo. This is Paolo's masterpiece. The greatly inferior Sant'Andrea near the Ponte Milvio (*fig. 125*) and its pavilion—the latter now replaced—also date from 1462–63.

After this Paolo seems to have returned to humbler tasks. On 16 September 1463 he received sums in connection with marble arms for the Vatican Palace, and for work on a fireplace, among other things. On 5 November 1467 came 100 florins for a tomb and altar for Lodovico Trevisan in San Lorenzo in Damaso. This is now destroyed.

On 29 March 1470 Paolo made his will, which mentions an unfinished tomb for Luca Filippo de Riccarducci of the Pincio and sculptures for the prothonotary Cesarini. In a codicil Paolo also left to Cardinal Francesco de' Todeschini-Piccolomini a block intended for a tomb effigy of Pius II, and he paid a debt of 10 ducats to "Petro marmorario de Neapoli," who could well be Pietro da Milano. By another codicil Paolo's son Francesco was to be cared for by one of the will's executors, Maestro Buonomo, *marmoraro,* until he reached the age of twenty. I have noted above, chap. 3, n. 10, the possibility that Buonomo may be connected with the Boymans drawing. The full documents for Paolo (except for Doc. 9 in this book) and a bibliography, have been carefully assembled by Anna Maria Corbo, "L'Attività di Paolo di Mariano a Roma," *Commentari, 17* (1966), 195–226.

Bertolotti, Antonio. "Urkundliche Beiträge zur Biographie des Bildhauers Paolo di Mariano." *Repertorium für Kunstwissenschaft, 4* (1881), 426–42.

Leonardi, V. "Paolo di Mariano Marmoraro." *L'Arte, 3* (1900), 264.

PERE JOAN

Pere Joan, or Pedro de Vallfagona (Raffaelo Causa says that R. Filangieri is mistaken when he says in "Gran Sala" that these are two different artists) was born in Tarragona, the son of Jordí de Deu, who was also a sculptor. A document in Sant Llorenç, Santa Coloma de Querault, states that Jordí, the father, executed the retable in that church.

In about 1400, with his father, Pere Joan began decorating the Casa del Consejo Municipal Barce-lona. Pere Joan's masterpieces here are the Archangel Raphael on the facade and the equestrian Saint George on an exterior balcony. The date is usually given as 1415–18. Pere Joan is also assigned the angels' heads on the balustrade overlooking the Calle del Obispo (Puig i Cadafalch).

In 1425 Pere Joan was called to Tarragona by Dalmacio de Mur, the archbishop, to execute the main altarpiece in the cathedral. He began work on 4 March 1426. In 1436 he stopped, and the retable was completed by his assistant Guillen de la Mota (Durán Sanpere; Vinaza).

In 1441, probably in April, Pere Joan began work on another retable, for the cathedral at Saragossa. This has led to some confusion: Puig i Cadafalch maintains that the work was actually by a different artist, Pedro de Vallfagona. But other scholarship convincingly identifies the two men (Bertaux; Durán Sanpere). In any case on 10 July 1441 there is a document which reads: "El 10 de Julio de dicho ano el maese Pascual empezó a parar los andianos para la obra de rejóla para respualdo al retablo sobre el altar mayor, ganando el, con su mozo y el chico 6 s. y su hieto Juan, que obra tan bien como el, 3 s. 8 d." According to Thieme-Becker, Pere Joan finished only the base relief of this work (the scenes from the life of Saints Lawrence, Valerius, and Vincent, and the patron's arms).

On 16 August 1445 Pere Joan reported sick. But in November of the same year he returned to work and documents suggest that he completed the retable in December. After this there are no more Spanish documents. But fragments of the altarpiece for the archbishop's chapel, Saragossa, now in the Metropoli-tan Museum, New York, are ascribed to the artist (Thieme-Becker).

On 7 October 1450 Pere Joan is mentioned as "mestre d'obres" in the Aragonese court at Naples, and a number of later documents record payments to him here (Docs. 9, 10; Filangieri, "Rassegna"). We also learn that in 1455–57 Pere Joan was renting houses (sculpture shops) near the Castel Nuovo (Filangieri, "Rassegna").

Pere Joan's name does not appear in any other known documents for the construction of the Arch. But on 31 January 1458, when the Arch workers received their first payment of 200 ducats each for the colossi, he is still present, and received 40 ducats as "mestre ymagniayre qui lavora les ymatges de pedra ops de la fabrica del dit. castell" (Fabriczy). R. Filangieri ("Gran Sala") assigns to him the relief on that side of the triumph portal in the Gran Sala that faces toward the royal apartments.

If Pere Joan was sixteen in 1400 when he began working with his father on the Casa de Consejo Municipal, Barcelona, he would have been seventy-four in 1458.

Bertaux, E. "Les primitifs espagnols," pt. 5. *Revue de l'art, 23* (1908), 349–50.

Causa, Raffaello. "Sagrera, Laurana e l'arco di Castelnuovo." *Paragone 55* (1954), 11–12.

Ceán Bermúdez, Agustín. *Diccionario de los mas illustres profesores de las bellas artes en España.* Madrid, 1800. 2, 350.

Durán Sanpere, Agustí. *Los Retablos de piedra.* Monumenta Cataloniae, 2. Barcelona, 1934. Pp. 37–67.

Fabriczy, C. von. "Der Triumphbogen Alphonsos I am Castel Nuovo zu Neapel." *Jahrbuch der preus-sischen Kunstsammlungen, 20* (1899), 149.

Filangieri, R. "La Gran Sala di Castel Nuovo." *Dedalo, 9* (1928–29), 152.

———. "Rassegna critica delle fonti per la storia di Castel Nuovo." *ASPN, 62* (1937), 305.

Puig i Cadafalch, J., and J. Miret y Sans. "El Palau de la Diputació General de Catalunya." Institut d'Estudis Catalans. Seccio historico-arqueologica. *Annuari, 3* (1909–10), 396–403.

Thieme-Becker (1932), s.v. Pedro Juan (A. L. Mayer).

Vinaza, Cipriano Muñoz y Manzano. *Arqueologia sagrada catalana.* Vich, 1933. *1,* 114 ff; 2, 510 ff.

PIETRO DA MILANO

Pietro da Milano, Pietro da Martino da Milano, or Pietro da Como, was probably born around 1410.

All of Fabriczy's references in his 1899 *Preussische Jahrbuch* article to the Pietro di Giovanni da Como who sculptured the Bishop Bartoli tomb in the cathedral at Siena, worked on the base of the Gattamelata statue, and designed and helped to execute the relief in the center tympanum of the cathedral at Orvieto, have been ignored in the following biography. They refer to a different individual, as was later admitted by Fabriczy himself (Fabriczy, "Pietro da Martino"). Fabriczy also conflates Pietro da Milano with Pere Joan ("Der Triumphbogen," p. 11), and a third confusion on Fabriczy's part identifies Pietro da Milano with Pietro di Giovanni da Varese, an architect who in Rome worked on the fortifications at the Campidoglio, the Church of San Teodoro, and Santa Maria Maggiore (Müntz; Fabriczy, "Triumph-bogen," p. 11; Rolfs).

We have noted the possibility that Pietro was in Naples in the 1440s in connection with the arcivescovado arch (p. 34). That Pietro was indeed then in Naples and enjoyed Alfonso's favor would also be indicated if he was the Pietro da Milano who was at that time castellan of the royal fort at Tropea in Calabria (Mazzoleni). A similar preferment was later granted to Onofrio di Giordano.

On 3 May 1452 the rectors of Ragusa gave Pietro permission to leave the city with his family, and on 2 June 1452 they dispensed him from work he had promised to do for the parish of San Biagio. This, I have assumed, involved the fontana San Biagio (Doc. 6a).

On 3 June 1452, presumably before he had heard of the rectors' decision, Alfonso wrote to them referring to previous letters and asking that Pietro come to work in Naples. By 17 July 1453 Pietro had arrived and begun his work on the Arch (Docs. 6b, 8, 9, 17, 18).

We next hear of Pietro in 1461, when he has transferred himself to France and the service of René of Anjou. There he made medals for René, one with a double portrait of the king and queen, while in 1463 "Maistre Pierre de Millain tailleur et ymageur du Roy de Sicile" created "les ymages et misteres de la Magdeleine de la Bausme" for the Church of Saint-Maxe, Bar-le-duc (Maxe-Werly). In the same year Pietro carved a relief of two fighting dogs for the castle hall of Bar-le-Duc (Maxe-Werly), which is now in the garden of a private house in that town. Pietro was given a new garment by René for a court festival on 4 December 1463, and in 1463–64 he made signed medals for René's son-in-law, Ferry of Lotharingia, and of his daughter Margaret, wife of Henry VI of England (Maxe-Werly).

"Mestre Pere marmoraro" was back in Naples on 18 May 1465 and received 33 ducats for work done as "capomestre de totes les obres de pedra del Castel nou." He thereafter worked on the inner portal, and during the following years finished the Arch (Docs. 21, 22, 23, 25, 27, 28, 29, 30, 31).

On 7 March 1468 Pietro was commissioned by Giovanni Caracciolo to carve ornament for the Caracciolo chapel in the cathedral; on the following 16 December he was asked to carve the marble ornament over the door of the *scrivania* in the Castel Nuovo along with other works including a heraldic group of weapons for which he received 13 ducats. On 14 April 1469, "Maestro Pietro de Martino di Milano, ad presens habitator Neapolis, regius magister marmorum, sculptor" married his sons Simplicius (or Simplicianus) De Martino and Giovanni Martino de Martino to the sisters Maria and Sforzina Talamanca. Ferrante gave the brides dowries of 200 ducats each (Strazzullo).

On 20 September 1469 the widow of Francesco Antonio Guindazzo commissioned a tomb for her late husband, to be placed in San Domenico [Maggiore], for 150 ducats, the work to be finished in eight months. This was destroyed by fire in 1506. On 19 January 1470 Pietro was paid 190 ducats for the tomb of Carlo Stendardo in Sant'Agostino ad Arienzo near Caserta, to be modeled on the tomb of Cardinal Angelo d'Anna (d. 1428) in Santa Maria in Cosmedin, Naples (Strazzullo). On 31 May 1470 Pietro bought marble mortar for unspecified projects in the royal works; and on 13 October 1470 he borrowed 5 onzi, 20 tarì, due in a month, from the notary Angelo Cifra.

In 1470 Pietro built a tomb in Santa Maria la Nova, inscribed:

PETRUS DE MARTINO MEDIOLANENSIS OB TRIUMPHALEM ARCIS NOVAE ARCUM SOLERTER STRUC-TUM ET MULTA STATUARIAE ARTIS SUO MUNERE HUIC AEDI PIAE OBLATA A DIVO ALPHONSO REGE IN EQUESTREM ADSCRIBI ORDINEM ET AB SUIS DONARI MERUIT MCCCCLXX

The tomb no longer exists (see above, p. 34).

In 1472 Pietro began making seven windows in the Gran Sala of Castel Nuovo, payments for which totaled 20 ducats and were recorded between 27 November and 6 April of the following year. On 17 December 1472 Guindazzo's widow was sued by Pietro for 20 ducats still owed for her husband's tomb (Strazzullo).

On 7 August 1473, 10 ducats were paid to Bernardino, son of Pietro, for work done by Pietro on the Arch, which makes us suppose that Pietro was now dead. If, as I think, Pietro was a mature artist who had worked for Onofrio di Giordano in Dalmatia, and had even possibly been associated with the arcivescovado arch of 1443, he might well have been in his sixties thirty years later. In any case he was surely dead when on 3 September 1474 his heirs sued Guindazzo's widow. On 9 March 1476 they received payments for the Carlo Stendardo tomb (55½ ducats). At the same time Pietro's heirs were listed as his widow, Giovanna, and his sons Simplicianus, Joannes Martinus, Bernardinus, Altobellus, and Jacobus. Altobellus and Bernardinus appear as minors (Strazzullo). Rolfs thinks the latter might possibly have been the "Mino" or "Dino" del Reame who appears in documents at this time.

Fabriczy, C. von. "Der Triumphbogen Alphonsos I am Castel Nuovo zu Neapel." *Jahrbuch der preussischen Kunstsammlungen*, 20 (1899), 8–21.

———. "Neues zum Triumphbogen Alphonsos I." *Jahrbuch der preussischen Kunstsammlungen, 23* (1902), 3–16.

———. "Pietro di Martino da Milano in Ragusa." *Repertorium für Kunstwissenschaft, 28* (1905), 192–93.

Maxe-Werly, A. "Un Sculpteur italien à Bar-le-duc en 1463." Academie des inscriptions et belles-lettres. *Comptes rendus des séances,* ser. 4, *24* (Paris, 1896), 54–62.

Mazzoleni, I., ed. *Fonti aragonesi.* Naples, 1957. *1,* 76–78.

Müntz, Eugène. *Les Arts à la cour des papes.* Paris, 1878. *1,* 89, 146, 200.

Rolfs, W. *Franz Laurana.* Berlin, 1907. *1,* 203–28.

Strazzullo, Franco. "Documenti sull'attività napoletana dello scultore milanese Pietro de Martino (1453–1473)." *ASPN, 81* (1963), 325–41.

SAGRERA, GUILLERMO

Sagrera was born in Inca, Mallorca, in the 1380s. In 1416–17 he is recorded as *magister* in the Church of San Joan, Perpignan, and he was called with eleven other architects to consult on the building of the nave of Gerona cathedral (Llaguno, *1,* doc. 28). In this document "Guillermus Sagrera magister operis sive fabricae ecclesiae Sancti Joanis Perpigniani" voted with others for a single-aisled solution; the idea was adopted by the chapter on 15 March 1417.

On 11 March 1426 in Palma, Mallorca, Sagrera signed a contract with the Colegio of the Lonja del Mar (exchange) agreeing to erect a building for them along the lines of a plan already in existence (Wethey). The text (translated from the Lemosino of the original by Llaguno) reads that Sagrera is to complete the building "en la forma que está commenzada, y segun las muestras dadas y entregadas a los honrados fabriqueros por el mismo Guillermo" in fifteen years. He is to be responsible for making statues for each facade and is to bear all expenses for materials and supplies with certain exemptions such as iron work. The payment is to be 22,000 Mallorcan libras (Llaguno, *1,* doc. 29).

From 1420–27, according to Thieme-Becker, Sagrera was also protomagister of the cathedral at Palma, and in 1422 he executed a Saint Peter and a Saint Paul for the Puerta del Mirador. These still exist. Next, in 1441, he made a window or windows and a holy water stoup for the chapel of San Guillermo (now dedicated to Saint Anthony of Padua).

In 1446 or 1447 Sagrera quarreled with the Colegio and went to Naples to plead his cause at court. His assistant, Guillermo Vilasolar, was left in charge of the Lonja. On 20 January 1449 King Alfonso sent a letter to the Colegio inquiring about the lawsuit (Llaguno, *1*, doc. 29). In the letter the king identified Sagrera as "protomagister" of the Castel Nuovo. On 21 October 1450 the case went against Sagrera, who thereafter remained in Naples.

On 6 March 1450 Alfonso wrote to a certain Juan Alvert asking him to send to Santani, Mallorca, for stone for the Castel Nuovo (Filangieri). By 1451 Sagrera was working on the Sala dei Baroni (above, p. 32), having been removed from the position of protomagister of the Castel Nuovo. Finally, in July 1453 he was paid 400 ducats as capomaestro of the Gran Sala (R. Filangieri). Causa also assigns to him, on stylistic grounds, a major responsibility for the Aragonese Arch.

On 19 August 1456 Sagrera died. The Sala was completed by his relatives, Johan and Jaume Sagrera (R. Filangieri).

Alomar, G. "Los Discipulos de Guillermo Sagrera en Mallorca, Napoles y Sicilia." *NN,* n.s. *3* (September–October 1963), 185–96; (November–December 1963), 125–35.

Causa, R. "Sagrera, Laurana e l'Arco di Castelnuovo." *Paragone 55,* (1954), 3–23.

Filangieri, Riccardo. "La gran Sala di Castel Nuovo in Napoli." *Dedalo, 9* (1928–29), 145–71.

Ilaguno y Amirola, E. *Noticias de los arquitectos y arquitectura de España.* Edited by J. A. Ceán-Bermúdez. Madrid, 1829. *1,* 93, 96–102, 276–81.

Pane, Roberto. "Note su Guillermo Sagrera architetto." *Napoli Nobilissima,* n.s. 4 (1961), 151–62.

Thieme-Becker (1935), s.v.

Wethey, H. "Guillermo Sagrera." *Art Bulletin, 21* (1939), 44–60.

NOTES

CHAPTER 1

1 G. B. Cantalicio, *De bis recepta Parthenope Gonsalviae libri quatuor,* in Giovanni Gravier, ed., *Raccolta di tutti i più rinomati scrittori della storia del regno di Napoli* (hereafter cited as Gravier, *Raccolta*), 6 (Naples, 1769–72), 65–67: "Moenia sed post hunc simul aspicis altera pontem, / Cumque triumphali consurgit fornice Porta / Regia, quae Alfonsi prisci monumenta figurat; / Qualis Septimii testatur in Urbe trophaeum, / Aut ibi quale decus demonstrat Flavius Arcus. / Felix porta quidem, Boreae quae cernit ab axe, / Montem apud Erasmi, cineres atque Maronis."

2 Angelo di Costanzo, *Istoria del regno di Napoli* [before 1591], 3 (Milan, 1805), 117–18: "fecero venire una gran quantità di marmi bianchi, e condussero i meglio [*sic*] Scultori di quel tempo, che facessero un Arco Trionfale per ponerlo avanti i gradi della porta picciola dell'Arcivescovado; e poichè fu fatto, volendo incominciare a ponersi avanti i gradi della porta . . . Cola Maria Bozzuto, che aveva molto ben servito il Re in quella guerra, andò a lamentarsi al Re, che quel' Arco impediva il lume alla casa sua; e' il Re, ridendo, disse ch'egli avea ragione; e dappoi mandò a ringraziare gl' Eletti della Citta, ed a dir loro, che avrebbe più caro che quell' Arco si trasferisse al Castello Nuovo, dove ancora si vede nell' entrare dell'ultima porta."

3 E.g. Pompeo Sarnelli, *La vera Guida de' forestieri* . . . (Naples, 1697), p. 33; Luigi d'Afflitto, *Guida per i curiosi e per i viaggiatori che vengono alla citta di Napoli . . . ,* 2 (Naples, 1834), 14. Carel von Fabriczy repeats the story of Giovanni da Nola's contribution, saying that some considered the river gods also to be of Cinquecento provenance; Fabriczy himself only says the tradition is impossible to verify ("Der Triumphbogen Alphonsos I am Castel Nuovo zu Neapel," *Jahrbuch der preussischen Kunstsammlungen,* 20 [1899], 132). Cf. also Wilhelm Rolfs, *Franz Laurana,* 1 (Berlin, 1907), 168.

4 The claim is discussed by W. R. Valentiner, "Andrea dell'Aquila, Painter and Sculptor," *Art Bulletin, 19* (1937), 503–36.

5 Angelo Battaglini, "Memoria sopra uno sconosciuto egregio scultore del secolo XV e sopra alcune sue opere," *Dissertazioni dell'Accademia romana di archaeologia, 1* (1821), 115–32. The best summary of the long controversy over responsibility for the Arch is in R. Filangieri, "L'Arco trionfale di Alfonso d'Aragona," *Dedalo, 12* (1932), 429–66.

6 Best published in Fausto Nicolini, ed., *L'Arte napoletana del rinascimento e la lettera di Pietro Summonte a Marcantonio Michiel* (Naples, 1925).

7 Vasari claims Giuliano da Maiano as the designer (*Vite,* Milanesi ed., *2,* 470–72 [hereafter cited simply as Vasari]), and Rolfs anticipates Filangieri in claiming that the king himself designed the Arch, and that Laurana executed the lower part and Pietro da Milano the upper ("Der Baumeister des Triumphbogens in Neapel," *Jahrbuch der preussischen Kunstsammlungen,* 25 [1904], 93).

8 Leopoldo Cicognara, *Storia della scultura dal suo risorgimento in Italia sino al secolo XIX,* 2 (Venice, 1816), 117–20.

9 Arnaldo Venditti, *Architettura neoclassica a Napoli* (Naples, 1961), p. 278.

10 J. B. L. G. Séroux d'Agincourt, *Histoire de l'art par les monumens . . . ,* 1 (Paris, 1823), 95–97.

11 Mariano d'Ayala, "Dell'Arco trionfale di re Alfonso d'Aragona in Castel Nuovo," *Annali civili del regno delle Due Sicilie, 12, fasc.* 23 (Sept.–Oct. 1836), 34–45. D'Ayala, however, oddly finds the upper arch more Roman-looking than the lower.

12 R. Liberatore, "L'Arco trionfale di Alfonso d'Aragona nel Castel Nuovo," *Real Museo Borbonico, 13* (1843), 1–35.

13 G. V. Fusco, *Degli Autori dell'arco di trionfo di Alfonso d'Aragona al Castel Nuovo* (Naples, 1850): a more intelligent account than H. W. Schulz's in *Denkmäler der Kunst des Mittelalters in Unteritalien,* 3 (Dresden, 1860), 113–17, who opts for Giuliano da Maiano on *stylistic* grounds!

14 Venditti, *Architettura neoclassica,* pp. 366–67. There was a discussion as to whether the Arch was to be kept at the Castel Nuovo or set up on the north side of the city at the Porta Costantinopoli. In 1872 the winning restoration project had been submitted by a group headed by Federico Travaglini (who had earlier restored the interior of San Domenico Maggiore, 1850–53). In his text Travaglini criticized the "due informi piloni che in gran parte nascondono le colonne corinzie del primo scompartimento dell'Arco e formano involucro alle stesse," and he accordingly designed heavy iron cages to surround or flank the paired columns. Adolfo Avena, in *Il Restauro dell'arco d'Alfonso d'Aragona in Napoli* (Rome, 1908), pp. 3–84, gives a full account of these mid- and late-nineteenth-century restoration plans; cf. also Giorgio Rosi, "Il Restauro di Castelnuovo di Napoli," *Le Arti, 4, fasc.* 4 (1942), 284–87.

15 Cf. F. Lacetti, "L'Arco trionfale di Alfonso d'Aragona," *Natura ed arte, 14* (1904–05), 2d semester, 98–104; L. Serra, "L'Arco di Alfonso d'Aragona," *L'Arte, 7* (1904), 408; Antonio Sacco,

"L'Arco trionfale del re Alfonso d'Aragona," *Arte e storia*, 24 (1905), 4–6; and Avena, *Il Restauro*.

16 Achille Stella, *Castelnuovo di Napoli alla luce dei documenti e della storia* [Reale commissione provinciale per la conservazione dei monumenti] (Naples, 1928); [idem?], *La Verità sui restauri di Castelnuovo* [Associazione per la tutela dei monumenti e del Paesaggio di Napoli], (Naples, 1931); idem, *Il Restauro di Castel Nuovo. Premesse e conseguenze di un irrazionale rifacimento* (Naples, 1931); [Commissione per l'isolamento e il restauro di Castel Nuovo], *Relazione sui criteri per un piano generale di restauro* (Naples, n.d.); R. Filangieri, *Critiche amene all' opera di Castel Nuovo* (Naples, 1931); idem, ed., *Relazione sull' isolamento e sui restauri di Castel Nuovo* (Naples, 1940). Cf. idem, "Rassegna critica delle fonti per la storia di Castel Nuovo," *Archivio storico per le provincie napoletane* (hereafter cited as *ASPN*), 62 (1937), p. 323 *n.* 1; and Rosi, "Il Restauro." I have not attempted to collect all the many other pamphlets and newspaper articles connected with this restoration. By contrast that of 1904–08 seems to have been fairly serene. The many attacks of 1931 and after centered around Filangieri's determination to expunge all pre- and post-Aragonese elements. Achille Stella maintained that the building (as we see it today) was in fact medieval and that the outer bastions, which Filangieri removed, had been erected by Alfonso I. This is untenable, but Stella does succeed in showing how intuitive some of Filangiéri's acts were; above all Filangieri seems not to have documented his conclusions with drawings, so that the modern visitor has little idea of precisely what changes were made.

17 G. Filangieri, *Documenti per la storia le arti e le industrie delle provincie napoletane* (Naples, 1883–97).

18 Iole Mazzoleni, *Fonti aragonesi, a cura degli archivisti napoletani* (Naples, 1957).

19 Fabriczy, "Der Triumphbogen," 1–30, 125–58.

20 Emile Bertaux, "L'Arco e la porta trionfale di Alfonso e di Ferdinando d'Aragona al Castel Nuovo," *ASPN*, 25 (1900), 27–63.

21 Fabriczy, "Neues zum Triumphbogen Alphonsos I," *Jahrbuch der preussischen Kunstsammlungen*, 23 (1902), 3–16.

22 Ettore Bernich, "Leon Battista Alberti e l'Architetto dell'arco trionfale di Alfonso d'Aragona," *Napoli Nobilissima* (hereafter cited as *NN*) *13* (1904), 148–55, with reply by Wilhelm Rolfs, "L'Architettura albertiana e l'arco trionfale di Alfonso d'Aragona," *NN, 13* (1904), 171–72. See also Bernich, "Leon Battista Alberti e l'arco trionfale di Alfonso d'Aragona in Napoli," *NN, 12* (1903), 114–18, 131–36. Bernich's whole point is based on his impression that Pietro da Milano did not arrive in

Naples until 1456. But Fabriczy had already established that Pietro was called, at least, in 1452 ("Neues zum Triumphbogen").

23 Wilhelm Rolfs, *Franz Laurana, 1*, 46–241. He counts the folds of drapery in statues and the flutes in columns and niches, and even gives the latitude and longitude of Domenico da Montemignaio's birthplace.

24 Fritz Burger, *Francesco Laurana: eine Studie zur italienische Quattrocento-Skulptur* (Strasbourg, 1907). Burger's importance seems to be that he is the first to have broached this possibility. Otherwise his monograph depends on secondary evidence and sources, but it is intelligent (see esp. pp. 20–70).

25 Giuseppe de Blasiis, "Le Case dei principi angioini nella piazza di Castelnuovo," *Racconti di storia napoletana* (Naples, 1908), n. 1.

26 Avena, *Il Restauro*, pp. 3–84.

27 Lionello Venturi, "Studii sul Palazzo Ducale di Urbino," *L'Arte, 17* (1914), 415–73, esp. 444–50.

28 R. Filangieri, "L'Arco trionfale," pp. 429–66, 594–626, 457 n. 10.

29 Leo Planiscig, "Ein Entwurf für den Triumphbogen am Castel nuovo zu Neapel," *Jahrbuch der Preussischen Kunstsammlungen, 54* (1933), 16–28; R. Filangieri, "Un più antico Progetto dell' arco trionfale di Alfonso d'Aragona," *Rassegna storica napoletana, 1*, no. 2 (1933), 75–80.

30 Raffaello Causa, "Sagrera, Laurana e l'Arco di Castel Nuovo," *Paragone, 55* (1954), 3–23.

31 Eileen R. Driscoll, "Alfonso of Aragon as a Patron of Art," in Lucy Freeman Sandler, ed., *Essays in Memory of Karl Lehmann* (New York, 1964), pp. 87–96. See also below, chap. 4, n. 8.

32 Gianni Carlo Sciolla, "L'Arco di Castelnuovo: il progetto architettonico," *Critica d'Arte, 19* (January–February 1972), 68–72.

CHAPTER 2

1 The most significant writings for the parts of Alfonso's career I have examined are: Jose Ametller y Vinyas *Alfonso V de Aragón en Italia y la crisis religiosa del siglo XV*, ed. Jaime Collell (Gerona, 1903); C. Marinesco, "Du Nouveau sur 'Tirant lo Blanch,'" *Estudios Romanics, 4* (1953–54), 127–203; P. E. Schramm, "Der König von Aragon, seine Stellung im Staatsrecht (1276–1410)," *Historisches Jahrbuch, 74* (1955), 99–123; Eugenio Dupré-Theseider, *La Politica italiana di Alfonso il Magnanimo* (Palma di Mallorca, 1955); Tammaro De Marinis, "La Liberazione di Alfonso V d'Aragona prigioniero dei Genovesi," *ASPN, 73* (1955), 101–06; A. Boscolo, "L'Attività storiografica sulle figure di Ferdinando I d'Aragona e di Alfonso il Magnanimo," *Medio Evo Aragonese*

(Padua, 1958), 149–65; Alan F. C. Ryder, "La Politica italiana di Alfonso d'Aragona (1442–1458)," *ASPN,* 77 (1959), 43–106; Emilio Saez, "Semolanza de Alfonso el Magnànimo," in Antonio Torraja, ed., *Estudios sobre Alfonso el Magnànimo* (Barcelona, 1960), pp. 25–41; Ernesto Pontieri, "Alfonso V d'Aragona nel quadro della politica italiana del suo tempo," *Atti dell'Accademia di scienze morali e politiche della società nazionale di scienze lettere ed arti di Napoli,* 71 (1960), 183–251; Alan F. C. Ryder, "Alfonso d'Aragona e l'avvento di Francesco Sforza al ducato di Milano," *ASPN,* 80 (1962), 9–46.

2 See De Marinis, "La Liberazione," the two Ryder articles cited in chap. 2, n. 1, and G. P. Bognetti, "Per la Storia dello stato visconteo. Un Registro di decreti della cancelleria di Filippo Maria Visconti, e un trattato segreto con Alfonso d'Aragona," *Archivio storico lombardo,* 54 (1927), 237–357.

3 "Captum navali pugna Alfonsum cum duobus fratribus, altero etiam rege, multis item regulis, non modo liberos esse voluit [F. M. Visconti], verum nullum liberalitatis, comitatis, mansuetudinis genus in eos praetermisit," G. G. Pontano, in Francesco Tateo, ed., *I Trattati delle virtù sociali* (Rome, 1965), p. 47. As to the later suggestion that Alfonso become Duke of Milan, Pontano discusses a memorial addressed to Alfonso (but possibly not sent) from Borso d'Este in 1445, which said in part: "Havendo questa [Milan], la Vostra Maesta po dire de havere la migliore parte de Italia, e non e dubio alchuno che la Vostra Maysta non sia re d'Italia" (p. 204).

4 Dupré-Theseider, *La Politica italiana,* p. 18.

5 Marinesco, "Du Nouveau," pp. 172–73; and Jaime Vicens i Vives, *Els Trastàmares* (Barcelona, 1956), pp. 132–36.

6 Dupré-Theseider claims that the lower arch's inscription, referring to Alfonso as "rex italicus," shows that about 1452, when it was carved, the king was still able to see himself as potentially King of Italy (*La Politica italiana,* pp. 12–13). But in fact Alfonso had given up all hopes of Milan by then. The phrase is more likely to mean simply "King with Italian possessions," just as, in the same inscription, "rex hispanicus" can only mean "King with Spanish possessions." See also, for the "Italian policy," Vicens i Vives, *Els Trastàmares,* pp. 136–39.

7 See G. Toffanin, Jr., "I Seggi di Napoli," *Il Fuidoro,* 3 (1956), 16–27, esp. pp. 21–23. The Seggio del Popolo's headquarters was in the Piazza Sellaria, near the Convent of Sant'Agostino. It was removed on 7 September 1456 by Alfonso I (Sarnelli, *Guida de' forestieri,* pp. 53–60).

8 G. A. Summonte, *Historia del regno di Napoli* [1597 ff.] *1* (Naples, 1749), 191–234.

9 Pietro Giannone, *Istoria civile del regno di Napoli,*

3 (Palmiria, 1762), 372. For the Spanish group see Benedetto Croce, "La Corte spagnuola di Alfonso d'Aragona a Napoli," *Atti dell'Accademia pontaniana,* 24, no. 2 (1894).

10 G. A. Summonte, *Historia, 1,* 127–90; and Everardo Gothein, *Il Rinascimento nell'Italia meridionale,* trans. and rev. Tommaso Persico (Florence, 1915), pp. 3–30.

11 Dupré-Theseider, *La Politica italiana,* pp. 13–14. The defeats of 1447–48 at Piombino and, in 1449, the Pyrrhic victory at Lodi and the defeat by the Venetians at sea would have confirmed Alfonso in his new concentration on domestic affairs.

12 This was in 1455. Dupré-Theseider, *La Politica italiana,* p. 29.

13 Francesco Colangelo, *Vita di Antonio Beccadelli* (Naples, 1820), p. 235.

14 Croce, "La Corte spagnuola."

15 Note the part played by the Florentine contingent in the triumph of 1443 (p. 14 below); and Ernesto Pontieri, "La Dinastia aragonese di Napoli e la casa de' Medici di Firenze," *ASPN,* 65 (1940), 274–342; 66 (1941), 217–73.

16 Croce, "La Corte spagnuola"; Tommaso Persico, *Gli Scrittori politici napoletani dal 1400 al 1700* (Naples, 1912), esp. pp. 44–94; Casimir von Chtedowski, *Neapolitanische Kulturbilder, XIV–XVIII Jahrhundert* (Berlin, 1920); Antonio Altamura, *L'Umanesimo nel mezzogiorno d'Italia* (Florence, 1941); Constantin Marinesco, "Notes sur la vie culturale sous le règne d'Alphonse le Magnanime, roi de Naples," *Miscel·lánia Puig i Cadafalch,* 1 (Barcelona, 1947–51) (p. 291–307); and Ottavio Morisani, *Letteratura artistica a Napoli* (Naples, 1958), pp. 44–61. Pontano writes: "Alphonsus, adulescentulos quosdam cum intellexisset ob parentum inopiam, quibus coeperant disciplinis continuare operam non posse, eos in Galliam ulteriorem Parisios misit, pecunia statuta, quae illis suo ex aerario suppeditaretur" (*De liberalitate* 21).

17 Giannone, *Istoria 3,* 372.

18 For all these Tammaro De Marinis, *La Biblioteca napoletana dei re d'Aragona* (Milan, 1947–52), s.v.

19 Roberto Pane, *L'Architettura del rinascimento a Napoli* (Naples, 1937), pp. 57–58.

20 Camillo Minieri-Riccio, "Alcuni Fatti di Alfonso I di Aragona," *ASPN,* 6 (1881), 243–44; Ettore Bernich, "Statue e frammenti architettonici della prima epoca aragonese," *NN, 15* (1906), 8.

21 C. Marinesco, "Les Affaires commerciales en Flandre d'Alphonse V d'Aragon, roi de Naples (1416–1458)," *Revue historique,* 221 (1959), 33–48.

22 Nicolini, *L'Arte napoletana del rinascimento e la lettera di Pietro Summonte a Marcantonio Michiel* (Naples, 1925), p. 163; Michael Baxandall, "Bartholomaeus Facius on Painting," *Journal of the*

Warburg and Courtauld Institutes, 27 (1964), 90–107, esp. pp. 102–03.

23 Cf. R. Filangieri, "Rassegna critica delle fonti per la storia di Castel Nuovo," *ASPN*, 62 (1937), 304–33; and Ottavio Morisani, "Gli Artisti nel 'De viris' di Bartolommeo Fazio," *ASPN*, 74 (1955), 107–17, esp. pp. 111–12. See also Vasari, 2, 567–69.

24 G. B. Cavalcaselle, *A History of Painting in Italy*, 4 (London, 1911), 156.

25 "Suis temporibus rex Alphonsus vicit omnes aetatis illius reges tum in iis comparandis atque exhibendis, quae ad sacrificiorum apparatum et sacerdotum spectarent ornatum, tum in deorum et dearum statuis, quas plurimas, et in iis duodecim Apostolorum ex argento conflatas, habuit." See also Tristano Caracciolo, *De varietate fortunae*: "Aulaeis exquisitissime elaboratis argento auroque adeo abundavit, ut repositoria in Turris effigiem substructa, vel erecta, sustinentibus animalibus eodem metallo fabricatis, suisque pretiosis armis instructa, multiplicibus vasibus non ad usum tantum, sed ad invidiosam ostentationem opplerentur" (Gravier, *Raccolta*, 6, 83).

26 For further information see Riccardo Filangieri, "La Peinture flamande à Naples pendant le quinzième siècle," *Revue belge d'archéologie et d'Histoire de l'art*, 2 (1932), 128–43; and Liana Castelfranchi-Vegas, "I Rapporti Italia-Fiandra," *Paragone*, n.s. 15 (May 1966), 9–24.

27 André Chastel, "Cortile et Théâtre," in *Le Lieu théâtrale à la renaissance* [*Colloques internationaux du centre national de la recherche scientifique*] (Paris, 1964), p. 99; and Pontano, who speaks of Alfonso's heavy debts occasioned by these spectacles (*De lib.* 10). The most complete account is still P. N. Signorelli, *Vicende della coltura nelle due Sicilie*, 3 (Naples, 1810), 530–59.

28 Gerònimo Zurita y Castro, *Anales de la corona de Aragòn*, 3 (Saragossa, 1610), 124. There is no truth in Giannone's assertion (*Istoria*, 3, 367, following Tutini) that Alfonso was never crowned at all.

29 The incident of the breached wall near the Porta del Carmine, through which Alfonso entered the city, may have been taken from Suetonius, *Nero*, 25. The elements of Alfonso's dress—golden wreath, curule chair, scepter, and embroidered toga and tunic adorned with palms—are in Livy, 30. 5–12.

30 For this see Fritz Saxl, "Pagan Sacrifice in the Italian Renaissance," *Journal of the Warburg and Courtauld Institutes*, 2 (1938–39), 346–67, esp. pp. 365–67; and Giovanni Caradente, *I Trionfi nel primo rinascimento* (Turin, 1963).

31 This latter seems to have been more a coronation than an actual triumph (Vasari, 2, 419). The triumph of Castruccio Castracane in Lucca, 1326,

was probably a mere literary convention (Caradente, *Trionfi*, n. 27), despite Fabriczy's assertion that "Seit dem antiken Triumphzug Castruccio Castracanes . . . ist dies [Alfonso's] die erste Veranstaltung solcher Art, die durch die Erinnerung an das antike Romertum bestimmt war" ("Der Triumphbogen," p. 4). See also Wilhelm Rolfs, *Franz Laurana*, p. 49, n. 2. Another famous triumph was Lodovico Scarampo's entry into Rome in 1459, after defeating the Turkish fleet at Metelino in 1457.

32 As depicted in R. Filangieri, ed., *Una Cronaca napoletana figurata del quattrocento* (Naples, 1956), e.g. opp. p. 92. For a bibliography of Renaissance triumphs in general see Caradente, *I trionfi*, n. 1.

33 See also Paul Schubring, *Cassoni*, 1 (Leipzig, 1923), pp. 58–60, nos. 111, 114, 116.

34 Amettler y Vinyas, *La Crisis religiosa*, 1, 103–07.

35 An analogous figure of Caesar appeared in the relief of the triumph procession that once adorned the outer face (toward the royal apartments and away from the Gran Sala) of the Porta del Trionfo in the Castel Nuovo. See E. Bernich, who describes it (it was mostly destroyed in the fire of 1919) but does not recognize the scene as Alfonso's 1443 triumph ("La Sala del trionfo in Castelnuovo," *NN*, 13 [1904], 167). For published descriptions of the procession see B. Croce, "I Teatri di Napoli del secolo XV–XVIII," *ASPN*, 14 (1889), 556–684, esp. pp. 562–64; V. Nociti, *Il trionfo di Alfonso I d'Aragona cantato da Porcellio* (Rossano, 1895); "Racconti di storia napoletana," *ASPN*, 33 (1908), 478–80; Marino Jonata, "Il Giardeno," in Fabriczy, "Der Triumphbogen," pp. 146–47; Gennaro Maria Monti, *Il Trionfo di Alfonso I di Aragona a Napoli in un inedita descrizione contemporanea* (Naples, 1931); Antonio Panormita, *De dictis et factis*, 1, 50, in Janus Gruterus, *Lampas, sive fax artium liberalium, hoc est thesaurus criticus . . .*, 2 (Florence, 1737), 39; Bartolommeo Fazio, *De rebus gestis ab Alphonso I*, 7, in Gravier, *Raccolta*, 4; Zurita, *Anales*, 3, 279; and an account by a correspondent from Barcelona, Antonio Vinyes, in Jose Maria Madurell Marimon, *Mensajeros barceloneses en la corte de Nápoles de Alfonso V de Aragón, 1435–1458* (Barcelona, 1963), no. 164 (see appendix I below, Doc. 1). Other writings are referred to in the following notes.

36 R. Filangieri, "Rassegna critica," *ASPN*, 62 (1937), 313, n. 2.

37 Fabriczy, "Triumphbogen," p. 147. See also Vincenzo Laurenza, "Il Panormita a Napoli," *Atti dell'Accademia pontaniana*, 42, no. 8 (1912), 9.

38 Fazio, *De rebus*, p. 157.

39 "un Arco corrispondente al carro trionfale, tutto

di legname inaurato e colorato. Questo carro passava disotto, fatta misura per tutte le strade dove avea a passare. E l'Arco eminente con 4 faccie e 4 archi, alla sommità di ogni angolo [aveva] li trombetti vestiti di seta all'arme di Napoli, et alla parete per ogni banda [erano] le inventione diverse e le tabelle per ogni banda [erano] maiuscole, con le laude della prospera e buona fortuna del Re Alfonso, narrando l'origine e regale prosapia, in la fè cattolica; oltra sopra d.o Arco sei giovani cantando come angeli vestiti alla ninfale con ali" ("Racconti di storia napoletana," p. 479).

40 Gaetano Filangieri, *La Chiesa el il convento di San Lorenzo Maggiore in Napoli* . . . (Naples, 1873). The car had cost the citizens 1,901 ducats (Summonte, *Historia, 4,* 9–11).

41 Ibid., p. 15.

42 Panormita, *De dictis, 1,* 50; this fact, at one time doubted because of all known witnesses only Panormita mentioned it, is confirmed by Antonio Vinyes in *Marimon, Mensajeros,* p. 219 (Doc. 1).

43 Cf. "Diario anonimo dall' anno MCXCII sino al MCCCCLXXXVII," in Gravier, *Raccolta, 1,* 217; also Rolfs, "Der Baumeister," p. 82. For Panormita's epigram, see his letter of 1 December 1447 to Francesco Martorelli, in Gruterus, *Lampas, 3,* 361–62.

44 Panormita, *De dictis,* in Gruterus, *2,* 39.

45 For later triumphs perhaps influenced by this one, see the medallion by Cristoforo de Geremia of a triumph of 1461 for Cardinal Lodovico Scarampo (Hill 756); C. Corvisieri, "Il Trionfo romano di Eleonora d'Aragona," *Archivio della Società romana di storia patria, 1* (1878), 475–91; Hérmann Egger, "Entwürfe Baldassare Peruzzis für den Einzug Karl V in Rom," *Jahrbuch der kunsthistorischen Sammlungen des . . . Kaiserhauses, 23* (Vienna, 1902), pt. 1, sec. 1, 1–44; and René Schneider, "Le Thème du triomphe dans les entrées solonnelles en France," *Gazette des Beaux-Arts, 9* (1913), 85–106. See also the descriptions given of the triumphal arches in Sannazaro's masques of the 1490's, as produced at Castel Capuano. For the Porcellio poem see U. Fritelli, *Giannantonio de'Pandoni, detto il Porcellio* (Florence, 1900), p. 84. Of the eye-witness accounts, so far as I know only Notar Giacomo speaks of a stylistic classicism, and he only says (giving the wrong date) that the king rode through the city with the lords of the kingdom "ad uso derima" (*Cronaca di Napoli* [Naples, 1845], p. 88). Even this may only refer to the breached wall and to the general idea. Fazio, in *De rebus gestis Alphonsi,* 7, stresses ways in which the procession was *un*-Roman: "Non de his, veteri Romanorum more, triumphare: nulli ante currum captivi ducti, nulla spolia praelata" (Gravier, *Raccolta, 4,* 157).

46 R. Filangieri, "Rassegna critica," *ASPN, 62* (1937), 272.

47 Carlos Sarthou Carreres, *Castillos de España* (Madrid, 1943), s.v.

48 For Tarascon, see Jean-Marie Floret, *Le Château de Tarascon,* 7th ed. (Tarascon, 1962).

49 Francisco Hueso Rolland, "El Castillo de los reyes de Aragòn en Nàpoles," *Revista española de arte* [Madrid], *3* (1934), 211–18; R. Filangieri, "La Citadella aragonese e il recinto bastionato di Castel Nuovo," *Atti dell'Accademia pontaniana,* ser. 2, *34* (1929), 49–73; idem, "L'Opera degli artisti spagnuoli nella ricostruzione quattrocentesca del Castel Nuovo di Napoli," *Spagna in Napoli* ([Madrid], 1950?), 43–52; idem, "Castelnuovo nel. '400," *Il Fuidoro, 3* (1956), 3–15; idem, *Castelnuovo, Reggia angioina ed aragonese* (Naples, 1934, 2d ed. 1964); and idem, "Rassegna critica delle fonti per la storia di Castel Nuovo," *ASPN, 62* (1937), 267–333, *63* (1938), 258–342, *64* (1939), 237–322. For Italian fortifications in general in this period, see E. Rocchi, *Le Origini della fortificazione moderna, 1* (Rome, 1894), 1–40; and A. Cassi-Ramelli, *Dalle Caverne ai rifugi blindati* (Milan, 1964), pp. 309–84.

50 Sarthou Carreres, *Castillos,* s.v.

51 R. Filangieri, "Rassegna critica," *ASPN, 62* (1937), 238.

52 A. Stella says that the ravelins could not possibly have been artillery emplacements (*Il Restauro,* pp. 31–32); indeed, one tends to agree, since they are so narrow and exposed. He also says that he discovered traces of the actual, very different firing emplacements in the fabric before Filangieri's reconstruction, and that these were even lower down in the parapet. Stella adds that the arcaded gallery which Filangieri built in the upper exterior wall had never existed on the outside of the castle (p. 38). Whatever the truth of this, how could the gallery have been a firing platform? How could its octagonal *pilastrini,* 2 *palmi* (.528 m.) thick, have protected the gunners?

53 R. Filangieri, "Rassegna critica," *ASPN, 62* (1937), 289.

54 This unusual form may just conceivably have been Italian: Jordi Rubió has published a letter of 2 June 1446 from Alfonso to Don Alfonso de Pimentel, Count of Benevente, in Barcelona, asking that Daniel Florentino, a specialist in "geometria e otras sciencias demuestrativas," be given permission from the King of Castile to come to Naples to work on the rebuilding of the Castel Nuovo ("Alfons 'el Magnanim' rei de Napols, i Daniel Florentino, Leonardo da Bisuccio i Donatello," *Miscel·lánia Puig i Cadafalch, 1* [Barcelona, 1947–51], 25–35). Daniel Fiorentino may

conceivably have been Vasari's Dello, or Daniello, Fiorentino, who, says Vasari, worked in Spain for a time (2, 147–53). But no Daniello seems to have appeared in the Castel Nuovo account books.

55 "Si aliud, quam Novi, loco nomen inesset, profecto ne quadrantem quidem in illius instauratione erogaturus esset" (T. Caracciolo, *De varietate fortunae*, in Gravier, *Raccolta*, 6, 84).

56 R. Filangieri, "Rassegna critica," *ASPN*, 62 (1937), 273–74, 280.

57 R. Filangieri, "La gran Sala di Castelnuovo," *Dedalo*, 9 (1928–29), 145–71; and Carlo Calzecchi, "La Sala del trionfo in Castelnuovo di Napoli," *Bollettino d'arte*, 18 (1924–25), 371–83. Sagrera began working exclusively on the Gran Sala after 20 December 1452 (R. Filangieri, "Gran Sala," p. 146). Filangieri says the room was completed (after Sagrera's death) in about 1456 (p. 150). It was partly destroyed by fire in 1919.

58 Juan Ainaud de Lasarte, *Alfonso el Magnànimo y las artes plàsticas de su tiempo* (Palma de Mallorca, 1955), p. 7.

59 R. Filangieri, "Rassegna critica," *ASPN*, 62 (1937), 305.

60 R. Filangieri, "L'Opera degli artisti spagnuoli," pp. 43–52.

61 See Pietro Summonte, in Nicolini, *L'Arte napoletana*, p. 160, which I think is the oldest published reference to this legend and which adds that René taught Colantonio "la pratica e la tempera" of Flemish painting. See also [E. Müntz?], *Notes sur l'influence artistique du roi René* (Paris, 1875), p. 483; O. Smital and E. Winkler, eds., René of Anjou, *Livre du cuer d'amours epris* (Vienna, 1926), esp. *1*, 327; Aldo De Rinaldis, *Naples angevine* (Paris, 1927); and Otto Pächt, "René d'Anjou et les van Eyck," *Cahiers de l'Association internationale des études françaises, 8* (1956), 111–67.

62 N. F. Faraglia, "Sepolcro di re Ladislao," *ASPN*, 7 (1882), 169–71; R. Filangieri, "La Scultura in Napoli nei primi albori del rinascimento," *NN*, n.s. *1* (1920), 65–69; E. Rigoni, "Notizie di scultori toscani a Padova nella prima metà del '400," *Archivio veneto*, 6 (1929), 119.

63 Antonio Filangieri, *La Chiesa e il monastero di San Giovanni a Carbonara*, ed. R. Filangieri (Naples, 1926), pp. 33–43; Elena Romano, *Saggio d'iconografia dei reali angioini di Napoli* (Naples, 1920), with a review [B. Croce], *NN*, n.s. *1* (1920), 62–63; W. R. Valentiner, *Tino da Camaino* (Paris, 1935), pp. 16–42; Harald Keller, "Die Entstehung des Bildnisses am Ende des Hochmittelalters," *Römische Jahrbuch für Kunstgeschichte*, 3 (1939), p. 306, n. 296; Erwin Panofsky, *Tomb Sculpture* (New York, 1964), pp. 67–96 (for a more general survey); and for the related tomb of René, A. De Rinaldis, "La

Tomba primitiva di Renato d'Angiò," *Belvedere—Kunst und Kultur der Vergangenheit, 3* (1923), 92–98.

64 "Miraris niveis pendentia saxa columnis, / hospes, et hunc, acri qui sedet altus equo" (Sannazaro, *Poemata*, [Padua, 1719], p. 170. See also in the same volume, Epigrams, 1, 4).

65 "Improba mors hominum, heu semper obvia rebus / Dum Rex magnanimus totum spe concipit orbem / En moritur, saxo tegitur rex inclytus isto / Libera sidereum, mens ipsa petivit Olympum" (noted in Carlo Celano, *Notizie del bello dell'antico e del curioso della città di Napoli*, ed. G. B. Chiarini, 2 [Naples, 1856], 485).

CHAPTER 3

1 HACTENUS EFFRENIS, DOMINI NUNC PARET HABENIS / REX DOMAT HUNC EQUUM PARTHENOPENSIS AEQUUS. Cf. Pandolfo Collenuccio (d. 1504), *Compendio de le istorie del regno di Napoli*, ed. A. Saviotti (Bari, 1929), p. 152. Pandolfo, after speculating that the horse may have been a symbol of Earth, adds: "Corrado li fece mettere un morso in bocca e sopra le redine questi due versi fece scolpire."

2 Ibid. Carlo Celano says a temple of Neptune stood behind the horse, and that the latter (without reins) symbolized the hiding of "a congeries of waters" beneath the earth (*Notizie, 2*, 311–14).

3 Scipione Mazzella, *Descrittione del regno di Napoli* (Naples, 1586), p. 482.

4 G. Ceci, "Il Palazzo dei Carafa di Maddaloni poi di Colubrano," *NN*, 2 (1893), 149–52; *Corpus nummorum italicorum*, 19 (Rome, 1940), pl. iv, figs. 6–7. Beneath Ferrante on the small coin with unreined horse (the *cavallo*) was inscribed EQUITAS REGNI, and on the obverse was a crowned portrait of the king. See also L. Volpicella, "Le Imprese della numismatica aragonese di Napoli," in M. Cagiati, *Le Monete del reame delle Due Sicilie*, (Naples, 1911–13), supplement.

5 See my *Alfonso II and the Artistic Renewal of Naples, 1485–95* (New Haven, 1969), pp. 82–95. For the Aragonese kings as military knights, see P. E. Schramm, "Der König von Aragon," pp. 99–123, esp. p. 118.

6 L. Planiscig, "Ein Entwurf für den Triumphbogen," pp. 16–28; R. Filangieri, "Un più antico progetto," pp. 75–80; B. Degenhart, *Antonio Pisanello* (Vienna, 1940), pp. 47–48; Harald Keller, "Bildhauerzeichnungen Pisanellos," *Festschrift Kurt Bauch* (Munich, 1957), pp. 139–52; *Italiaanse Tekeningen in Nederlands Bezit* (Paris, Rotterdam, Haarlem, 1962), no. 14, pp. 24–25; Maria Fossi-Todorow, *I Disegni di Pisanello e della sua cerchia* (Florence, 1966), 408, no. 165; and G. L. Hersey, "The Arch of Alfonso in Na-

ples and its Písanellesque 'Design,' " *Master Draw-ings*, 7 (1969), 16–24.

7 O. Morisani, "Considerazioni sulle sculture della Porta di Capua," *Bollettino di storia dell'arte dell'istituto universitario di magistero, Salerno, 3* (January 1953), 1–20, (March 1953), 1–4, (September–December 1953), 1–76; for fifteenth-century knowledge of this monument, see also Giacomo de Nicola, "Un Disegno della Porta di Capua di Federigo II," *L'Arte, 11* (1908), 384–85.

8 Cf. Bertaux, "L'Arco e la porta trionfale," p. 27. For Ciriaco in Athens, see E. W. Bodnar, *Cyria-cus of Ancona and Athens* (Brussels / Berchem, 1960). Bodnar says that Ciriaco saw the Arch of Hadrian in 1436 and made a drawing of it (p. 39); in October, 1443, he was with Alfonso (p. 50).

9 Luigi Rossini, *Gli Archi trionfali onorarii e fune-bri degli antichi romani . . .* , (Rome, 1836), pp. 4–5, restores the Porta Marzia, Perugia, as a two-story gate with upper *civitas* figure, as in the Boymans pavilion, but with no discussion of his reasons for doing so.

10 This "Bonanu" may have been one of the *proto-magistri* of Castel Nuovo in the 1440s, a man named Francis Bonshoms, or, possibly, the uncle of one of the sculptors of the Arch, Paolo Romano. Romano's uncle, Bonomo de Rione Pinee, was an executor of Paolo's will and a sculptor in Rome. There are several documents on him in Antonio Bertolotti, "Paolo di Mariano scultore del secolo XV," *Archivio storico . . . della città e provincia di Roma*, anno 8, 4 (1882), fasc. 7, 291–317, esp. pp. 307–08. If the Boymans inscription is a later hand, as some have thought, it could still be an annotation as to a former owner of the draw-ing. The original "R°pine," shall we say, would have been misread as "Ravena" by a later tran-scriber who annotated the Boymans drawing.

11 See Aldo Neppi Modona, *Gli Edifici teatrali greci e romani: teatri, odei, anfiteatri, circhi* (Florence, 1961), p. 128 (for Orange), and (for Lyon) Pierre Wuilleumier, *Fouilles de Fourvière à Lyon* [Supplement to *Gallia, 4*] (Paris, 1951). For Naples see Minervini, "Antico teatro a Napoli," *Bullettino archeologico napoletano*, n.s. 7 (135–36); and M. Napoli, *Napoli greco-romana* (Na-ples, 1959), pp. 183–90.

12 No doubt some relation to the famous Diomede, possibly a brother. Diomede was the sixth son of that "valoroso Antonio Carafa, detto Malizia, che imitando il padre, servì così bene Alfonso I, ed egli fu capo de' soldati, che per l'aquedotto en-traron in Napoli, e furono cagione di farla venire in potere di Alfonso" (Celano-Chiarini, *Notizie, 3,* 684). Fazio mentions a Giovanni Carafa who took the fort at Barletta for Alfonso I, and this may be the one Valla means (*De rebus*

gestis Alphonsi primi, in Gravier, *Raccolta, 4,* 108–09). Diomede's second son, Giovanni An-tonio, father of Pope Paul IV, was appointed cas-tellan of Castel Capuano on 29 October 1487, which at least indicates that it may have been a family post (Iole Mazzoleni, ed., *Regesto della Cancelleria aragonese di Napoli* [Naples, 1951], p. 162).

13 "Ioannes Carrapha strenuus Decurio Neapolitanus, cum in arce, quae dicitur Capuana, imaginem regis armati, equoque insidentis pingendam curas-set, et circum eam quatuor virtutes Iustitiam, Charitatemque, sive Largitatem, Prudentiam, ac Temperantiam, sive Fortitudinem (est enim am-bigua pictura) a me contendit, ut versus totidem facerem, singulos in singularem [*sc.* singulatim] libellis, quos manutenebant, scribendos: addi-ditque, ut duos saltem [*sc.* saltim] eo biduo, qui superioribus imaginibus iam prope absolutis ad-scriberentur." Valla continues: "A pictore enim se deceptum, qui non praemonuisset scribere su-periores versus antequam ad inferiores pingendas descenderet imagines, ideoque tempus compo-nendorum versuum spe sua brevius esse: alioqui non ita commode postea scribi. Ego etsi febrire in-cipiebam, tamen me facturum recepi, ac plus ex-olui, quam promisi. Tres enim versus Iustitiae, Largitatis, Temperantie, eodem die ad hominem misi, quos cum pictor esset descripturus, et plurimi homines lectitarent" (Lorenzo Valla, *In Bartolo-maeum Facium Ligurem, invectivarum seu recri-minationum*, lib. iv, in *Opera omnia*, ed. Eugenio Garin, *1* (Turin, 1962), 597–99). See also C. M. Tallarigo, *Giovanni Pontano e i suoi Tempi* (Naples, 1874), pp. 117–18, who notes the Valla passage. Valla was Alfonso's secretary only in 1435–44, but he remained in Naples until Febru-ary 1447. For Valla in Naples see Luciano Barozzi, *Studi sul Panormita e sul Valla* (Florence, 1891), pp. 74–118; and, more especially, Michael Baran-dall, *Giotto and the Orators* (Oxford, 1971).

14 "Parthenope, multos bello vexata per annos, / Nunc opera Alphonsi parta iam quiesco" (Panor-mita). "Parthenope virgo diuturno exercita Marte, / Martius Alphonsus dat, requiesce tibi" (Valla) (ibid.).

15 "E por que con el verdadero amigo todas cosas se deven comunicar vos notifico mi pensiamento e invencion de la colocacion de aquella por sentir vuestro pareçer que yo fago aquella que repre-sente la statua de la ciudad de Napols la qual cansada por mucho tiempo de guerra agora opte-nida paz se repose

Enbio vos aqui interclusos los versos que le fechos fazer.

Illa ego Parthenope bello vexata tot annos
Nunc opera Alphonsi parta iam pace quiesco."

Cf. B. Croce, "Una Lettera inedita di Alfonso

d'Aragona," *NN, 1* (1892), 127–28; and A. Giménez Soler, *Itinerario del rey don Alfonso de Aragón y de Nápoles* (Saragossa, 1908), pp. 224–25. The statue or image sent from Rome might have been the work of Bonomo de Rione Pinee, the name possibly written at the base of the Boymans drawing. Bonomo was a fellow-sculptor with Paolo Romano, who made the cardinal's tomb.

16 Costanzo Angelini, in a letter to a group competing in the 1852 restoration project, notes the long-standing tradition that there had been an arch in the Castel Capuano; he even maintains that the Castel Nuovo Arch was originally constructed for this other building, but gives no evidence. Cf. Avena, *Il Restauro,* p. 10.

17 For contemporaneous accounts of Parthenope see Fabio Giordano, *Descriptio Campaniae,* a manuscript in the Biblioteca Nazionale, Naples, XIII.B.26. Cf. esp. fols. 3r–6r; Collenuccio, *Compendio* (Basel, 1572), pp. 10–11; and G. C. Capaccio, *Historiae neapolitanae* (1565) in Gravier, *Raccolta, 22,* bk. 1, 11–35. Cf. also Vittorio Spinazzola, "Il Nome di Napoli," *NN, 1* (1892), 33–35, 49–51.

18 Philargyrius on the *Georgics* 3.564. The text has an unfortunate lacuna: "Lutatius lib. IIII dicit, Cumanos incolas a parentibus digressos Parthenopen urbem constituisse, dictam a Parthenope Sirena, cuius corpus etiam [. . . .] postquam ob locorum ubertatem amoenitatemque magis coepta sit frequentari, veritos ne Cymaeam desererent, inisse consilium Parthenopen diruendi. Post etiam pestilentia affectos ex responso oraculi urbem restituisse sacraque Parthenopes cum magna religione suscepisse, nomen autem Neapoli ob recentem institutionem imposuisse." Cf. Richard Buttner, *Porcius Licinus und der litterarische Kreis des Q. Lutatius Catulus* (Leipzig, 1893), p. 187. For Parthenope's genealogy, see Summonte, *Historia, 1,* 28.

19 The tomb is mentioned in Pliny, *Historia Naturalis* 3. 5. 22.; Strabo, *Geographia* 1. 83. 93, 2. 449, Lycophron, *Alexandra* 717. See Julius Beloch, *Campanien* (Berlin, 1879), p. 77; and Bartolommeo Capasso, *Napoli greco-romana* (Naples, 1905), pp. 92–93; There is a tradition that it stood near the site of the present San Giovanni Maggiore (Summonte, *Historia, 1,* 29–30.) Statius presents Parthenope as follows: "ridetque benigna. Parthenope gentile sacrum nudosque virorum / certatus et parva suae simulacra coronae" (*Sylvae* 3. 1. 151 ff.); and "Una [camera] tamen cunctis, procul eminet una diaetis, / qua tibi Parthenopen de recto limite ponti / ingerit: hic Grais penitus delecta metallis saxa" (ibid. 2. 2. 83 ff.) A copy of the *Sylvae* appears as no. 99 in an inventory of the library of Alfonso I (De Marinis, *La Biblioteca napoletana, 2,* 194). Cf. also Paolo Savi-Lopez, "Napoli nelle descrizioni dei poeti. Le

Selve di Stazio," *NN, 6* (1897), 45–46.

20 Cf. Hermann Schrader, *Die Sirenen nach ihrer Bedeutung und Kunstlerischen Darstellung im Alterthum* (Berlin, 1868), esp. pp. 53 ff., and G. de Petra, *Le Sirene del mar tirreno* (Naples, 1911).

21 Emanuele Ciaceri discusses whether the nymph's head that appears on so many of these coins could represent Parthenope (*Storia della Magna Grecia, 1* [Rome, 1928], 331). Beloch, records an obol with a youth's head and the motto ΣΕΒΕΙΘΟΣ and, on the reverse, a winged woman seated on an urn, under which is [N]ΕΟΠΟΛΙΤΕ (Beloch, *Campanien,* p. 38). A similar figure on a type of didrachm from Syracuse has been called Nike (G. E. Rizzo, *Monete greche della Sicilia, 1* [Rome, 1946], fig. 48). For the whole controversy cf. Ettore Gàbrici, *Problemi di numismatica greca della Sicilia e Magna Grecia* (Naples, 1959), pp. 75–97. A coin issued by Ferrante, and also by Alfonso II during the later years of the century, became known as the *Sirena* (Summonte, *Historia, 5,* 17–18; L. Salazar, ed., "Racconti di storia napoletana," *ASPN, 33* [1908], 507–08). But this name was apparently a misreading of the motto SERENA OMNIA. For this see Arturo Sambon, "I 'Carlini' e la medaglia trionfale di Ferdinando I d'Aragona Re di Napoli," *Rivista italiana di numismatica, 4* (1891), 481–88.

22 F. K. von Duhn, "Der Dioskurentempel in Neapel," in *Sitzungsberichte der Heidelberger Akademie der Wissenschaften, 1* (1910), 1–20, esp. p. 11.

23 L. de la Ville sur-Yllon, "Il Corpo di Napoli e la 'capa' di Napoli," *NN, 3* (1894), 23–26. Domenico Antonio Parrino says that the Viceroy Don Parafan de Ribera, Duke of Alcalà, who reigned from 1559–71, being a collector of antiquities, returned to Spain with a statue of Parthenope that had stood opposite the Church of Santo Stefano. On the way the vessel carrying it was captured by pirates and the statue was dumped into the sea (*Teatro eroico e politico de' vicere del regno di Napoli . . .* [in Gravier, *Raccolta, 9,* 177]).

24 For Eumelos see Hyginus, *Fabulae* 243. G. C. Capaccio quotes Pontano as having said that Eumelos was also a king, a collector of pictures, and founder of a tribe, as is attested (says Capaccio) by a Greek inscription: ΕΥΜΗΛΟΝ ΘΕΟΝ ΠΑΤΡΩΩΝ / ΥΡΙΤΟΡΣΙΝ ΕΥΜΗΛΕΙΔΩΝ / Τ. ΦΛΑΤΙΟΣ ΠΙΟΣ / ΦΡΟΝΥΙΣΤΗΣ ΑΝΕΘΗΚΕΝ (*Historiae neapolitanae,* pp. 31–32). This Eumelos may also have been conflated with Eumelius Falerus, also described as a founder of Naples and an argonaut (Celano-Chiarini, *Notizie, 1,* 9).

25 The motif of a rearing horse, in 1447, would clearly precede the equestrian statue with rearing horse in Filarete (Magl. 172r) which has been claimed as the introduction of the idea (J. R.

Spencer, "Filarete and Central Plan Architecture," *Journal of the Society of Architecutral Historians,* 17 [1958], 10). In the same context one must of course refer to Leonardo's design for such a statue, mounted on a quadrifrons arch (Windsor 12354). For the question of Parthenope's identity, see Gàbrici, *Problemi,* pp. 75–97.

26 Angelo di Costanzo, *Istoria del regno di Napoli, 3,* 119; G. A. Summonte, *Historia, 4,* 75.

27 Many such temporary arches, decorated with figure sculpture, were erected in Naples. For example in 1470 a certain Giosuè Anselmo, painter, was paid for nineteen days of work constructing "un arco trionfale con un bastimento di legno con quattro colonne e quattro immagini grandi a simiglianza delle quattro virtù, sul quale arco era raffigurato il monte Calvario con tre croci, e sotto una rupe ove stava il monumento." This was erected in the Sala dei Baroni for Holy Thursday (N. Barone, "Le Cedole di tesoreria dell' Archivio di Stato di Napoli," *ASPN,* 9 [1884], 228–29). Summonte says it was suggested after Ferrante's death in 1494 that another such arch be erected in front of the cathedral (*Historia, 4,* 624). This was not done, but Alfonso II's planned Porta Reale of the following year may have been a permanent result of this plan for a temporary arch. See my *Alfonso II,* chap. 7. Similar structures were erected for Sannazaro's masques as produced in the Castel Capuano in the 1490s (B. Croce, "I Teatri di Napoli," pp. 556–684, esp. pp. 562–80).

28 R. Filangieri, "Rassegna critica delle fonti per la storia di Castel Nuovo," *ASPN,* 62 (1937), 272.

29 Cf. n. 6, above. The only real connection is through a tradition linking Pisanello with the Arch itself, which I noted in chap. 1, and which goes back at least as far as Fritz Burger, who thinks Pisanello actually made a sketch of the proposed Castel Nuovo structure (*Franz Laurana,* p. 70). On the other hand, if this had happened, it is more than likely that Fazio would have mentioned it in the biography of Pisanello in his *De viris illustribus,* which he does not, though he does mention the medals.

30 See Adolfo Venturi, ed., [G. Vasari], *Le Vite de' più eccellenti pittori scultori e architetti. I. Gentile da Fabriano e il Pisanello* (Florence, 1896), p. 49.

31 This we know from a letter to Pisanello from the Marchese Guglielmo Gonzaga in Mantua, dated 11 March 1444 (ibid.).

32 This could be implied by the language of the *privilegium* mentioned below, n. 35.

33 Degenhart, *Pisanello,* p. 78; Keller, "Bildhauerzeichnungen Pisanellos," pp. 145, 149–50.

34 G. Marinelli, "Il Codice Vallardi e i disegni del Pisanello al Louvre (verso una nuova attribuzione?)," *Emporium, 133* (1961), 251–59; Maria

Fossi-Todorow, "Un Taccuino di viaggi del Pisanello e della sua bottega," *Scritti di storia dell'arte in onore di Mario Salmi, 2* (Rome, 1959), 133–61.

35 Venturi, *Gentile da Fabriano,* pp. 59–61. For the nonexistent artist "Enea Pisano" who resulted from a misreading by Schülz and Gaetano Filangieri of the text of the privilegium, see ibid., and G. Ceci, *Saggio di una bibliografia per la storia delle arti figurative* (Bari, 1911), p. 97.

36 G. F. Hill interprets the book and the motto VIR SAPIENS as possibly a reference to Alfonso's interest in astronomy. He identifies the wounded animal as a fawn. The three larger birds below are vultures, says Hill, and the fourth an indeterminate bird of prey. He quotes Leonardo on the eagle as the symbol of *Liberalitas,* and mentions the Agrigentine coin-type that I illustrate (*fig.* 37) as the possible source of the conception (*Pisanello* [London, 1905], pp. 196–201). Cf. also Mario Salmi, "Riflessioni sul Pisanello medaglista," *Annali dell' istituto italiano di numismatica, 4* (1957), 13–23.

37 Schramm, "Der König von Aragon," p. 103.

38 Filarete, MS Magl., 45v.

39 See Dupré-Theseider, *La Politica italiana,* p. 13.

40 For Pisanello's later whereabouts and death, see Enio Sindona, *Pisanello* (New York, 1961), p. 24 and n. 57, with earlier bibliography.

41 See H. W. Janson, *The Sculpture of Donatello, 2* (Princeton, 1957), 90, with earlier bibliography; and Ottavio Morisani, "Per una Rilettura del monumento Brancacci," *NN,* ser. 3, 4 (May-August 1964), 3–11.

42 E. Bertaux, *La Renaissance en Italie et en France à l'époque de Charles VIII* (Paris, 1885), p. 424. Bertaux gives the tomb to "Ciccione" (Andrea di Nofri da Firenze). See N. F. Faraglia, "La Tomba di Ser Gianni Caracciolo in San Giovanni a Carbonara," *NN,* 8 (1899), 20–23; Antonio Filangieri, *La Chiesa e il Monastero di San Giovanni a Carbonara,* ed. R. Filangieri (Naples, 1926); R. Filangieri, "La Scultura in Napoli," pp. 89–94.

43 Filangieri, "Primi albori." Valla (*Opera,* pp. 597–99) mentions a competition between himself and Panormita for the inscription on the Caracciolo tomb.

CHAPTER 4

1 Collenuccio, *Compendio,* p. 191.

2 Eileen R. Driscoll, "Alfonso of Aragon," p. 92. Rolfs is equally gratuitous in identifying the relief as depicting Constantine (*Franz Laurana, 1,* 74), while Ettore Bernich has identified it as Alberti ("Leon Battista Alberti," pp. 148–55).

3 Bernich, "La Sala del trionfo," pp. 165–68.

4 Not only did he need the text, but he needed a royal edition, says Panormita (*De dictis et factis Alphonsi Aragonum, 1. 50,* in Gruterus, *Lampas,*

2, 38): "Cum inclytam illam arcem Neapolitanam instaurare instituisset, Vitruvii librum, qui de architectura inscribitur, afferri ad se iussit. Allatus est, quandoquidem impromptu[s] erat Vitruvius meus, sine ornatu aliquo, sine asseribus; quem rex simul atque inspexit, non decere hunc potissimum librum, qui nos quomodo contegamur, tam belle doceat, detectum incedere, eumque mihi perquam polite ac subito cooperiri mandavit." There was a local tradition, known to Alfonso, that Vitruvius's tomb was in nearby Gaeta (G. C. Capaccio, *Historiae neapolitanae*, 2, 212).

5   Vitruvius, *De Architectura* 1.5. Regarding what I call "diamond-cut" masonry, he actually says: "pectinatum disposita quemadmodum serrae dentes solent esse conlocentur."

6   Archivo de la Corona de Aragòn, Privilegiorum cancellariae Neapolis, tom. 16, regestro 2914. Dmni Regis Alfonsi 4 [i.e. of Catalonia], 1450–53. Magnifici Arnaldi Sans Castellani Castri novi Neapolis construendis domorum (fols. 102v, 103r, xvj [October 1450]).

7   It is interesting, too, that the scaenae frons of the Roman theater at Pula was still apparently semi-erect in the fifteenth century, forming part of a castle called the Palas Rotondi. It was described as such by Georg Pfistring in 1436–40: see Anton Gnirs, *Pola: Ein Führer durch die antiken Baudenkmäler und Sammlungen* (K. K. Osterreichisches Archaologisches Institut) (Vienna, 1915), p. 104.

8   There is no mention of Alberti in the old checklists published in Tammaro De Marinis, *La Biblioteca napoletana*, nor, apparently, has De Marinis's research turned up a copy of the work that can be connected with Alfonso. There is one possibility: University of Chicago Manuscript Latin 1 (Edgar J. Goodspeed, *A Descriptive Catalogue of Manuscripts in the Libraries of the University of Chicago* [Chicago, 1912], pp. 3–4). This is probably fifteenth-century. At the foot of fol. 150b is written: "Scriptum Manu Cancelarii Extis Regni Siciliae Cancelarii," which could mean an Aragonese provenance.

9   Driscoll publishes a drawing showing proportional divisions of the upper and lower Castel Nuovo arches, which she says correspond to Alberti's prescriptions in *De re aedificatoria*. But in the lower arch these proportions result mostly from the fact that it is copied from the Pula model; and the main vertical proportions of the upper arch, in turn, are established by those of the lower. Driscoll's only remaining "Albertian" proportion is in the height of the upper attic, which is one-half that of the nicchione stage—a commonplace relationship.

10 For all this see Torgil Magnuson, *Studies in Roman Quattrocento Architecture* (Rome-Stock-

holm, 1958), pp. 144, 157–59, with earlier bibliography. The description of the planned Vatican gate, which with "duae magnae turres erigebantur, in quarum meditullio porta cum fornice triumphali condebatur, unde in palatium introibatur" dates from 1452, the same year in which the Neapolitan Arch was planned in its present form.

11 This contract is exhaustively discussed, with earlier bibliography, by R. Filangieri "Rassegna critica delle fonti per la storia di Castel Nuovo," *ASPN*, 62 (1937), 275–78.

12 There is no reason to agree with Rolfs that here the two corner towers of the castle front are meant, and that the central tower on this facade did not yet exist (*Franz Laurana*, 1, 56–57). The text clearly says "Li doe torri de la porta."

13 See Alessandro Dudan, *La Dalmazia nell'arte italiana*, 1 (Milan, 1921), 166–77; Ottavio Morisani, *Michelozzo architetto* (Florence[?], 1951), pp. 97–98; Ljubo Karaman, *Umjetnost u Dalmaciji XV i XVI Vijek* (Zagreb, 1933), pp. 64–68.

14 Carlo L. Ragghianti, "Tempio Malatestiano," *Critica d'arte*, 12 (May 1965), 23–31, and 13 (October 1965), 27–39. See also Dudan, *La Dalmazia*, 1, 172.

15 Avena, *Il Restauro*, p. 93.

16 Cf. above, chap. 1, n. 21. It is perhaps also worth noting that in the fifteenth century the arch at Pula formed part of the city walls, though there seem to have been no flanking towers (Gnirs, *Pola*, s.v.). There is a drawing from the period, an elevation and details attributed to Francesco di Giorgio, in the Uffizi, Drawing Cabinet, A2058. Despite this conventional attribution the drawing could actually have been made for the Arch in Naples.

17 Cf. Cvito Fisković, *Nasi Graditelji i Kipari XV i XVI Stoljeća u Dubrovniku* (Zagreb, 1947), fig. 30.

18 Summonte, *Historia*, 4, 16. In this connection, too, Bernich implies the existence of documentation that the arcivescovado arch was ordained on 28 February 1443 by the rulers of the seggi; but he does not identify the document ("Leon Battista Alberti," p. 115, n. 2).

19 Pietro is quite likely the artist responsible for a drawing in the Codex Vallardi of Pisanello's LIBERALITAS obverse, which in turn he would have used for his own medal based on this design for René of Anjou (Hill, *Corpus*, 54). Cf. Maria Fossi-Todorow, *I Disegni del Pisanello e della sua cerchia* (Florence, 1966), no. 160.

20 R. Filangieri, "Rassegna critica," *ASPN*, 62 (1937), 305.

21 Ibid., pp. 284–85.

22 R. Filangieri, "La gran Sala," pp. 145–71, esp. p. 170.

23 Cf. Gnirs, *Pola,* s.v. The same was true of Agostino di Duccio's very Albertian Porta San Pietro, Perugia, of 1475.

24 Rolfs finds the nearest prototype in the capitals of the outer wall of the left aisle of Santa Maria in Cosmedin; but these are not as close as the ones I cite (*Franz Laurana, 1, 126*).

25 Cf. Leo Planiscig, "Ein Bildhauer am Hofe Alfons' I. von Neapel," *Jahrbuch der Kunsthistorischen Sammlungen in Wien,* n.s. 8 (1934), 65–78, esp. p. 72.

26 Cf. R. Filangieri, who sees the right-hand ressaut as an (unspecified) Hippolytus scene, linked to a Hippolytus sarcophagus in Constantinople (*Castel Nuovo,* p. 92; see also Rolfs, *Franz Laurana, 1,* 79). Bertaux identifies the right-hand incident, properly I think, as Hercules and Phaedra, and the left-hand one, improperly, as Hercules and Omphale ("L'Arco e la porta trionfale," pp. 27–63). Pisanello's other medal for Alfonso has on its obverse a youth with dog, killing a boar (Hill, *Corpus,* 42). The slaying of the Calydonian boar by Meleager is frequently represented in this manner in myth (e.g. Apollodorus 1. 8), and Meleager is also, of course, Oeneus's son and a fellow-huntsman with Hercules. Thus this medal would be linked to the Hercules imagery of the Arch. The boar, which had laid waste the kingdom of Calydon, would represent René, and the *venator intrepidus,* Alfonso.

27 The style of these reliefs anticipates those on the imposts of the portal of the Rector's Palace at Dubrovnik, dated 1465 by Dudan (*La Dalmazia, 1,* 166–77) and given to Giorgio da Sebenico or Paolo de Ragusa.

28 Cf. Massimo Pallottino, *Il grande Fregio di Traiano* (Rome, 1938); and Hans Peter L'Orange, *Der spätantike Bildschmuck des Konstantinsbogens* (Berlin, 1939).

29 Some fanciful interpretations of these scenes, all lacking documentation or even basic credibility, have been made. Fabriczy says the central figure in each is of Alfonso, and sees "den Auszug des Königs an der rechten Wand des Thoreingangs, uber dem letzteren seinen Siegestriumph und an der linken Thorwand gleichsam die Begründung seiner staatlichen Macht" ("Der Triumphbogen," pp. 135–36). Rolfs sees the left-hand figure as Alfonso of Calabria, grandson of Alfonso I, after the battle of Otranto in 1481—a chronological impossibility (*Franz Laurana, 1,* 147–49). On p. 153 he says more correctly that the right-hand central figure does not resemble Ferdinand enough to have been intended to represent him. Fritz Burger simply says both central figures portray Alfonso (*Francesco Laurana,* pp. 28–29). W. R. Valentiner sees the young (left-hand) figure as Alfonso after his conquest of Naples in 1442, even

though Alfonso was forty-four at this time ("Andrea dell'Aquila," p. 522).

30 For other portraits of Ferrante, see my *Alfonso II,* figs. 25–30. For Ferrante's acclamation as heir, cf. Dupré-Theseider, *La Politica italiana,* p. 22. Panormita (Gruterus, *Lampas, 3,* 314–15) speaks of both Alfonso and Ferrante as Hercules figures. Classical Hercules statuettes similar to these Arch figures exist (e.g. British Museum 1261, 1266).

31 Noted by Fabriczy, "Triumphbogen," p. 136.

32 Rolfs claims that the Aragonese kept lions as pets (*Franz Laurana, 1,* 151–52).

33 This Herculan imagery is noted but not explored by Burger, *Francesco Laurana,* p. 31.

34 [Nicaise?], *Les Sirènes, on discours sur leur forme et figure* (Paris, 1691), p. 21. For the substantial cult of Hercules in Naples cf. G. C. Capaccio, *Historiae neapolitanae, 1,* s.v., in Gravier, *Raccolta, 22,* 196–97.

35 Pontano mentions Hercules' voyage from Calydon, where the River Acheloos flows, to Campania (*De bello neapolitano,* in Gravier, *Raccolta, 5,* 144; G. A. Summonte, *Historia, 1, 23*).

36 Identified as Medusa by Filangieri, *Castel Nuovo,* p. 92; he makes it analogous to the Medusa head on the Gattamelata's breastplate. The head of Acheloos may relate to a drawing by one of Pisanello's circle now in the Museum Boymans-van Beuningen, Rotterdam (I.521). See Fossi-Todorow, *I Disegni del Pisanello,* no. 203r. The Medusa or Parthenope head is also of much the same type as that on sarcophagus 23.36, Walters Art Gallery, Baltimore.

37 According to Capaccio, Parthenope played the lyre and the other two sirens, Leucosia and Ligea, respectively played the tibia and sang (*Historiae, 1,* p. 24). For other variations by Renaissance artists on nereid images see Phyllis Bober, "An Antique Sea-Thiasos in the Renaissance," *Essays in Memory of Karl Lehmann* (New York, 1964), pp. 43–48.

38 R. Filangieri, *Castel Nuovo,* p. 96. For the funeral significance of such figures see Jan Białostocki, "The Sea-Thiasos in Renaissance Sepulchral Art," *Studies in Renaissance and Baroque Art Presented to Anthony Blunt* (London–New York, 1967), pp. 69–74.

39 See above, n. 2, for earlier identifications.

40 For this and its symbols see Luigi Volpicella, "Le Imprese della numismatica aragonese di Napoli," in M. Cagiati, *Le Monete del Reame delle Due Sicilie* (Naples, 1911–13), supplement; G. M. Fusco, *Intorno all'Ordine dell'Armellino* (Naples, 1844); and idem, *I Capitoli dell'Ordine dell'Armellino* (Naples, 1845).

41 These coffers have Dalmatian parallels in the Chapel of Saint John, Trogir cathedral, ca. 1468, probably by Andrea Alessi, Ivan Duknović, and

Niccolò Fiorentino. See Karaman, *Umjetnost u Dalmaciji*, pp. 78–94.

42 Almost all authorities agree that the upper relief originally depicted Ferrante's coronation. But Mariano d'Ayala mentions a story to the effect that it represents Ferrante's legitimization on 3 March 1443 ("Dell'Arco trionfale, " pp. 34–45).

43 See my "Alfonso II, Benedetto e Giuliano da Maiano e la Porta reale," *NN*, ser. 3, *4* (1964), 77–95. Rolfs speculates unconvincingly that the statue of Alfonso I mentioned by Pietro Summonte in his letter to Michiel could instead have been of Ferrante, and intended for this niche (*Franz Laurana, 1*, 165).

44 One thinks here also of Sannazaro's lines on Ferrante's brother, "In Laudes Federicum Regem": "Cinxerit sacra meritum corona / Et caput; Gallos quoniam feroces / Contudit: totas revocarit Orci ex Faucibus urbes: / Nil tamen majus, nihil egit umquam / Fortius; quam quod titubante regno, / Quum sibi sceptrum, et diadema posset /Sumere tutus" (*Poemata*, Epigrams, 2, ed. G. A. Vulpio [Padua, 1719], 11. 29 ff.).

45 According to Eugene Müntz, *Histoire de l'art pendant la Renaissance, 1* (Paris, 1889), 579. For the doors, see Filippo Baldinucci, *Opere, 5* (Milan, 1811), annotation by Giuseppe Piacenza, pp. 525–28; Leopoldo Cicognara, *Storia della scultura, 2*, 191–92; Mariano d'Ayala, "Dell'Arco trionfale," pp. 39–44; H. W. Schülz, *Denkmäler der Kunst, 3*, 120–23; E. Nunziante, *I primi Anni di Ferdinando d'Aragona . . .* (Naples, 1898), pp. 737 ff.; Fabriczy, "Triumphbogen," pp. 140–45; Antonio Maresca di Serracapriola, "Battenti e decorazione marmorea di antiche porte esistenti in Napoli," *NN, 10* (1901), 17–25; M. Biancale, "Le Porte di bronzo di Castelnuovo in Napoli," *L'Arte, 10* (1907), 423–35; L. Volpicella, "Le Porte di Castelnuovo e il bottino di Carlo VIII," *NN*, ser. 2, *1* (1920), 153–60; and R. Filangieri, "Rassegna critica," *ASPN, 62* (1937), 327–33.

46 This is Filangieri's reasoning (in "Rassegna critica," *ASPN, 62* [1937], 332), since there is a lacuna in the *cedole* from mid-1474 through the end of 1475, and since there are also no records of payments in the existing cedole. For his explanation of the various holes, and of the cannonball still embedded in the left-hand valve, see ibid., pp. 328–30. The best description of the military clothing, weapons, and gear is in D'Ayala, "Dell'Arco trionfale."

47 As to other attributions of the doors, Cicognara assigns them to Giuliano da Maiano, but strangely adds that they look more like thirteenth-century work than fifteenth (*Storia della scultura*). Biancale tries to distinguish three hands in the design or execution of the scenes: Sculptor A did the middle left-hand panel, the surrender of Troia

(*fig. 63*); Sculptor B the two upper panels, the meeting at Calvi and the attempt on Ferrante's life (*figs. 58, 59*), as well as *fig. 61*, the entry of the Aragonese, and *fig. 62*, the Battle of Troia. Sculptor C did the left-hand lower panel, *fig. 60*, the retreat from Accadia. A is identified as Pietro da Milano ("Le Porte di bronzo"). I see no merit in the analysis.

48 "Andrea dell'Aquila," p. 509.

49 Sarnelli tells the legend of a contest between two of the Arch masters, in which they agreed that the man who made the better of the two inner reliefs could knock the noses off the loser's figures (*Guida de' forestieri*, pp. 32–33). The loser was apparently Pietro, the master of the left-hand relief, since several noses in this panel are damaged. The story has been pooh-poohed as an unworthy jape— yet, of course, there are the two other pairs of roughly coeval "competition reliefs" in Rome, also connected with Arch masters: the pedestals of the two colossal Radio Vaticana statues (Paolo Romano and "Mino del Reame"), and the two angels over the door of San Giacomo degli Spagnuoli, which involved the same two artists. Cf. Müntz, *L'Art pendant la renaissance, 1*, 576–78.

CHAPTER 5

1 As noted by Rolfs, *Franz Laurana, 1*, 199. This must mean that during June and July Andrea had received monthly payments of 12 ducats, and the odd remainder in August (16 ducats, 3 tari, 6½ grani).

2 "Testis et Eugenii mirabilis urna sepulcri, / testis et Alphonsi regius arcus erit, / ille triumphali virtute et fortibus armis / Parthenope tot legit ab orbe virum." Cf. Angelo Battaglini, "Memoria sopra uno sconosciuto egregio scultore del secolo XV," *Dissertazioni [Atti] dell'Accademia romana di archeologia, 1* (1821), 115–32.

3 Mariano d'Ayala ("Dell'Arco trionfale," pp. 34–45, esp. p. 44) thinks this, as does Ettore Bernich ("Leon Battista Alberti," p. 154). The "Parthenope" of the fourth line was possibly intended as an ablative of cause, which would link Isaia with the proposed statue of Parthenope mentioned in chap. 3.

4 The drawing of the arch in fig. 66, from the Vatican *Libro di Giuliano da San Gallo* (fol. 36v) is I think the only view showing it in its relatively unruined state. But I admit that Giuliano may have restored a ruinous original.

5 Alfonso was in Algeria from June through September of this year but I do not know that he visited Cuicul (A. Giménez Soler, *Itinerario*, pp. 30–37). For the arch at Cuicul, see Albert Ballu, *Ruines de Djemila* (Algiers, 1921), pp. 54–55; and Louis Leschi, *Djemila, antique Cuicul* (Algiers, 1950), p. 28, with earlier bibliography.

6   Cf. especially G. Ceci's reconstruction of the Seggio di Portanova, which stood at the meeting point of the vico dei Chiodarelli, the largo Portanova, and the vico Santa Maria dei Muschini. This was a cruciform arched structure, about sixteen meters square, dating from Angevin times and rebuilt in the sixteenth century ("Il Seggio di Portanova," *NN, 2* [1893], 77–78).

7   According to Summonte the *baldacchino* was held by twenty-four youths, four from each of the six seggi (*Historia, 4,* 13). Aside from such documented (but to me unidentifiable) figures as Giovanni Antonio del Balzo Orsini, Prince of Taranto; Pietro Trotto, Ambassador from Milan; Antonio Sanseverino, Duke of San Marco; Trojano Caracciolo, Duke of Melfi; and Count Giacomo Piccinino, son of Nicolò, the group may include Ferrante. He would be the headless man behind the far left-hand baldacchino carrier who has lost his pole (*fig. 72*).

8   Noted by Giovanni Caradenti, *I Trionfi,* figs. 6, 7. This relief was in Santa Martina presso il Foro Romano before 1515. The female figure has been fancifully identified as Alfonso's friend Lucrezia d'Alagno (E. Bernich, "Madama Lucrezia," *NN, 15* [1906], 69–70).

9   Noted by Driscoll, "Alfonso of Aragon," p. 91. Cf. also Doc. 1, which says that the car is "fet a manera de cadafal."

10 Both inscriptions are by Panormita, according to R. Filangieri, "Rassegna critica," *ASPN, 62* (1937), 267.

11 Sheldon Nodelman, "Mino del Reame" (Master's thesis, Yale University, 1959), p. 14; and Charles Seymour, Jr., *Sculpture in Italy: 1400–1500* (Harmondsworth, Mddx., 1966), pp. 138, 243, n. 6. W. R. Valentiner conflates Mino with Domenico da Montemignaio, charged in 1455 with making images—not necessarily statues—of Alfonso and John the Baptist ("A Portrait Bust of Alfonso I of Naples," *Art Quarterly, 1* [1938], 61–88). It may be that Mino is Domenico, or even that he is Mino del Reame as well. The latter name appears in Vasari, and this is Nodelman's suggestion. But if so it is surprising that a Florentine as famous as Mino da Fiesole was not mentioned as an important contributor to the Arch by such subsequent pro-Florentine writers as Pietro Summonte and Vasari.

12 Keller, "Bildhauerzeichnungen Pisanellos," pp. 139–52. See also Fossi-Todorow, *I Disegni del Pisanello,* nos. 245, 250.

13 See Valentiner's comparison with those in Donatello's Casa Martelli arms in Florence, ca. 1440, in "Andrea dell'Aquila," pp. 503–36, and figs. 22, 23.

14 Fritz Burger concludes that by 1459 "muss der Skulpturenschmuck des Bogens bis zum Nischen-

geschoss und wohl auch noch der architektonische Teil desselben d.h. nahezu der ganze ursprüngliche geplante Bogen fertiggestellt worden sein!" (*Francesco Laurana,* p. 60). He thus gratuitously assumes that the 3,800 ducats was for finishing the whole monument and not merely for the statues. Burger then subtracts all the money paid to Pietro in the 1460s (Docs. 21–23, 25, 27–30), with the result that 2,800 ducats are unaccounted for. But Burger's arithmetic leaves no money to pay for the inner arch. Further, it is not clear whether Burger thinks this unaccounted-for sum of 2,800 ducats was paid but recorded on lost documents, or whether he thinks the budget for the colossi was cut. It seems more likely that the budget was reduced by Ferrante after his father's death. The reliefs of the upper arch would already have existed at this time; they are exquisitely finished. Then, in 1465, Ferrante would have seen to it that due care was expended on the inner arch, which was in his own honor, but would have abandoned the colossal figures, honoring Alfonso, for the outer nicchione. It is also likely that he then asked Pietro da Milano to make do with *disiecta membra* (*figs. 101, 106, 107, 112*) for the upper figures.

15 Adolfo Avena, *Il Restauro,* pp. 30, 93.

16 Fabriczy notes the fact ("Triumphbogen," p. 128, n. 1) as have many since. There are of course innumerable possibilities for classical sources, but I have found none that are exact. As to the architectural application of the niche-sarcophagus, one thinks of Donatello's tomb of John XXIII in the Florence baptistry, that of Nicholas V in the Grotte Vaticane, the Lateran sacristy altar, etc.—but this Neapolitan instance may be the earliest large-scale exterior employment of the form.

17 The third pair in from the left has been restored. Cf. also the griffins on the Loggia della Mercanzia, Siena, and the later (1484) and those in the pavement of the Siena cathedral—though these are semi-recumbent. Another parallel is the terracotta frieze in the Museo Nazionale, Ravenna, taken from a facade in via G. Guaccimanni. See Piero Sanpaolesi, *Aspetti dell'architettura del 400 a Siena e Francesco di Giorgio* (Urbino, 1949 [?]), p. 22.

18 Valentiner, "Andrea dell'Aquila," pp. 514–21.

19 Friedrich Karl von Duhn discusses the tympanum sculpture of this building and suggests (along with other possibilities) that two reclining river gods, possibly both representing the Sebeto, appeared on it ("Der Dioskurentempel," p. 11). Cf. above, chap. 3, n. 22. Lodovico de la Ville sur-Yllon, in "Il Sebeto," *NN, 11* (1902), 113–16, describes an archaic Greek Neapolitan coin showing a seated winged figure with a broken vase at its feet on the

reverse, and on the obverse a youth's head crowned with leaves, from whose forehead emerges a horn. It is inscribed ΝΕΟΠΟΛΙΤΕ. The same critic also quotes from Sannazaro's *Arcadia,* where the god Sebeto, crowned with herbs, is seated by a stone vessel with water pouring from it, as on the Arch tympanum. Sannazaro's god looks off to where the river splits in two, one branch running through open country and the other diving beneath the city. Here the poet may well be retailing the original significance of the Arch's twin river gods. Another possible classical source for the sculptures was the statue of the river mentioned by Michelangelo Schipa, "Napoli greco-romana," *NN, 14* (1905), 100. There is little merit to Rolfs's contention that the figures are derived from the spandrels of the Arch of Septimius (*Franz Laurana, 1,* 141).

20 Avena, *Il Restauro,* p. 94.

21 Fabriczy identifies it as Ferrante, though it looks to me like a female ("Der Triumphbogen," p. 133). Rolfs says it may be the figure of Justice that once stood over the oriel of the Gran Sala (*Franz Laurana, 1,* 132). Without base it is 2.42 meters high, and therefore about .20 meters shorter than the upper three left-hand Virtues.

22 Saint Michael and Saint George were Alfonso's patrons (Giménez Soler, *Itinerario,* p. 276). For a classical prototype for the Saint Anthony, see Guido della Valle, "La Villa sillana ed augustea Pausilypon," *Campania romana, 1* (1938), 207–67, esp. fig. 10.

23 Rolfs rejects the possibility that a free-standing group, including such a bronze equestrian portrait, was originally intended (*Franz Laurana, 1,* 118). But cf. Hans Semper, *Donatello, seine Zeit und Schule* (Vienna, 1875), pp. 306–09.

24 A. Filangieri, "La colossale Testa di cavallo in bronzo del Museo Nazionale di Napoli," *Arte e storia,* 15 October 1901, pp. 127–28. The transfer was made in 1809.

25 G. Ceci. "Il Palazzo dei Carafa di Maddaloni poi di Colubrano," *NN, 2* (1893), 149–52, 168–70, esp. p. 151. Cf. also Sarnelli, *La vera Guida,* s.v. Castel Nuovo.

26 A. Filangieri, "La colossale Testa"; Ceci, "Palazzo Carafa"; and, earlier, Vasari (*2,* 409), who says it is by Donatello but so beautiful some think it antique. G. B. Celano says the Museo Nazionale sculpture is the Conradian horse and not Donatello's, but that Donatello did make the *bozzetto* based on the large bronze. However Celano also says that this bozzetto represented Ferrante rather than Alfonso I (*Notizie, 2,* 311–14, *3,* 683–84). Benedetto Croce repeats the attribution of the Nazionale piece to Donatello ("Per la settima Edizione del 'Cicerone' del Burckhardt, lettera aperta al Dr. G. Bode," *NN, 6* [1897], 53). Rolfs says

only that it is of "nebensächlicher Bedeutung" "Der Baumeister," pp. 81–101, esp. p. 84). Dr. Cornelius Vermeule, who has kindly examined a photograph of it for me, suggests that the head is antique but that large sections of it—the area around the eyes, the nostrils, and the mane—were completely reworked in postantique times.

27 A secondary link between Donatello and Alfonso would be Porcellio, who composed an inscription for the Gattamelata tomb inside the Santo (H. W. Janson, *The Sculpture of Donatello, 1* [Princeton, N.J., 1957], p. 157).

28 See Jordi Rubió, "Alfons 'el Magnánim' rei de Napols, i Daniel Florentino, Leonardo da Bisuccio i Donatello," *Miscel·lània Puig i Cadafalch, 1* (Barcelona, 1947–51), 25–35. According to Janson the Gattamelata had been completed but not installed in June 1453, though by September it was on its pedestal (*Donatello, 1,* 155).

29 "Ipse autem puro celsum caput aere saeptus / templa superfulges et prospectare videris, / an nova contemptis surgant Palatia flammis / pulchrius." Aside from the general development of equestrian figures, on or off tombs (for which see John Pope-Hennessy, *Italian Renaissance Sculpture* 2nd ed. [New York, and London, 1971], pp. 52–60; and Panofsky, *Tomb Sculpture,* pp. 83–85), one should mention Alberti's judging of the equestrian monuments of Niccolò III d'Este in 1444 for the Arco del Cavallo, Ferrara. Here again we have a memorial portrait on an arch base. Among the unquestionably antique horses' heads that are fairly close to that in the Nazionale, there are two in the Museo Nazionale in Ancona and one in the Museo Archeologico, Florence. For the former see Sandro Stucchi, "Gruppo bronzeo di Cartoceto," *Bollettino d'arte, 45* (1960), 7–44, esp. 7–10.

30 Possibly the group of drawings of horses' heads in the Codex Vallardi could be tied in with all this. See Fossi-Todorow, *Pisanello,* nos. 286, 287–90.

31 For the equestrian monument as cenotaph, see Harald Keller, "Ursprünge des Gedächtnismals," *Kunstchronik, 7* (1954), 134–37. There is some confusion as to where Alfonso I's body actually lies. There is a coffin said to contain his remains in the sacristy of San Domenico Maggiore, Naples. But J. E. Martínez Ferrando gives a wealth of detail on how, on 23 August 1671 don Pedro Antonio de Aragón y de Cardona had the body reburied at Poblet, pantheon of the kings of Aragon. According to this account Alfonso had previously lain in San Pietro Martire, Naples ("Consideraciones en torno a la exposición documental sobre Alfonso el Magnánimo, organizada en el Archivo de la corona de Aragón," in Antonio Torraja, ed., *Estudios sobre Alfonso el Magnánimo* [Barcelona,

1960], pp. 213–32, esp. p. 214). Summonte, on the other hand, agrees with the present theory that Alfonso's body is in San Domenico (*Historia, 4,* 257). For memorial containers for hearts, including those of Francis I and Louis, Cardinal of Bourbon and Archbishop of Reims, cf. Panofsky, *Tomb Sculpture,* pp. 79–80.

32 Cf. the medal by Cristoforo de Geremia, with Alfonso I between Mars and Bellona (Hill, *Corpus,* 754), which is inscribed on the obverse, ALFONSUS REX REGIBUS IMPERANS ET BELLORUM VICTOR. Both scene and inscription could thus be expansions of the Arch iconography.

33 Laurentii Schrader, *Monumentorum italiae, quae hoc nostro saeculo et a christianis posita sunt libri quatuor* (Haberstadien, 1592), lib. 2, fol. 248.

34 See chap. 3, n. 14.

CHAPTER 6

1 Driscoll, "Alfonso of Aragon," p. 88.

2 See Mariano d'Ayala, "Intorno alle Sculture nella chiesa di San Domenico ed in espezialità sulle tombe di Malizia Carafa e dei d'Aquino," *Annali civili del regno delle Due Sicilie, 41* (1846), 99–105; Raffaello Maria Valle, *Descrizione storica artistica letteraria della chiesa e convento di San Domenico Maggiore continuata da B. Minichini* (Naples, 1853–54); N. F. Faraglia, "La Tomba di ser Gianni Caracciolo," pp. 20–23; Antonino Maresca di Serracapriola, "Battenti e decorazione," pp. 51–58; Giuseppe Cosenza, "La Chiesa e il convento di San Pietro Martire IV," *NN, 9* (1900), 104–09; Luigi Serra, "Due Scultori fiorentini del 400 a Napoli," *NN, 14* (1905), 181–85, *15* (1906) 4–8; Antonio Muñoz, "Studii sulla scultura napoletana del rinascimento," *Bollettino d'arte, ser. 1, 3* (1909), 55–73, 83–98; R. Filangieri, "La Scultura in Napoli," 65–69, 89–94; A. Filangieri, San Giovanni a Carbonara"; Ottavio Morisani, *Saggi sulla scultura napoletana del cinquecento* (Naples, 1941); idem, "Considerazioni sui Malvito di Como," in Edoardo Arslan, ed., *Arte e artisti dei laghi lombardi, 1* (Como, 1959), 265–74; Bruno Molajoli, ed., *Sculture lignee nella Campania* (Naples, 1950); Oreste Ferrari, "Per la Conoscenza della scultura del primo quattrocento a Napoli," *Bollettino d'arte, 39* (1954), 11–24; Franco Strazzullo, "Documenti sull'attività napoletana dello scultore milanese Pietro de Martino (1453–1473)," *ASPN, 81* (1963), 325–41.

3 For this and other Neapolitan architectural ornament possibly influenced by the Arch, consult Giuseppe Castaldi, "Il Palazzo di Giulio de Scorziatis," *NN, 12* (1903), 180–83; L. Catalani, *I Palazzi di Napoli* (Naples, 1845); Giuseppe Ceci, "Il Palazzo dei conti di Maddaloni poi di

Colubrano," *NN, 2* (1893), 149–52, 168–70; L. de la Ville sur-Yllon, "La Chiesa di S. Barbara in Castelnuovo," *NN, 2* (1893), 70–74, 118–22, 170–73; A. de Rinaldis, "Forme tipiche dell' architettura napoletana nella prima metà del quattrocento," *Bollettino d'arte, 18* (1924–25), 162–83; and Roberto Pane, *L'Architettura del rinascimento.*

4 For this see R. Langton Douglas, " 'Mino del Reame,' " *Burlington Magazine, 87* (1945), 217–24.

5 Kindly pointed out to me by Roberto Pane. Cf. Fondazione Salvator Romano, Cenacolo dello Santo Spirito, Florence, *Catalogo.*

6 P. D. Roussel, *Description du Château d'Anet* (Paris, 1875), p. 143. Roussel suggests Philibert de l'Orme as designer and Goujon as sculptor; But cf. Pierre du Colombier, *Jean Goujon* (Paris, 1949), pp. 24–30.

7 Strazzulo, "Documenti"; P. Trabaud, "Le Retable de Saint-Didier à Avignon," *Gazette des beaux-arts,* ser. 2, 23 (1881), 175–80.

8 Cf. Trabaud, "Le Retable"; Louis Courajod, "Un Fragment du rétable de Saint-Didier d'Avignon, sculpté par Francesco Laurana au musée du Louvre," *Gazette des beaux-arts,* ser. 2, 29 (1884), 182–87; L. Barthélemy, *François Laurana auteur du monument de Saint-Lazare dans l'ancienne cathédrale de Marseille* (Marseilles, 1885); Maxe-Werly, "Francesco da Laurana Fondeur-ciseleur à la cour de Lorraine," *Réunion des sociétés des beaux-arts des départements* (Paris, 1899), pp. 276–85; Lisetta Motta Ciaccio, "Francesco Laurana in Francia," *L'Arte, 11* (1908), 409–18.

9 For these copies see W. R. Valentiner, "A Madonna Statuette by Domenico Gagini," *Art in America, 25* (1937), 104–17.

10 Cf. Anna Maria Corbo, "L'Attività di Paolo di Mariano a Roma," *Commentari, 17* (1966), 195–226.

11 Valentiner, "Andrea dell'Aquila," pp. 503–36.

12 C. Gnudi suggests that Niccolò dell'Arca may have been influenced by the Arch (*Niccolò dell'Arca* [Turin, 1942], p. 13).

13 R. Filangieri, "Rassegna critica," *ASPN, 62* (1937), 300–02.

14 For this see Rodolphe Pfnor, *Monographie du château d'Anet* (Paris, 1867); Roussel, *Anet,* pp. 35–37; and Alphonse Roux, *Le Château d'Anet* (Paris, 1911), esp. pp. 24–25. Sir Anthony Blunt's assertion that the tower of San Biagio, Montepulciano, by the elder Antonio da Sangallo, is a "close parallel" and "model" for the Anet frontispiece, is patently incorrect (*Philibert de l'Orme* [London, 1958], p. 33). Sangallo's campanile is a very different object architecturally, being simply a slight enrichment of a typical, age-old tower formula. No real allusion is made to the

triumphal arch scheme, nor to the idea of the palace frontispiece.

15 Robert Willis and J. W. Clark, *The Architectural History of the University of Cambridge,* I (Cambridge, 1886–87), 177–90.

16 Nikolaus Pevsner, *The Buildings of England. Cambridgeshire* (Harmondsworth, Mddx. 1954), p. 64.

17 See chap. 1, n. 9. As this book was going to press, Philip Foster, who had kindly pointed out to me the Rothschild drawing reproduced in figure 118, has also brought to my attention a brief description of the sketchbook in which the drawing is found (*Dessins d'architecture du XVᵉ au XIXᵉ siècle dans les collections du Musée du Louvre* [Paris: Réunion des Musées nationaux, 1972], p. 10).

BIBLIOGRAPHY

This bibliography does not list standard reference works or well-known texts such as Vasari in the Milanesi edition. It also omits some of the articles listed in appendix 2. Additional matter will be found in Giuseppe Ceci, *Bibliografia per la storia delle arti figurative nell'Italia meridionale . . .* , 2 vols. (Naples, 1937).

MANUSCRIPTS

Barcelona. Archivo de la Corona de Aragòn. Privilegiorum. Cancellariae Neapolis. Registro 2915.
"Parthenope capta" [Porcellio de' Pandoni]. Naples. Biblioteca nazionale. V.F. 26.

CATALOGUES

Florence. Fondazione Salvator Romano. Cenacolo dello Santo Spirito. *Catalogo.*
Naples. Gallerie Nazionali di Capodimonte. *Sculture lignee nella Campania.* Edited by Bruno Molajoli. Naples, 1950.
Rotterdam. Museum Boymans–van Beuningen. *Italiaanse Tekeningen in Nederlands Bezit.* Paris, Rotterdam, Haarlem, 1962.

OTHER STUDIES

Aeschlimann, E. *See* Bisticci.

Ainaud de Lasarte, Juan. *Alfonso el Magnánimo y las artes plásticas de su tiempo.* IV Congreso de Historia de la Corona de Aragón. Palma de Mallorca, 1955.

Alomar, G. "Los Discipolos de Guillermo Sagrera en Mallorca, Napoles y Sicilia." *Napoli Nobilissima,* n.s. 3 (September–October 1963), 85–96; (November–December 1963), 125–35.

Altamura, Antonio. *L'Umanesimo nel mezzogiorno d'Italia.* Florence, 1941.

Amettler y Vinyas, José. *Alfonso V de Aragón en Italia y la crisis religiosa del siglo XV.* Edited by Jaime Collell. Gerona, 1903.

Armand, Alfred. *Les Médailleurs italiens des quinzième et seizième siècles.* 2d ed. Paris, 1883.

Arslan, G. C. *See* Morisani.

Avena, Adolfo. *Monumenti dell'Italia meridionale.* Rome, 1902.

———. *Il Restauro dell'Arco d'Alfonso d'Aragona in Napoli.* Rome, 1908.

[Associazione per la tutela dei monumenti e del paesaggio di Napoli.] *La Verità sui restauri di Castelnuovo.* Naples, 1931.

Baldinucci, Filippo. *Opere.* With additions by Giuseppe Piacenza. Milan, 1811.

Ballu, Albert. *Ruines de Djemila. Algiers,* 1921.

Barbier de Montault, X. "Le Château neuf de Naples." *Mémoires de l'Académie des sciences et belles-lettres d'Anger,* n.s. 3 (1898), 1–73.

Barini, Concetta. *Triumphalia: imprese ed onori militari durante l'impero romano.* Turin, 1952.

Barone, Nicola. "Le Cedole di tesoreria dell'Archivio di stato di Napoli dal 1460 al 1504." *ASPN,* 9 (1884), 5–34, 205–48, 387–429, 601–37; *10* (1885), 5–47.

Barozzi, Luciano, and R. Sabbadini. *Studi sul Panormita e sul Valla.* Florence, 1891.

Barthélemy, L. *François Laurana, Auteur du monument de Saint-Lazare dans l'ancienne cathédrale de Marseille.* Marseilles, 1885.

Battaglini, Angelo. "Memoria sopra uno sconosciuto egregio scultore del secolo XV e sopra alcune sue opere." *Dissertazioni [Atti] dell'Accademia romana di archeologia, I* (1821), 115–32. [For text of Porcellio's poem on Isaia da Pisa.]

Baxandall, Michael. "Bartholomaeus Facius on Painting. A Fifteenth-Century Manuscript of the 'De viris illustribus.'" *Journal of the Warburg and Courtauld Institutes,* 27 (1964), 90–107.

———. *Giotto and the Orators: Humanist Observers of Painting in Italy and the Discovery of Pictorial Composition, 1350–1450.* Oxford, 1971.

Beccadelli, Antonio. *See* Panormita.

Beloch, Julius. *Campanien.* Berlin, 1879; 2d ed., Breslau, 1890.

Bernardy, Amy A. *Zara e i monumenti italiani della Dalmazia.* Bergamo, 1928.

Bernich, Ettore. "Di due altri Vedute di Castelnuovo nel secolo XVI." *NN, 13* (1904), 129.

————. "Leon Battista Alberti e l'architetto dell' arco trionfale di Alfonso d'Aragona a Napoli." *NN, 12* (1903), 114–19, 131–36.

————. "La Sala del trionfo in Castelnuovo." *NN, 13* (1904), 165–68.

————. "Madama Lucretia." *NN, 15* (1906), 69–70.

————. "Statue e frammenti architettonici della prima epoca aragonese." *NN, 15* (1906), 8.

Bertaux, Emile. "L'Arco e la porta trionfale di Alfonso e di Ferdinando d'Aragona al Castel Nuovo." *ASPN, 25* (1900), 27–63.

————. "Magistri Johannes et Pacius de Florentia marmorarii fratres." *NN, 4* (1895), 134–38.

Bertolotti, Antonio. "Paolo di Mariano scultore del secolo XV." *Archivio storico . . . della città e provincia di Roma,* anno 8, vol. 4, fasc. 7 (1882), 291–317.

————. "Urkundliche Beiträge zur Biographie des Bildhauers Paolo de Mariano." *Repertorium für Kunstwissenschaft, 4* (1881), 426–42.

Białostocki, Jan. "The Sea-Thiasos in Renaissance Sepulchral Art." In *Studies in Renaissance and Baroque Art Presented to Anthony Blunt,* pp. 69–74. London and New York, 1967.

Bisticci, Vespasiano [da]. *Vite di uomini illustri del secolo XV.* Edited by P. d'Ancona and E. Aeschlimann. Milan, 1951.

Blunt, Anthony. *Philibert de l'Orme.* London, 1958.

Bodnar, E. W. *Cyriacus of Ancona and Athens.* Brussels and Berchem, 1960.

Bognetti, G. P. "Per la Storia dello stato visconteo. Un Registro di decreti della cancelleria di Filippo Maria Visconti, e un trattato segreto con Alfonso d'Aragona." *Archivio storico lombardo, 54* (1927), 237–357.

Bologna, Ferdinando. "Il Maestro di San Giovanni da Capestrano." *Proporzioni, 3* (1950), 86–98.

Boscolo, A. "L'Attività storiografica sulle figure di Ferdinando I d'Aragona e di Alfonso il Magnanimo." In *Medio Evo aragonese,* pp. 149–65. Padua, 1958.

Bottari, Stefano. "Per Domenico Gagini." *Rivista d'arte, 17* (1935), 77–85.

————. "Una Scultura di Nino Pisano a Trapani." *Critica d'arte, 3* (1956), 555–56.

Bucarelli, Palma. "Questioni lauranesche. Una Statua nella chiesa della Maddalena in Roma." *Bollettino d'arte, 26* (1932–33), 90–95.

Burger, Fritz. *Francesco Laurana: eine Studie sur italienischen Quattrocento-Skulptur.* Strasbourg, 1907.

————. *Geschichte des florentinischen Grabmal von den ältesten Zeiten bis Michelangelo.* Strasbourg, 1904.

————. "Isaia da Pisas plastische Werke in Rom." *Jahrbuch der preussischen Kunstsammlungen, 27* (1906), 228–44.

Buttner, Richard. *Porcius Licinus und der litterarischen Kreis des Q. Lutatius Catulus.* Leipzig, 1893.

Cagiati, M. *See* Volpicella.

Calzecchi, Carlo. "La Sala del trionfo in Castel Nuovo di Napoli." *Bollettino d'arte, 18* (1924–25), 371–83.

Cantalicio, Gonsalvo. *De bis recepta Parthenope.* 1506. In Gravier, *Raccolta, 6,* 65–67.

Capaccio, G. C. *Il Forestiero.* Naples, 1634.

————. *Historiae napoletanae.* 1565. Naples, 1771.

Capasso, Bartolommeo. *Le Fonti della storia napoletana. . . .* Naples, 1902.

————. *Napoli greco-romana.* Naples, 1905.

Caracciolo, Tristano. "De varietate fortunae." *Opuscula historica,* in Gravier, *Raccolta, 6.*

Caradente, Giovanni. *I Trionfi nel primo rinascimento.* Turin, 1963.

Carletti, N. *Topografia universale della città di Napoli.* Naples, 1786.

Carrotti, Guido. "L'Arco trionfale di Alfonso di Aragona e di Ferrante I in Napoli." *Arte italiana decorativa e industriale, 14* (1905), 11.

Cassi-Ramelli, A. *Dalle Caverne ai rifugi blindati.* Milan, 1964.

Castaldi, Giuseppe. "Il Palazzo di Giulio de Scorziatis." *NN, 12* (1903), 180–83.

Castelfranchi Vegas, Liana. "I Rapporti Italia-Fiandra." *Paragone,* n.s. *15* (May 1966), 9–24.

Catalani, L. *I Palazzi di Napoli.* Naples, 1845.

Causa, Raffaello. "Contributi alla conoscenza della scultura del '400 a Napoli." In *Sculture lignee nella Campania,* B. Molajoli, pp. 105–21. Naples, 1950.

———. "Sagrera, Laurana e l'Arco di Castelnuovo." *Paragone 55* (1954), 3–23.

Cavalcaselle, G. B. *A History of Painting in Italy.* London, 1911.

Ceán-Bermúdez, J. A. *See* Llaguno.

Ceci, Giuseppe. "Il Palazzo dei Carafa di Maddaloni, poi di Colubrano." *NN, 2* (1893), 149–52.

Celano, Carlo. *Notizie del bello dell'antico e del curioso della città di Napoli.* 1962. Edited by G. B. Chiarini. Naples, 1856.

Cerino, P. "I Monumenti d'Italia. L'Arco ed il trionfo di don Alfonso I d'Aragona." *L'Italia imperiale.* 17 December 1911.

Cerone, F. "La Politica orientale di Alfonso di Aragona." *ASPN, 37* (1902), 414–15.

Cerretto, Luigi Augusto. *I Gaggini da Bissone. Loro Opere in Genova ed altrove.* Genoa, 1903.

Chastel, André. "Le Lieu théâtrale à la renaissance." In *Colloques internationaux du Centre national de la recherche scientifique,* pp. 41–47. Paris, 1964.

———. *Studios and Styles of the Renaissance.* New York, 1965.

Chiarini, G. B. *See* Celano.

Chierici, Gino. *Castel del Monte.* Rome, 1934.

Chtedowski, Casimir von. *Neapolitanische Kulturbilder XIV–XVIII Jahrhundert.* Berlin, 1920.

Ciaccio, Lisetta. "Scultura romana del rinascimento." *L'Arte, 9* (1906), 165–84, 433–41.

Ciaceri, Emanuele. *Storia della Magna Grecia.* Rome, 1928.

Cicognara, Leopoldo. *Storia della scultura dal suo risorgimento. . . .* Venice, 1813–18.

Cinquini, Adolfo. *See* Panormita.

Clark, Kenneth. "Transformations of Nereids in the Renaissance." *Burlington Magazine, 97* (1955), 214–17.

Colangelo, Francesco. *Vita di Antonio Beccadelli.* Naples, 1820.

Collenuccio, Pandolfo. *Compendio delle istorie del regno di Napoli.* edited by A. Saviotti. Bari, 1929.

Colonna di Stigliano, Ferdinando. *Notizie storiche di Castelnuovo in Napoli.* Naples, 1822.

[Commissione per l'Isolamento e il restauro di Castel Nuovo.] *Relazione sui criterî per un piano generale di restauro.* Naples, n.d.

Corbo, Anna Maria. "L'Attività di Paolo di Mariano a Roma." *Commentari, 17* (1966), 195–226.

Correra, Luigi. *Il Castello nuovo di Napoli.* Trani, 1904.

Corvisieri, C. "Il Trionfo romano di Eleonora d'Aragona nel giugno del 1473." *Archivio storico della società romana di storia patria, 1* (1878), 475–91.

Croce, Benedetto. "La Corte spagnuola di Alfonso d'Aragona a Napoli." *Atti dell'Accademia pontaniana, 24* (1894), no. 2.

———. "Una Lettera inedita di Alfonso d'Aragona." *NN, 1* (1892), 127–28.

———. *La Spagna nella vita italiana durante la rinascenza.* Bari, 1917.

———. "I Teatri di Napoli del secolo XV–XVIII." *ASPN, 14* (1889), 556–684.

Cronia, Arturo. "Relazioni culturali tra Ragusa e l'Italia negli anni 1358–1526." *Atti e memorie della Società dalmata di storia patria, 1* (1926), 1–39.

D'Afflitto, Luigi. *Guida per i curiosi e per i viaggiatori che vengono alla città di Napoli. . . .* Naples, 1834.

D'Alos, R. *Documenti per la storia della biblioteca di Alfonso d'Aragona.* Rome, 1924.

D'Ancona, P. *See* Bisticci.

Davies, Gerald Stanley. *Renascence: The Sculptural Tombs of the Fifteenth Century in Rome.* London, 1910.

D'Ayala, Mariano. "Dell'Arco trionfale di re Alfonso d'Aragona in Castel Nuovo." *Annali civili del regno delle Due Sicilie, 12* (September–October 1836), 34–45.

———. "Intorno alle Sculture nella chiesa di San Domenico ed in espezialità sulle tombe di Malizia Carafa e de' D'Aquino." *Annali civili del regno delle Due Sicilie, 41* (1846), 99–105.

De Blasiis, Giuseppe. "Le Case dei principi angioini nella piazza di Castel Nuovo." In *Racconti di storia napoletana,* edited by F. Torraca. Naples, 1908.

Degenhart, Bernhard. *Antonio Pisanello.* Vienna, 1940.

———. "Di una Pubblicazione su Pisanello e di altri fatti." *Arte veneta, 7* (1953), 182–85.

———, and Annegrit Schmitt. "Gentile da Fabriano in Rom und die Anfänge des Antikenstudiums." *Münchner Jahrbuch der bildenden Kunst, 11* (1960), 59–151.

De la Ville sur-Yllon, Lodovico. "La Chiesa di S. Barbara in Castelnuovo." *NN, 2* (1893), 70–74, 118–22, 170–73.

———. "Il Corpo di Napoli e la 'capa' di Napoli." *NN, 3* (1894), 23–26.

———. "Il Sebeto." *NN, 11* (1902), 113–16.

Della Valle, Guido. "La Villa sillana ed augustea pausilypon." *Campania romana, 1* (1938), 207–67.

De Marinis, Tammaro. *La Biblioteca napoletana dei re d'Aragona.* 4 vols. Milan, 1947–52.

———. "La Liberazione di Alfonso V d'Aragona prigioniero dei Genovesi." *ASPN, 73* (1955), 101–06.

De Nicola, Giacomo. "Un Disegno della Porta di Capua di Federico II." *L'Arte, 11* (1908), 384–85.

Deonna, W. "La Sirène femme-poisson." *Revue archéologique,* ser. 5, 7 (1928), 18–25.

De Petra, G. *Le Origini di Napoli. Memorie della R. Accademia di archeologia lettere e belle arti, 23* (Naples, 1905), 39–66.

———. *Le Sirene del mar Tirreno.* Naples, 1911.

De Rinaldis, Aldo. "Forme tipiche dell'architettura napoletana nella prima metà del quattrocento." *Bollettino d'arte, 18* (1924–25), 162–83.

———. *Naples angevine.* Paris, 1927.

———. "La Tomba primitivia di Renato d'Anjou." *Belvedere—Kunst und Kultur der Vergangenheit, 3* (1923), 92–98.

De Tummulillis, Angelo. "Notabilia temporum."

In *Fonti per la storia d'Italia, 7.* Leghorn, 1890.

"Diario anonimo dall'anno MCXCII sino al MCCCCLXXXVII." In Gravier, *Raccolta, 1.*

Di Costanzo, Angelo. *Istoria del Regno di Napoli.* 1581. Milan, 1805.

Di Marzo, G. *I Gagini e la scultura in Sicilia nei secoli XV e XVI.* 2 vols. Palermo, 1880–83.

———, and E. Mauceri. "L'Opera di Domenico Gagini in Sicilia." *L'Arte, 6* (1903). 147–58.

Di Stefano, R. "La Chiesa di Sant'Angelo a Nilo e il seggio di Nido." *NN,* n.s. 4 (May–August 1964), 12–21.

Driscoll, Eileen R. "Alfonso of Aragon as a Patron of Art." In *Essays in Memory of Karl Lehmann,* edited by Lucy Freeman Sandler, pp. 87–96. New York, 1964.

Du Colombier, Pierre. *Jean Goujon.* Paris, 1949.

Dudan, Alessandro. *La Dalmazia nell'arte italiana.* 2 vols. Milan, 1921–22.

Dupré-Theseider, Eugenio. *La Politica italiana di Alfonso il Magnanimo.* IV Congreso de Historia de la corona de Aragón. Palma de Mallorca, 1955.

Durán Sanpere, Agustí. *Los Retablos de piedra. Monumenta cataloniae,* vol. 2. 2 Barcelona, 1934.

Egger, Hermann. "Entwürfe Baldassare Peruzzis für den Einzug Karl V in Rom." *Jahrbuch des kunsthistorisches Sammlungen des Kaiserhauses, 23* (Vienna, 1902), pt. 1, sec. 1, pp. 1–44.

Fabriczy, Carel von. "Antonio di Chellino da Pisa?" *Repertorium für Kunstwissenschaft, 29* (1906), 380–84.

———. "Antonio di Chellino da Pisa," *L'Arte, 9* (1906) 442–45.

———. "Domenico Gaggini in Neapel." *Repertorium für Kunstwissenschaft, 28* (1905), 193–94.

———. "Neues zum Triumphbogen Alphonsos I." *Jahrbuch der preussischen Kunstsammlungen, 23* (1902), 3–16.

———. "Onofrio Giordano della Cava." *Repertorium für Kunstwissenschaft, 28* (1905), 188–90.

———. "Pietro da Martino da Milano in Ragusa." *Repertorium für Kunstwissenschaft, 28* (1905), 192–93.

———. "Toscanische und oberitalienische Künstler in Diensten der Aragonesen zu Neapel." *Repertorium für Kunstwissenschaft*, 20 (1897), 85–120.

———. "Der Triumphbogen Alphonsos I am Castel Nuovo zu Neapel." *Jahrbuch der preussischen Kunstsammlungen*, 20 (1899), 1–30, 125–58.

Faraglia, N. F. "Le Memorie degli artisti napoletani. . . . *ASPN*, 8 (1883), 83–110, 259–86.

———. "Il Sepolcro di re Ladislao." *ASPN*, 7 (1882), 169–71.

———. *Storia della lotta tra Alfonso V. d'Aragona e Renato d'Angiò*. Lanciano, 1908.

———. "La Tomba di Sergianni Caracciolo in San Giovanni a Carbonara." *NN*, 8 (1899), 20–23.

Fazio, Bartolommeo. "De rebus gestis ab Alphonso primo." In Gravier, *Raccolta, 4*.

———. *De viris illustribus liber* [1455–56]. Florence, 1745.

Ferraiolo. *See* Filangieri, R.

Ferrari, Giulio. *La Tomba nell'arte italiana*. Milan, 1916.

Filangieri, Antonio. *La Chiesa e il monastero di San Giovanni a Carbonara*. Naples, 1924.

———. "La colossale Testa di cavallo in bronzo del Museo nazionale di Napoli." *Arte e storia*, 15 October 1901.

Filangieri, Gaetano. *Documenti per la storia le arti e le industrie delle provincie napoletane*. 5 vols. Naples, 1883–97.

———. "La Testa di cavallo in bronzo già di Casa Maddaloni." *ASPN*, 7 (1882), 407–20.

Filangieri, Riccardo. "L'Architettura della reggia aragonese di Napoli." *L'Arte, 31* (1928), 32–35.

———. "Architettura e scultura catalana in Campania nel secolo XV." *Boletín de la Sociedad castellonese de cultura, 11* (1930), 121–36.

———. "L'Arco trionfale di Alfonso d'Aragona." *Dedalo, 12* (1932), 439–66, 594–626.

———. "Castelnuovo nel '400." *Il Fuidoro, 3* (1956), 3–15.

———. *Castelnuovo, reggia angioina ed aragonese di Napoli*, Naples, 1934; 2d ed., 1964.

———. "La Citadella aragonese e il recinto bastionato di Castelnuovo." *Atti dell'Accademia pontaniana*, ser. 2, 34 (1929), 49–73.

———. *Critiche amene all'opera di Castel Nuovo*. Naples, 1931.

———. ed. *Una Cronaca napoletana figurata del quattrocento ca. 1490*. Naples, 1956.

———. "La gran Sala di Castel Nuovo in Napoli." *Dedalo, 9* (1928–29), 145–71.

———. "L'Opera degli artisti spagnuoli nella ricostruzione quattrocentesca del Castel Nuovo di Napoli." *In Spagna in Napoli* pp. 43–52. Madrid, 1950.

———. "La Peinture flamande à Naples pendant le quinzième siècle." *Revue belge d'archéologie et d'histoire de l'art, 2* (1942), 128–43.

———. "Un più antico Progetto dell'arco trionfale di Alfonso d'Aragona." *Rassegna storica napoletana, 1*, no. 2 (1933), 75–80.

———. "Rassegna critica delle fonti per la storia di Castel Nuovo." *ASPN*, 62 (1937), 327–33.

———. *Relazione sull'isolamento e sui restauri di Castel Nuovo*. Naples, 1940.

———. "La Scultura in Napoli nei primi albori del rinascimento." *NN*, ser. 2, 1 (1920), 65–69, 89–94.

Fisković, Cvito. *Naši graditelji i Kipari XV. i XVI. Stoljeća u Dubrovniku*. Zagreb, 1947.

Floret, Jean-Marie. *Le Château de Tarascon*. 7th ed. Tarascon, 1962.

Folnesics, Hans, and Leo Planiscig. *Bau- und Kunstdenkmale des Küstenlandes*. Vienna, 1916.

Fossi-Todorow, Maria. *I Disegni del Pisanello e della sua cerchia*. Florence, 1966.

———. "Un Taccuino di viaggi del Pisanello e della sua bottega." In *Scritti di storia dell'arte in onore di Mario Salmi, 2*, 133–61. Rome, 1959.

Foucard, C., ed. "Descrizione della città di Napoli e statistica del regno nel 1444." *ASPN, 2* (1877), 715–57.

Fritelli, U. *Giannantonio de' Pandoni, detto il Porcellio*. Florence, 1900.

Fusco, G. M. *I Capitoli dell'Ordine dell'armellino*. Naples, 1845.

———. *Degli Autori dell'arco di trionfo di Alfonso d'Aragona al Castel Nuovo*. Naples, 1850.

Gàbrici, Ettore. *Problemi di numismatica greca della Sicilia e. Magna Grecia*. Naples, 1959.

Garin, Eugenio. *See* Valla.

Garzilli, Paolo. *See* Notar Giacomo.

Gentile, P. *La Politica interna di Alfonso V. nel regno di Napoli dal 1443 al 1450.* Montecassino, 1909.

Giannone, Pietro. *Historia civile del regno di Napoli.* Palmiria, 1762.

Gnirs, Anton. "Grabungen und antike Denkmale in Pola." *Jahreshefte des österreichischen archäologischen Instituts,* 15 (1912–13), appendix, 214–71.

Gnudi, C. *Niccolò dell'Arca.* Turin, 1942.

Gothein, E. *Die Kulturentwicklung Suditaliens in Einzeldarstellungen.* Breslau, 1886.

Graef, Paul. "Triumph- und Ehrenbogen." In *Denkmäler des classischen Alterthums,* edited by A. Baumeister, 3, 1865–1900. Munich and Leipzig, 1888.

Gravier, Giovanni. *Raccolta di tutti i più rinomati scrittori dell'istoria generale del regno di Napoli.* 22 vols. Naples, 1769–72.

Grayson, Cecil. *An Autograph Letter from Leon Battista Alberti to Matteo de' Pasti, November 18, 1454.* New York, 1957.

———. "The Composition of L. B. Alberti's 'Decem libri de re aedificatoria.' " *Münchner Jahrbuch der bildenden Kunst,* 11 (1960), 152–61.

Habler, K. "Der Streit Alphonsos von Aragon mit den Päpsten um die Krone von Neapel." *Zeitschrift für allgemeine Geschichte,* 1 (1884), 828–49.

Heiss, A. *Les Médailleurs de la renaissance.* Paris, 1882.

Hersey, G. L. *Alfonso II and the Artistic Renewal of Naples, 1485–1495.* New Haven, 1969.

———. "Alfonso II, Benedetto e Giuliano da Maiano, e la Porta reale." *NN,* ser. 3, 4 (1964), 77–95.

———. "The Arch of Alfonso in Naples and Its Pisanellesque 'Design.' " *Master Drawings,* 7 (1969), 16–24.

Hill, G. F. "New Light on Pisanello." *Burlington Magazine,* 13 (April–September 1908), 288.

———. *Pisanello.* London, 1905; 2d ed., 1920.

Huelson, Christian, and Henri Jordan, eds. *Topographie der Stadt Rom in Alterthum.* Berlin, 1871–1907. *See also* Sangallo.

Hueso Rolland, Francisco. "El Castillo de los reyes de Aragón en Napoles." *Revista española de arte,* 3 (1934), 211–18.

Ingal Úbeda, Antonio. *Iconografía de Alfonso el magnánimo.* Valencia, 1950.

Ivekovic, C. M. *Dalmatiens Bau- und Kunstdenkmäler. I. Zara.* Vienna, 1927.

Jackson, T. G. *Dalmatia, the Quarnero and Istria, with Cettigne in Montenegro and the Island of Grado.* 3 vols. Oxford, 1887.

Janson, H. W. *The Sculpture of Donatello.* 2 vols. Princeton, 1957.

Jonato, M. "Il Giardeno." In Fabriczy, "Der Triumphbogen," p. 140.

Jordan, Henri. *See* Huelsen.

Karaman, Ljubo. *Umjetnost u Dalmaciji XV i XVI Vijek.* Zagreb, 1933.

Kastner, Georges. *Les Sirènes. Essai sur les principaux mythes relatifs à l'incantation, etc.* Paris, 1858.

Keller, Harald. "Bildhauerzeichnungen Pisanellos." In *Festschrift Kurt Bauch,* pp. 139–52. Munich, 1957.

———. "Die Entstehung des Bildnisses am Ende des Hochmittelalters." *Römische Jahrbuch für Kunstgeschichte,* 3 (1939), 229–334.

———. "Ursprünge des Gedächtnismals." *Kunstchronik,* 7 (1954), 134–37.

Krinsky, Carol Herselle. "Seventy-eight Vitruvius Manuscripts." *Journal of the Warburg and Courtauld Institutes,* 30 (1967), 36–70.

Lacetti, F. "L'Arco trionfale di Alfonso di Aragona." *Natura ed Arte,* 14 (1904–05), pt. 2, pp. 98–104.

Lanciani, Rodolfo Amedeo. *The Ruins and Excavations of Ancient Rome.* Boston, 1897.

Langton Douglas, R. " 'Mino del Reame.' " *Burlington Magazine,* 87 (1945), 217–24.

Laurenza, Vincenzo. "Il Panormita a Napoli." *Atti dell'Accademia pontaniana,* 42, (1912), no. 8.

Lavagnino, Emilio. "L'architetto di Sisto IV." *L'Arte,* 27 (1924), 4–13.

Lawrence, Elizabeth Baily. "The Illustrations of the Garrett and Modena Manuscripts of Marcanova." *Memoirs of the American Academy in Rome,* 6 (1927), 127–31.

Leonardi, V. "Paolo di Mariano Marmoraro." *L'Arte,* 3 (1900), 86–106, 259–74.

Leschi, Louis. *Djemila, antique Cuicul.* Algiers, 1950.

Liberatore, R. "L'Arco trionfale di Alfonso d'Aragona nel Castel Nuovo." *Real Museo borbonico, 13* (1843), 1–35.

Llaguno y Amirola. *Noticias de los Arquitectos y arquitectura de España.* . . . Edited by J. A. Ceán-Bermúdez. 4 vols. Madrid, 1829.

Madurell Marimón, José Maria. *Mensajeros barceloneses en la corte de Nàpoles de Alfonso V de Aragón, 1435–1458.* Barcelona, 1963.

Magnuson, Torgil. *Studies in Roman Quattrocento Architecture.* Rome and Stockholm, 1958.

Malaguzzi Valeri, Francesco. *La Corte di Lodovico il Moro.* 4 vols. Milan, 1913–23.

Mancini, Girolamo. *Vita di Lorenzo Valla.* Florence, 1891.

Marchini, G. "Il Palazzo ducale d'Urbino." *Rinascimento [La Rinascita],* 9 (1958), 43–78.

Marinelli, G. "Il Codice Vallardi e i disegni del Pisanello al Louvre (verso una nuova attribuzione?)." *Emporium, 133* (1961), 251–59.

Marinesco, Constantin. "Les Affaires commerciales en Flandre d'Alphonse V d'Aragon, roi de Naples (1416–1458)." *Revue historique, 221* (1959), 33–48.

———. "Notes sur la vie culturelle sous le règne d'Alphonse le Magnanime, roi de Naples." *Miscel·lania Puig i Cadafalch,* vol. 1, pp. 291–307. Barcelona, 1947–51.

———. "Du nouveau sur *Tirant lo Blanch.*" *Estudis romanics,* 4 (1953–54), 137–203.

Marletta, Fedele. "Per la Biografia di Porcellio dei Pandoni." *La Rinascita,* 3 (1940), 842–81.

Martínez Ferrando, J. E. "Consideraciones en torno a la exposiciòn documental sobre Alfonso el Magnànimo, organizada en el Archivo de la corona de Aragóna." In *Estudios sobre Alfonso el Magnànimo,* edited by Antonio Torraja, pp. 213–32. Barcelona, 1960.

Mauceri, Enrico. "Caratteri dell'arte siciliana del rinascimento. Suo Origine e sviluppo." *Rassegna d'arte antica e moderna,* 6 (1919), 210–22.

———. "Nuovi Documenti intorno a Domenico Gagini." *Rassegna bibliografica dell'arte italiana,* 6 (1903), 170–74. *See also* Di Marzo.

Maxe-Werly, A. "Un Sculpteur italien a Bar-le-Duc en 1463." *Comptes rendus des séances de l'Académie des inscriptions et belles-lettres,* ser. 4, 24, (Paris, 1896), 54–62.

Mazzella, Scipione. *Descrittione del regno di Napoli.* Naples, 1586.

Mazzoleni, Iole, ed. *Fonti aragonesi, a cura degli archivisti napoletani.* Vol. 1. Naples, 1957.

———, ed. *Regesto della cancelleria aragonese di Napoli.* Naples, 1951.

Middledorf, Ulrich, and Hanno-Walter Kruft. "Three Male Portrait Busts by Francesco Laurana." *Burlington Magazine, 113* (1971), 264–67.

[Milanesi, Gaetano.] *Catalogo delle opere di Donatello e bibliografia degli autori che ne hanno scritto.* Florence, 1887.

Minervini. "Antico teatro a Napoli." *Bullettino archeologico napoletano,* ser. 2, 7 (1858–59), 135–36.

Minieri-Riccio, Camillo. "Alcuni Fatti di Alfonso I. d'Aragona." *ASPN,* 6 (1881).

———. *Gli Artisti ed artefici che lavorarono in Castelnuovo a tempo di Alfonso I e Ferrante I di Aragona.* Naples, 1876.

Miret y Sans, J. *See* Puig i Cadafalch.

Molajoli, Bruno. *See* Causa.

Montalto, Lina. "Vesti e gale alla corte aragonese." *NN,* ser. 2, *1* (1920), 25–29, 41–44, 70–73, 127–30, 142–47. Republished as *La Corte di Alfonso I di Aragona. Vesti e gale.* Naples, 1922.

Monti, Gennaro Maria. *Il Trionfo di Alfonso I di Aragona a Napoli in un inedita descrizione contemporanea.* Naples, 1931.

Morisani, Ottavio. "Gli Artisti nel 'De viris' di Bartolommeo Facio." *ASPN,* 74 (1955), 107–17.

———. "Considerazioni sui Malvito di Como." In *Arte e artisti dei laghi lombardi,* edited by Edoardo Arslan. Como, 1959.

———."Considerazioni sulle sculture della porta di Capua." *Bollettino di storia dell'arte dell'istituto universitario di magistero, Salerno, 3* (January 1953), 1–20; (March 1953), 1–4; and (September–December 1953), 1–76.

———. *Letteratura artistica a Napoli.* Naples, 1958.

————. *Michelozzo architetto*. Florence(?), 1951.

————. "Per una Rilettura del monumento Brancacci." *NN*, ser. 3, 4 (May–August 1964), 3–11.

Mormile, Giuseppe. *Descrittione della città di Napoli*. Naples, 1625.

Müntz, Eugène. *Les Arts à la cour des papes pendant le XVe et XVIe siècle*. Paris, 1878.

————(?). *Notes sur l'influence artistique du roi René*. Paris, 1875.

Napoli, Mario. "Napoli antica" and "Realtà storica di Partenope." *La Parola del Passato*, 7 (1952), 243–85.

————. *Napoli greco-romana*. Naples, 1959.

Neppi Modona, Aldo. *Gli Edifici teatrali greci e romani: teatri, odei, anfiteatri, circhi*. Florence, 1961.

[Nicaise?] *Les Sirènes, ou discours sur leur forme et figure*. Paris, 1691.

Nicolini, Fausto. *L'Arte napoletana del rinascimento e la lettera di Pietro Summonte a Marcantonio Michiel*. Naples, 1925.

Noack, Ferdinand. *Triumph und Triumphbogen*. Leipzig, 1928.

Nociti, V. *Il Trionfo di Alfonso I d'Aragona cantato da Porcellio*. Rossano, 1895.

Nodelman, Sheldon. "Mino del Reame." Master's thesis, Yale University, 1959.

Notar Giacomo. *Cronaca di Napoli*. Edited by P. Garzilli. Naples, 1845.

Nunziante, Emilio. I primi Anni di Ferdinando d'Aragona e l'invasione di Giovanni d'Angiò. Naples, 1892.

Nunziante, Ferdinando. "Castel Capuano Sede dei tribunali." *NN*, 2 (1893), 113–18.

Orsini, Gaetano d'Amico. "Francesco Laurana e la sala della Jole nel palazzo ducale d'Urbino." *Archivio storico per la Dalmazia*, 2 (1927), fasc. 9, 3–12.

Pächt, Otto. "René d'Anjou et les van Eyck." *Cahiers de l'Association internationale des études françaises*, 8 (1956), 111–67.

Pane, Giulio. "La Villa Carafa e la storia urbanistica di Pizzofalcone." *NN*, ser. 3, 4 (September–December 1964), 133–48.

Pane, Roberto. *L'Architettura del rinascimento in Napoli*. Naples, 1937.

Panofsky, Erwin. *Tomb Sculpture*. New York, 1964.

Panormita, Antonio. "De dictis et factis Alphonsi regis." In *Lampas, sive fax artium liberalium hoc est thesaurus criticus . . .*, edited by Janus Gruterus. Vol. 3. Lucca(?), 1747.

————. *Poesie latine inedite di A. Beccadelli*. Edited by Adolfo Cinquini and Roberto Valentini. Aosta, 1907.

Papini, Roberto. *Francesco di Giorgio architetto*. Florence, 1946.

Parrino, Domenico Antonio. *Teatro eroico e politico de' vicerè del regno di Napoli dal tempo del re Ferdinando il cattolico. . . .* In Gravier, *Raccolta*, 9.

Patera, B. "Sull'attività di Francesco Laurana in Sicilia. . . . *Annuale del Liceo classico 'G. Garibaldi' di Palermo*, 2 (1965), 526–50.

Persico, Tommaso. *Diomede Carafa, uomo di Stato e scrittore del secolo XV*. Naples, 1899.

Pfnor, Rodolphe. *Monographie du Château d'Anet*. Paris, 1867.

Piacenza, Giuseppe. *See* Baldinucci.

Pirro, Alberto. *Le Origini di Napoli*. Salerno, 1905.

Planiscig, Leo. "Ein Bildhauer am Hofe Alfons' I. von Neapel." *Jahrbuch der kunsthistorischen Sammlungen in Wien*, n.s. 8 (1934), 65–78.

————. "Ein Entwurf für den Triumphbogen am Castelnuovo zu Neapel." *Jahrbuch der preussischen Kunstsammlungen*, 54 (1933), 16–28.

————. "Riflessioni ed ipotesi intorno a una statua di re Alfonso d'Aragona." *Bollettino d'arte*, 27 (1933–34), 293–98.

Pontieri, Ernesto. "Alfonso V d'Aragona nel quadro della politica italiana del suo tempo." *Atti dell'Accademia di scienze morali e politiche della Società nazionale di scienze lettere ed arti di Napoli*, 71 (1960), 183–251.

————. "La Dinastia aragonese di Napoli e la casa de' Medici di Firenze." *ASPN*, 65 (1940), 274–342; 66 (1941), 217–73.

————. "La Giovinezza di Ferrante I d'Aragona." In *Studi in onore di Riccardo Filangieri*. Vol. 1, pp. 531–601. Naples, 1959.

Pope-Hennessy, John. *Italian Renaissance Sculpture*. New York, 1958; 2d ed., New York and London, 1971.

Porcellio. *See* Battaglini.

Puig i Cadafalch, Josep, and J. Miret y Sans. "El Palau de la Diputacio General de Catalunya." Institut d'Estudis Catalans, *Annuari, 3* (1909–10), 385–480.

"Racconti di storia napoletana." *ASPN, 33* (1908), 478–80.

Radetti, Giorgio. *See* Valla.

Ragghianti, C. L. "Tempio Malatestiano." *Critica d'arte, 12* (May 1965), 23–31; (October 1965), 27–39.

René of Anjou. *Livre du cuer d'amours epris.* Edited by O. Smital and E. Winkler. Vienna, 1926.

Requin, H. "Documents inédits sur le sculpteur François Laurana." *Réunion des sociétés des beaux-arts des départements, 25* (Paris, 1901), 498–508.

Riccoboni, A. *Roma nell'arte. La Scultura nell'evo moderno.* Rome, 1942.

Rigoni, E. "Notizie di scultori toscani a Padova nella prima metà del '400." *Archivio veneto, 6* (1929), 118–36.

Rizzo, Giulio Emanuele. *Monete greche della Sicilia.* Rome, 1946.

Rolfs, Wilhelm. "L'Architettura albertiana e l'arco trionfale di Alfonso d'Aragona." *NN, 13* (1904), 171–72.

———. "Der Baumeister des Triumphbogens in Neapel." *Jahrbuch der preussischen Kunstsammlungen, 25* (1904), 81–101.

———. *Franz Laurana.* 2 vols. Berlin, 1907.

Romano, Elena. *Saggio d'iconografia dei reali angioini di Napoli.* Naples, 1920.

Romano, G. "L'Origine della denominazione 'Due Sicilie' e un'orazione inedita di L. Valla." *ASPN, 22* (1897), 397–403.

Rosi, Giorgio. "La Cinta bastionata cinquecentesca di Castel Nuovo." *Atti del V convegno di storia dell'architettura, 1948,* pp. 317–26. Florence, 1957.

———. "Il Restauro di Castelnuovo di Napoli." *Le Arti,* 4, fasc. 4 (1942), 284–87.

Rossini, Luigi. *Gli Archi trionfali onorarii e funebri degli antichi romani sparsi per tutta Italia.* Rome, 1836.

Rotondi, Pasquale. *Il Palazzo ducale di Urbino.* Urbino, 1950.

Roussel, Pierre-Désiré. *Histoire et description du château d'Anet.* Paris, 1875.

Roux, Alphonse. *Le Château d'Anet.* Paris, 1911.

Rubió, Jordi. "Alfonso 'el Magnánim' rei de Napols, i Daniel Florentino, Leonardo da Bisuccio i Donatello." *Miscel·lánia Puig i Cadafalch,* Vol. 1, pp. 25–35. Barcelona, 1947–51.

Rumpf, Andreas. *Die Meerwesen.* In *Die antiken Sarcophagreliefs,* edited by Carl Robert and Gerhart Rodenwaldt. Vol 5. Berlin, 1939.

Ryder, Alan F. C. "La Politica italiana di Alfonso d'Aragona (1442–58)." *ASPN, 77* (1959), 43–106.

———. "Alfonso d'Aragona e l'Avvento di Francesco Sforza al ducato di Milano." *ASPN, 80* (1962), 9–46.

Sabbadini, R. *See* Barozzi.

Sacco, A. "L'Arco trionfale del re Alfonso d'Aragona." *Arte e storia, 24* (1905), 4–6.

Saez, Emilio. "Semblanza de Alfonso el Magnánimo." In *Estudios sobre Alfonso el Magnánimo,* edited by Antonio Torraja, pp. 25–41. Barcelona, 1960.

Salazar, L., ed. "Racconti di storia napoletana." *ASPN, 33* (1908), 507–08.

Salmi, Mario. "Riflessioni sul Pisanello medaglista." *Annali dell'Istituto italiano di numismatica, 4* (1957), 13–23.

Sambon, Arturo. "I 'Carlini' e la medaglia trionfale di Ferdinando I d'Aragona re di Napoli." *Revista italiana di numismatica, 4* (1891), 481–88.

———. *Monnaies de la Grande-Grèce et de la Sicile.* Paris, 1927.

Sangallo, Giuliano [da]. *Il Libro di Giuliano da San Gallo.* Edited by Christian Huelsen. Leipzig, 1910.

Sannazaro, Jacopo. *Poemata.* Padua, 1719.

Sanpaolesi, Piero. *Aspetti dell'architettura del '400 a Siena e Francesco di Giorgio.* Urbino, 1949(?).

Sarnelli, Pompeo. *La vera Guida de' forestieri.* . . . Naples, 1697.

Sarthou Carreres, Carlos. *Castillos de España.* Madrid, 1943.

Saviotti, A. *See* Collenuccio.

Saxl, Fritz. "Pagan Sacrifice in the Italian Renaissance." *Journal of the Warburg and Courtauld Institutes, 2* (1938–39), 346–67.

Schmitt, Annegrit. "Gentile da Fabriano und der Beginn der Antikennachzeichnung." *Münchner Jahrbuch der bildenden Kunst, 11* (1960), 91–146.

Schneider, René. "Le Thème du triomphe dans les entrées solennelles en France à la Renaissance." *Gazette des beaux-arts,* ser. 4, 9 (1913), 85–106.

Schrader, Hermann. *Die Sirenen nach ihrer Bedeutung und kunstlerischen Darstellung im Alterthum.* Berlin, 1868.

Schrader, Laurentio. *Monumentorum italiae, quae hoc nostro saeculo et a christianis posita sunt libri quatuor.* Halberstadien, 1592.

Schramm, P. E. "Der König von Aragon. Seine Stellung im Staatsrecht (1276–1410)." *Historische Jahrbuch,* 74 (1955), 99–123.

Schubring, Paul. *Cassoni.* Leipzig, 1923.

Schülz, Heinrich Wilhelm. *Denkmäler der Kunst des Mittelalters in Unteritalien.* 4 vols. Dresden, 1860.

Sciolla, Gianni Carlo. "L'Arco di Castelnuovo: il progetto architettonico." *Critica d'Arte, 19* (January–February 1972), 68–72.

Semper, Hans. *Donatello, seine Zeit und Schule.* Vienna, 1875.

Séroux d'Agincourt, J. B. L. G. *Histoire de l'art par les monumens. . . .* 6 vols. Paris, 1823.

Serra, Luigi. "L'Arco di Alfonso d'Aragona." *L'Arte,* 7 (1904), 408–10.

Seymour, Charles, Jr. *Sculpture in Italy: 1400 to 1500.* Harmondsworth, Mddx., 1966.

Shearer, Cresswell. *The Renaissance of Architecture in Southern Italy: A Study of Frederick II of Hohenstaufen and the Capua Triumphator Archway and Towers.* Cambridge, 1935.

Sherman, Frederick Fairchild. "Laurana's Bust of Alfonso I, King of Naples." *Art in America,* 26 (1938), 120–21.

Signorelli, Pietro Napoli. *Vicende della Coltura nelle Due Sicilie.* Naples, 1810.

Sindona, Enio. *Pisanello.* New York, 1961.

Smital, O. *See* René of Anjou.

Soergel, Gerda. "Die Proportionslehre Albertis und ihre Anwendung an der Fassade von S. Francesco in Rimini." *Kunstchronik, 13* (1960), 348–51.

Sorgente, M. A. *De neapoli illustrata.* Naples, 1597.

Soria, A. *Los Humanistas de la corte de Alfonso el Magnánimo,* Granada, 1958.

Spadetta, Pietro. "La Lanterna del Molo." *NN, 1* (1892), 109–11.

Spinazzola, Vittorio. "Il Nome di Napoli." *NN, 1* (1892), 33–35, 49–51.

———. "Paleopolis." *NN, 1* (1892), 161–64.

Stella, Achille. *Castelnuovo di Napoli alla luce dei documenti e della storia.* Associazione per la tutela dei monumenti e del paesaggio di Napoli. Naples, 1928.

———. *Il Restauro di Castel Nuovo.* Naples, 1931.

Strazzullo, Franco. "Documenti sull'attività napoletana dello scultore milanese Pietro de Martino (1453–1473)." *ASPN, 81* (1963), 325–41.

Stucci, Sandro. "Gruppo bronzeo di Cartoceto." *Bollettino d'arte,* 45 (1960), 7–44.

Summonte, Giovanni Antonio. *Historia della città e regno di Napoli* [1601–43]. Naples, 1748.

Summonte, Pietro. *See* Nicolini.

Tesorone, G. "Una Porta del rinascimento a Napoli." *Arte italiana decorativa e industriale, 11* (1902), 61–62.

Toffanin, G., Jr. "I Seggi di Napoli." *Il Fuidoro, 3* (1956), 16–27.

Torraca, F. *See* De Blasiis.

Torraja, Antonio, ed. *Estudios sobre Alfonso el Magnánimo.* Barcelona, 1960.

Tschudi, Hugo von. "Giovanni Dalmata." *Jahrbuch der preussischen Kunstsammlungen,* 4 (1883), 169–90.

Valentiner, W. R. "Andrea dell'Aquila, Painter and Sculptor." *Art Bulletin, 19* (1937), 503–36.

———. "Andrea dell'Aquila in Urbino." *Art Quarterly, 1* (1938), 275–88.

———. "A Madonna Statuette by Domenico Gagini." *Art in America,* 25 (1937), 104–17.

———. "A Portrait Bust of Alphonso I of Naples." *Art Quarterly, 1* (1938), 61–88.

———. *Tino da Camaino.* Paris, 1935.

Valentini, R. *See* Panormita.

Valla, Lorenzo. *Opera omnia.* Edited by Eugenio Garin. Turin, 1962.

———. *Scritti filosofici e religiosi.* Edited by Giorgio Radetti. Florence, 1953.

Valle, Raffaello Maria. *Descrizione storica artistica letteraria della chiesa e convento di San Domenico maggiore.* Continued by B. Minichini. Naples, 1853–54.

Vasari, Giorgio. *See* Venturi, A.

Venditti, Arnaldo. *Architettura neoclassica a Napoli.* Naples, 1961.

Venturi, Adolfo. *La Data della morte di Vittor Pisano* [per l'Albo nuziale Rovighi-Valcari]. Modena, 1883.

————. "La Scultura dalmata del XV secolo." *L'Arte,* 11 (1908), 30–46, 113–29.

————, ed. [Giorgio Vasari.] *Le Vite de' più eccellenti pittori scultori e architetti. I. Gentile da Fabriano e il Pisanello.* Florence, 1896.

Venturi, Lionello. "Studii sul palazzo ducale di Urbino." *L'Arte,* 17 (1914), 415–73.

Vicens i Vives, Jaime. *Els Trastámares.* Barcelona, 1956.

Vinaza, Cipriano Muñoz y Manzano. *Arqueologia sagrada catalana.* Vich, 1933.

Volpicella, Luigi. "Le Imprese della numismatica aragonese di Napoli." In *Le Monete del reame delle Due Sicilie,* edited by M. Cagiati. Naples, 1911–13. Supplement.

Wegner, Ingeborg. *Studien zur Ikonographie des Greifen im Mittelalter.* Leipzig, 1928.

Wethey, Harold. "Guillermo Sagrera." *Art Bulletin,* 21 (1939), 44–60.

Willemsen, Karl Arnold. *Castel del Monte, die Krone Apuliens.* Wiesbaden, 1955.

————. *Kaiser Friedrich's II Triumphtor zu Capua.* Wiesbaden, 1953.

Winkler, E. *See* René of Anjou.

Wölfflin, Heinrich. "Die antiken Triumphbogen in Italien. Eine Studie zur Entwicklungsgeschichte der römischen Architektur und ihr Verhaltnis zur Renaissance." *Repertorium für Kunstwissenschaft,* 16 (1893), 11–27.

Wuilleumier, Pierre. *Fouilles de Fourvière à Lyon.* Supplement to *Gallia,* 4. Paris, 1951.

Zippel, G. "Artisti alla corte degli Estensi nel quattrocento." *L'Arte,* 5 (1902), 405–07.

Zurita y Castro, Gerónimo. *Anales de la corona de Aragón.* Zaragoza, 1610.

INDEX

ILLUSTRATIONS

1. Naples. The Aragonese Arch, 1443–1475.

3. The same. (From Séroux d'Agincourt, *Histoire de l'art.*)

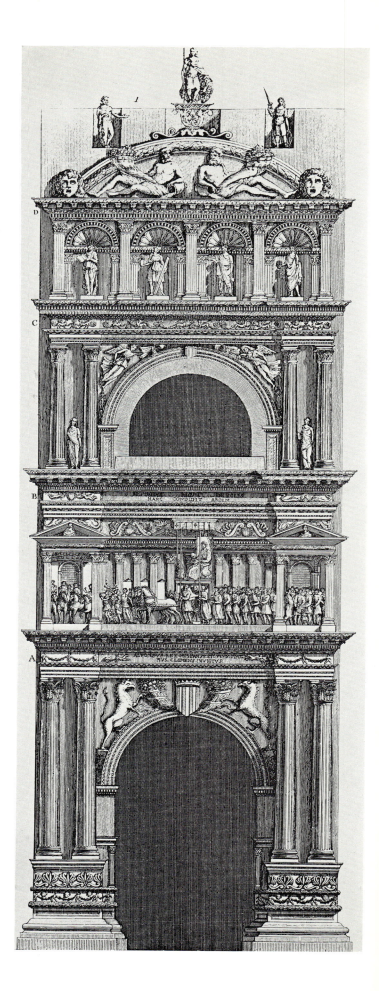

2. The same. (From Sarnelli, *Guida de' Forestieri.*)

4. The same, triumph frieze. (From Cicognara, *Storia della Scultura.*)

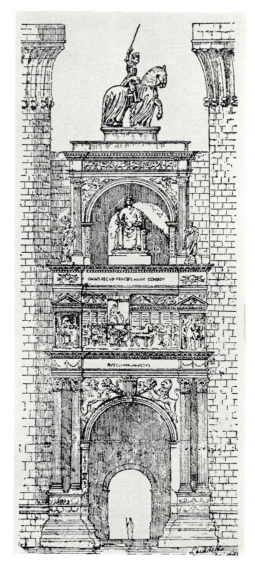

5. Ettore Bernich, "restoration" of the Arch, 1903.

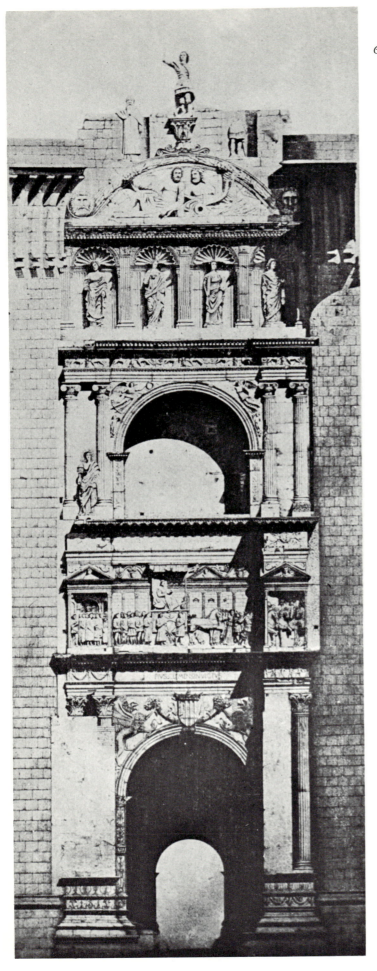

6. Avena and Mazzanti, drawing of the Arch at restoration of 1902–04. (From Avena, *Il Restauro dell'Arco d'Alfonso d'Aragona in Napoli*.)

7. Florentine School, a triumph, mid-fifteenth century. (London, Courtauld Institute Galleries.)

9. Miniature of the triumph of Alfonso I, from Valla, *De rebus gestis Ferdinandi primi.* (Rome, Vatican Library.)

8. Engraving of the triumph of Alfonso I, after a drawing formerly owned by M. A. Cavalieri. (From Summonte, *Historia della città e regno di Napoli.*)

10. Drawing of fortifications at Senigallia, from Codex Escurialensis, 5r. (Escorial, Library.)

11. Castel del Monte, Apulia, 1240–ca. 1250

12. Naples. Castel Nuovo, detail from anonymous fifteenth-century painting. (Naples, Museo di San Martino.)

13. Naples. Castel Nuovo.

14. The same, Sala dei Baroni, by Guillermo Sagrera, 1451–56 ff., vault.

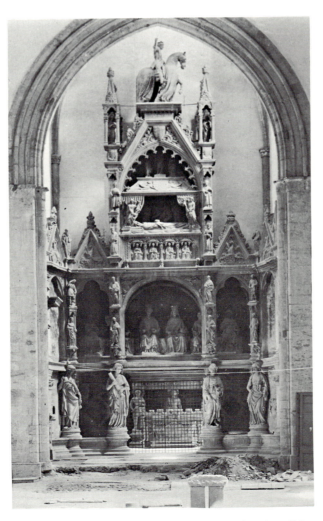

15. Naples. San Giovanni a Carbonara, tomb of Ladislas, 1414(?)–28, by Andrea di Nofri da Firenze and others.

16. Naples. Castel Capuano, project for festival arch, 1446(?).
(Rotterdam, Museum Boymans–van Beuningen.)

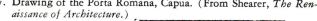

17. Drawing of the Porta Romana, Capua. (From Shearer, *The Renaissance of Architecture.*)

18. Detail of drawing of the *scaenae frons* of the Roman theater,
Orange. (From Neppi Modona, *Edifici teatrali.*)

19. Pisanello, medal for Alfonso I, 1448
(?), obverse. (Madrid, Museo Arque-
ologico Nacional.)

21. Hemidrachm   from   Agrigento.
(From Sambon, *Monnaies de la
Grande-Grèce et de Sicile.*)

20. The same, reverse.

22. Naples. Sant'Angelo a Nilo, tomb of Rinaldo Brancacci, 1427–30, by Donatello and Michelozzo.

23. Naples. San Giovanni a Carbonara, tomb of Gianni Caracciolo, 1441.

24. Dubrovnik. Fontana San Biagio, 1452
(?), by Pietro da Milano(?), detail.

25. Tarragona. Cathedral, detail of reredos of
Santa Tecla, by Pere Joan.

26. Pula. Arch of the Sergii, 29–27 B.C.,
restoration. (From Rossini, *Archi trionfali*.)

27. Naples. Aragonese Arch, lower arch.

28. The same, capital on extreme right.   29. Rome. San Lorenzo fuori le Mura, capital.   30. Pula. Arch of the Sergii, capital.

31. Naples. Aragonese Arch, lower arch, spandrel griffins.

32. Drawing of bombards, detail of muzzle. (Codex Vallardi 2293, Paris, Louvre.)

33. Naples. Aragonese Arch, lower arch, putti from left-hand ressaut.

34. Drawing after a Roman prototype, naiads and tritons, fifteenth century. (Rotterdam, Museum Boymans–van Beuningen.)

35. Naples. Aragonese Arch, left-hand inner relief.

36. Rome. Arch of Constantine, Trajanic relief.

37. Naples. Aragonese Arch, lower arch, right-hand inner relief.

38. The same, left-hand inner relief, detail.

39. The same, right-hand inner relief, detail.

40. The same, right-hand outer pedestal face, detail.

41. The same, right-hand inner relief, detail.

42. The same, left-hand inner pedestal face with roundel of Caesar.

43. The same, left-hand inner pedestal, head of Acheloos.

44. The same, right-hand inner pedestal, detail.

45. The same, right-hand outer pedestal, detail.

46. The same, vault.

47. The same, vault keystone.

48. Naples. Aragonese Arch, elevation of inner arch, 1465.
(M. Bernard Boyle and Author.)

49. Pietro da Milano, medal of René and Jeanne d'Anjou, 1462(?). (From G. F. Hill, *A Corpus of Italian Medals*.)

50. Rome. Arch of Domitian, from the *Libro di Giuliano da San Gallo*. (Rome, Vatican Library.)

51. Naples. Aragonese Arch, inner arch.

52, The same, putti with shield.

53. The same, upper niche, left-hand group.

54. The same, upper niche, right-hand group.

55. The same, left-hand group, heads.

56. Avignon, St.-Didier, relief of Christ carrying the Cross, 1479–81, by Francesco Laurana, detail.

57. Naples. Castel Nuovo, bronze doors, 1474–75, by Guglielmo Lo Monaco.

58. The same, detail, the meeting at Calvi.

59. The same, detail, the attempt on Ferrante's life.

HINC   TROIANI
CASTRA MOVENT

VERSVS · MAGNO · CONCVSSA · TIMORE
HOSTES · NE · CVBITO · PEREANT

60. The same, detail, the retreat from Accadia.

61. The same, detail, the entry of the Aragonese.

62. The same, detail, the Battle of Troia.

63. The same, detail, the surrender of Troia.

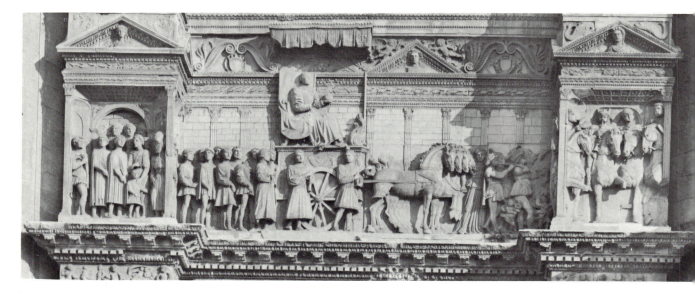

64. Naples. Aragonese Arch, triumph frieze.

65. The same, showing division of blocks. (After Avena.)

66. Rome. Detail from "Arco di Malborghetto," from the *Libro di Giuliano da San Gallo.* (Rome, Vatican Library.)

67. Djemila. Arch of Caracalla.

68. Naples. Aragonese Arch, triumph frieze, left-hand pavilion.

69. The same, detail of "People."

70. The same, Moors.

71. The same, detail of Moors.

72. The same, barons.

73. The same, detail of barons.

74. The same, detail of barons.

75. The same, portrait of Alfonso.

76. Isaia da Pisa, Madonna and saints, 1438, detail. (Rome, Grotte Vaticane.)

77. Naples. Aragonese Arch, triumph frieze, baldacchino bearer.

78. Mino da Fiesole, bust of Piero de' Medici, 1453. (Florence, Bargello.)

79. Naples. Aragonese Arch, baldacchino bearer.

80. The same, triumph frieze, horses and genius.

81. The same, triumph frieze, musicians.

82. The same, detail.

83. The same, musicians in right-hand tabernacle.

84. The same, left-hand pediment head.

85. The same, central pediment head.

86. The same, right-hand pediment head.

87. The same, upper arch.

88. Fano. Triumphal arch-gate, from the *Libro di Giuliano da San Gallo*. (Rome, Vatican Library.)

89. Naples. Aragonese Arch, upper arch, left-hand spandrel victory.

90. The same, putto beneath.

91. The same, right-hand spandrel victory.

92. The same, putto beneath.

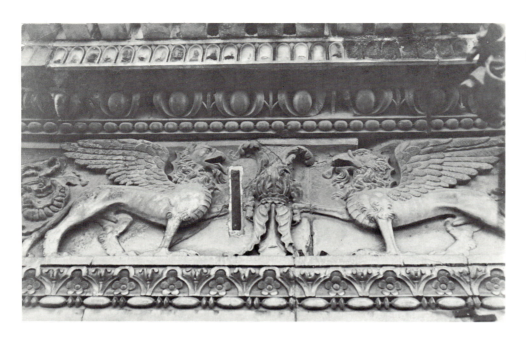

94. The same, detail of capitals.

95. Drawing of river god, Italian, fifteenth century. (Berlin, Staatliche Museen.)

96. Naples. Aragonese Arch, upper tympanum.

97. The same, upper arch, pediment, head of right-hand god.

98. Head of Jupiter, from Porta Romana, Capua, ca. 1239–47. (Capua, Museo Campano.)

99. Naples. Aragonese Arch, upper arch, nicchione vault, keystone.

100. Roman sarcophagus, detail. (Rome, Deutsche Archaeologisches Institut.)

101. Naples. Aragonese Arch, upper arch, statue to right of nicchione.

102. The same, detail.

104. The same, detail.

103. The same, upper niches, Justice.

105. Drawing of antique statue, from *Codex Escurialensis,* 47 v. (Escorial, Library.)

106. Naples. Aragonese Arch, upper
arch, Temperance.

107. The same, detail.

108. The same, Fortitude.

109. The same, Prudence.

110. The same, tympanum figure of Saint Anthony (now inside nicchione).

111. The same, tympanum figure of Saint George (now inside nicchione).

112. The same, tympanum figure of Saint Michael.

113. Pere Joan, sculpture from Old Cathedral, Lérida, before 1445. (Lérida, Museo Provincial.)

114. Castle entrance, from Filarete, *Treatise on Architecture,* ca. 1460–64. (Valencia, University Library.)

115. Colossal antique bronze horse's head (reworked in Renaissance?). (Naples, Museo Nazionale.)

116. Padua. Gattemelata monument, 1447–53, by Donatello, detail of horse's head.

117. Rouen. Cathedral, tomb of Louis de Brézé, 1535–44, by Jean Goujon(?). (From Roussel, *Description du Château d'Anet.*)

118. Drawing in the Cabinet Rothschild, 1424, detail. (Paris, Louvre.)

119. Anet. Frontispiece in Cour d'Honneur, begun 1548, by Philibert de l'Orme.

120. Ecouen. Frontispiece, 1555–60, by Jean Bullant. (From Du Cerceau, *Les Plus excellents bastiments de France.*)

121. Louvre. Square Court, 1546 ff., by Pierre Lescot (the third floor is later).

122. Hatfield House, Hertfordshire, 1608–12, by Robert Lyminge. (Copyright © *Country Life,* London.)

123. Antonio Niccolini, detail from project for re-erecting the Aragonese Arch in a marina in the harbor at Naples, mid-eighteenth century. (Naples, Museo San Martino.)

DATE DUE

DEMCO 38-297